Richard H. Spencer

GENEALOGICAL AND MEMORIAL

ENCYCLOPEDIA

OF THE

STATE OF MARYLAND

A Record of the Achievements of Her People in the Making
of a Commonwealth and the Founding of a Nation

Under the Editorial Supervision of

RICHARD HENRY SPENCER, LL.B.

Corresponding Secretary of The Maryland Historical Society; Author of
"Carlyle Family"; "Thomas Family of Talbot County,
Maryland, and Allied Families," etc., etc.

ILLUSTRATED

CLEARFIELD COMPANY

Reprinted for Clearfield Company, Inc.
by Genealogical Publishing Company Inc.
Baltimore, Maryland 1992

PREFACE

EACH State should have, if possible, its own distinctive Genealogical and Memorial Encyclopedia, which should include the names of prominent citizens of the State, both living and dead, embracing genealogical and biographical sketches, not only of those well known in the church, at the bar, and other professions, but also of those who have been foremost in contributing to the commercial and industrial progress and welfare of the State. It is with this view that the Genealogical and Memorial Encyclopedia of Maryland has been undertaken.

It is almost impossible not to have a laudable desire to know something of the departed, and curiosity about our progenitors seems quite natural. If they were honored in any way above their fellows, it was because they were entitled to some distinction for having led honorable and useful lives, and had left their impress upon the history of their times.

There is inspiration in a rounded, well-spent life, therefore their lives are more interesting and instructive to us because they had accomplished something in the drama of life.

An able writer has well said: "To gather up the Memorials of those who have gone before us, to reconstruct their living portraits from historical fragments so widely scattered, is a work of time, of patience and unremitting toil; but, once completed, the ancestral line, reaching down the vista of the past, will stand out clearly before us, the images of our fathers will tenderly live in our minds, and we shall reverently cherish their memories, as will likewise the generations to come." For as Edmund Burke emphatically exclaimed, "Those who do not treasure up the memory of their ancestors do not deserve to be remembered by posterity." By a higher authority we are commanded to honor our forefathers, that our days may be long.

The cultivation of family history, therefore, is one of the essentials to the welfare of society. The history of a State is best told in a record of the lives of its people.

The genealogical and biographical sketches, it is hoped, will prove of interest and value, not only to members of the various families, but to the general reader as well. The aim of the work has been to give the genealogies of the subjects, so far as they could be obtained, their births, marriages and deaths, and full and accurate information as to their lives, from original sources or from the immediate family, whose family name represented either direct descent from the early settlers of Maryland, from Revolutionary ancestors, or marked success through intelligent and honest labor for the benefit of his State, whose influence and example are worthy of the greatest emulation. The story of their lives might perish, if not preserved by some method of research, as has been adopted by the publishers of this work. No similar work of this scope, concerning Maryland families, has ever been published. It contains ancestral lines never before printed, and a faithful chronicle of people who have made Maryland in part what it is. It gives, in a lucid and dignified manner, all the important facts regarding the ancestry, personal careers and matrimonial alliances of those who, in each succeeding generation, have been accorded leading positions in the social, professional and business life of the State.

"Than Maryland, no other State or region offers so peculiarly interesting a field for such research. Its sons, 'native here and to the manner born,' and of splendid ancestry, have attained distinction in every field of human endeavor."

The early settlers of the Province of Maryland brought with them some of the best traits and traditions of those who were accustomed to English country life, many of them being of ancient lineage, scions of the Landed Gentry, and some even of Knightly Families, and now, after a lapse of two hundred and fifty years, not a few of the landed estates are in the possession of the descendants of the original proprietors.

Much valuable information has been obtained from original sources; and, in the case of recent lives, important aid has been given by the friends and relatives of the subjects.

As portraiture is the demand of the times and contributes so much to the interest of biography, it has been made a feature of the work to have every sketch, as far as possible, embellished with a portrait.

It has been the aim and desire of the Editor and Publishers to render the Encyclopedia a comprehensive and authentic historical memorial.

RICHARD HENRY SPENCER.

PUBLISHER'S NOTE.—This work is paged continuously through the volumes, and the Index will be found at the close of Volume II.

The narratives contained herein have been submitted to the persons in interest, for verification and revision.

Charles Carroll Fulton.

CHARLES CARROLL FULTON

WITH the passing of Charles Carroll Fulton, a life of rare fullness and activity closed and journalism was bereft of one of its most shining lights. His life began in 1816, but two years after the roar of British and American cannon fired with deadly intent had ceased to echo across the harbor of the city he grew to love so well, and the smoke from those guns had barely cleared away, revealing the fact that the "star spangled banner in triumph did wave." It closed in 1883, his dying vision resting on a nation great and prosperous, hardly yet done with recounting the glories of the greatest of national or international expositions which celebrated its one hundredth birthday, held in the city which gave him birth. Those two cities, Philadelphia and Baltimore, witnessed the beginning and the ending of the life and illustrious career of one of the remarkable men of a remarkable period in the nation's history, and of one of the commanding figures in American journalism, Charles Carroll Fulton, a printer and newspaper man from boyhood, and editor of the "Baltimore American," from 1853 until his death in 1883.

And what a wonderful period in American history he lived in, and aided to make glorious! His active life witnessed Texas achieving independence from Mexican rule, and he followed with anxious breath the fortunes of an elder brother, George Washington Fulton, who fought with the Texans. And he saw Texas after achieving that independence voluntarily surrender it to enter the sisterhood of states and merge her "Lone Star" with the galaxy of stars which form the starry emblem. He saw the war with Mexico and the great territorial expansion which followed it; the discovery of gold in California, the invention of the telegraph and its application to the gathering of news from all parts of the world. He saw the death of the old Whig party and the blasting of the ambitions of his chief, Henry Clay; the birth of the Republican party and the rise of the great Lincoln, whom he also followed. He saw the North and the South locked for four years in deadly armed conflict, and he saw them again united in bonds which shall never be broken; and in all these historical events he bore a part, not a passive, but an active part. He saw his adopted city expand to commercial greatness and in that, too, he bore his part. As news editor of the "Baltimore Sun" (1842-1853) he won his first enduring fame as journalist, and as half owner, then as sole owner and editor of the "Baltimore American," he added to the lustre of that name which shall never fade in journalism.

Yet, though he lived for so many years at the head of a great journal and although his name was familiar to hundreds of thousands, his circle of intimate and personal friends was not large. His journalistic and domestic life absorbed his time and his thoughts, he cared but little for social or political honors, and thus was seen but little in public. Yet in all parts of Maryland and the neighboring States, lifelong readers of the "American" came to regard him with almost affectionate reverence as a guide and a friend. With tall, erect form, determined, pale, thoughtful countenance, full, white beard and firm set brow betokening the energy and force of his character, his was a figure that might well arrest attention; yet comparatively few of those who leaned upon his advice knew his person. But the glance of his eye was very kindly and genial, his smile most winning. All who came in contact with him respected him; all who knew him loved him.

Mr. Fulton was of Scotch ancestry paternally, his father, George Fulton, coming from the banks of the River

Tweed, to settle in Philadelphia, Pennsylvania. He obtained a position in Bioren's book store, then a Philadelphia literary center, but later he became a dry goods merchant. He married Ann Ware, of the well-known Ware family of the State of Delaware, who was early orphaned. She became a ward of the famous Benjamin Chew, whose Germantown residence figured so prominently during the battle fought October 4, 1777. She became a very warm friend of her guardian's daughter, Harriet Chew, who, in 1779, married Charles Carroll, "of Carrollton." When the third son of George and Ann (Ware) Fulton was born, the mother, in memory of her younger days, chose for her son the name of the husband of her girlhood friend, thus the name, Charles Carroll Fulton.

Both George and Ann (Ware) Fulton died in 1826, leaving five sons: George Washington, William Ware, Charles Carroll, Edington and Alexander, the eldest fourteen and the youngest six years of age. The family fortunes had gone awry during the last years of George Fulton's life, and the sole inheritance of those boys was energy and brains. Their early lives were closely bound together, all being taken into the home of their nearest relative, their mother's sister, Mrs. Eliza Freeman, who taught a private school. Under her kindly care and tuition the boys acquired the good foundation of an English education, but the time soon came when they must go out into the world and build their own fortunes. The eldest, George Washington, went to Texas, then a province of Mexico, took part with the Texans in achieving their independence, later settling and becoming one of the cattle barons of the State. He married a daughter of Henry Smith, provisional governor of Texas in 1835, while the struggle with Mexico was in progress.

The other four boys all chose the printer's trade and

became apprentices in the office of the "Philadelphia Gazette," later the "North American." The "Gazette" was then published by William Fry; the editor, Robert Walsh, a Baltimorean by birth, one of the most prominent editors of his day and a shining literary light. The "Gazette" offices were located on Second street, below Chestnut, and there the four brothers learned their trades, and although a hard school, it was a good one, and they acquired complete knowledge of the printing business from its very foundation. Their lives flowed in this similar channel for several years, when they separated, each going his own way.

Charles Carroll Fulton was born in Philadelphia, Pennsylvania, September 20, 1816, died in the city of Baltimore, Maryland, June 7, 1883. His parents died when he was ten years of age, and from that age until nearing his majority, his experiences were those of his brothers, as outlined in the foregoing paragraphs. He absorbed all the printer's lore the Fry offices in Philadelphia could afford him, then in 1830 started out on an independent career as an expert journeyman printer. His first venture was in New York City, where for a few months, he was employed in a printing office. In the same year, 1836, he came to Baltimore, was soon afterward married, and began working as a journeyman printer in the offices of John Toy, then the leading printer of the city. He continued with Mr. Toy for several years, carefully husbanding his resources and providing for the time he was determined should come when he would own his own printing establishment.

His next move was to the National Capital, where he was employed on that famous newspaper of the period, "The Washington Intelligencer," then the foremost journalistic agency in the country for moulding and directing political thought. The office of the paper was a headquarters for the politicians of that era, the proprietors, Messrs. Gates and Seaton, enjoying confidential relations with Clay, Webster, Benton, Calhoun and other statesmen whose genius illuminated the struggle in Congress which was the forerunner of the Civil War. In such an atmosphere Mr. Fulton could not avoid the study of men and manners; it was favorable to the cultivation of thought upon the serious issues then beginning to divide the nation, and amid such surroundings his political views were developed and confirmed with regard to the value of the Union, the sacrifices that should be made to perpetuate it, the moral wrong and economic blunder embraced in slavery and slave-labor. Inclined to the tenets of the Whig party in his budding manhood, his convictions were fixed in the midst of his Washington associations.

There then came to him the chance for independent publishing for which he had so long been waiting and preparing. "The Advocate," a paper published at Georgetown, D. C., was offered for sale, and the price being within the means at his command he purchased it, and for five years was its editor and proprietor, bringing it up to a respectable standing and carrying its circulation into Washington and the adjacent country. The National Capital being so near at hand, his political connections remained unbroken, and in his columns he was a sturdy champion of the Whig cause, being thoroughly imbued with the teachings of Henry Clay and having the highest admiration for that eminent man. For five years he edited and published the "Georgetown Advocate," developing with the years and really "finding himself." With the consciousness of intellectual power, the heritage of his Scotch father and American mother, and with the experiences that convinced him journalism was his true sphere, came the conviction that he must seek a wider field of action. With that conviction quickly came decision, the "Advocate" was sold and Baltimore determined upon as his new location.

On arriving in Baltimore he sought employment in the composing room of the "Baltimore Sun," a successful newspaper founded in 1837 by Swan, Abell & Simmons, Mr. Abell being in charge of the paper. Mr. Fulton was not long allowed to remain in the composing room, however, his experience and demonstrated capacity for a higher department causing Mr. Abell to press him into service as a reporter. This was altogether to Mr. Fulton's liking, and although the reporter's art or profession was then in its infancy, the "local column" of the "Sun" soon took shape and substance. In this, and as one of the earliest legitimate reporters, he found congenial occupation, his ready pen, tireless energy in the collection of news, and his perseverance marking him in the eyes of his chief for further promotion. After further demonstration of his readiness to avail himself of opportunities to embrace new features not hitherto considered within the scope of a reporter's duty and his perfect adaptability to newspaper work, Mr. Abell in 1842 promoted him to the desk of news editor. He administrated the affairs of this responsible desk for nearly eleven years, 1842-1853, a period which in the interest it possesses for the historian is surpassed by no decade lying between the last war with Great Britain and the civil conflict. Within this time occurred the war with Mexico and the annexation of Texas, the invention of the electric telegraph, the struggle for and against the extension of slavery into the territories and new states, the decline of the Whig party and the rise of the Republican party, the short-lived predominence of the Know-Nothing party, the discovery of gold in California, a comparatively vast extension of the railroad system, and improvement of steam transportation upon the ocean and inland waters. There was also the Seminole War in Florida, and the contest over the tariff, which was settled in 1842 by the passage of a protective act. It was a time when the nation was growing like a lusty young giant.

While the slavery question kept the political temper at fever heat, a spirit of adventure was prompting the people to enterprise. The newspapers kept pace with, or rather led the popular movement. It was Mr. Fulton's duty to co-operate with his employers in maintaining for the "Sun" that place in the front rank which it had already won. In 1838, Mr. Abell had achieved some notable victories in procuring news by employing horsemen to carry intelligence between breaks in railway communication, and later the plan was further elaborated. In this way the "Sun" was the first paper in the country, outside of Washington, to print the messages of Presidents Van Buren and Harrison on the days they were delivered, and from this there came the famous "pony express." Although the system was to some extent in use prior to Mr. Fulton's administration of the "Sun," it remained for him to have a part in its enlargement into that comprehensiveness which made it forever memorable in the chronicles of journalism. Mr. Fulton was one of the first to recognize that the telegraph was to be the prime auxiliary of the newspaper, and he helped to bring it into requisition as frequently and to the full extent that circumstance would permit. He suggested its use for bringing reports of the proceedings of Congress, this first being done during the session of 1844-1845.

Henry J. Rogers, the able assistant of Professor Morse and superintendent of the Baltimore office, had facilitated the work by the invention of a cipher code, and with the economy of time this secured, it was possible to obtain a fair account of congressional debate and action. Mr. Fulton was the interpreter of the cipher as it was received at the Baltimore end of the wire and made up the reports for the printers. On May 24, 1846, the message of President Polk was transmitted to Baltimore and published in full the next day. While continuing to hold the position of news editor of the "Sun," Mr. Fulton gave part of his time and effort to the organization of telegraph reporting, generally his plans being so acceptable that he gradually enlisted into the organization all the leading papers of the cities reached by the wires. The telegraph and newspaper offices became news exchanges, and the next step, a natural consequence of what had so far been accomplished, was that journalistic combination which, under the name of the Associated Press, has reached every source of information in all continents and subjected them to its ends. Mr. Fulton was the first agent of the Associated Press in Baltimore, handling its interests, at the same time that he was Mr. Abell's chief subordinate in the "Sun" office. But the double work became too arduous for him, and he brought into the agency of the Associated Press his youngest brother, Alexander Fulton. This arrangement lasted until 1853, in which year he severed his connection with the "Sun," and purchased an interest in "The American," a step which to him was the consummation of his most sanguine hopes.

The old firm of Dobbin, Murphy & Bose, which had for half a century published the "Baltimore American," was dissolved on the 30th of June, 1853, Mr. Dobbin purchasing the interest of Mr. Murphy, and Mr. Fulton that of Mr. Bose. For the following eleven years the "American" was owned and published by Messrs. Dobbin and Fulton. With the infusion of new blood in the management of the "American," a commendable spirit of enterprise was adopted in the gathering of news from distant points, in giving a faithful record of local events, and in bold and fearless editorials during the most exciting times. The political agitation that sought to sever the Union in 1861 did not cause the "American" to swerve from its love for the old flag. It circulated among the commercial classes, who had the largest interests at stake, and the most to lose by the disruption of the Union. The public sentiment was at times opposed to its teaching, and through the whole of the revolutionary period the "American" was able to give a calm, steadfast and effectual support to the Union and the National government. Many of its old friends dropped away and powerful interests were arrayed against its editor, but the paper was too deeply rooted in the great commercial heart of the Monumental City to be seriously crippled. Charles Carroll Fulton was, in those troublous times, the pilot who kept the "American" out of the current of public opinion when it set too strongly toward the breakers of disunion. Mr. Robert A. Dobbin died in September, 1862, leaving his interests in the "American" to his son, Joseph Dobbin, from whom Mr. Fulton purchased it. By that time social order had resumed its sway in the city, and the turbulent elements had been subdued. The "American" had become a power in the State, and a widely-read journal throughout the section that remained faithful to the flag. It became the recognized leader of the loyal public opinion of Maryland. Its "special correspondence" during the war was extensively copied, and the signature of "C. C. F." was a warranty that the writer gave expression to what he knew, and described what he saw.

Mr. Fulton was with the Army of the Potomac during two of its most important campaigns, and the readers of the "American" got the benefit of his candor, his accurate habits of observation, and his indomitable enterprise in gathering news and dispatching his letter while the incidents were fresh, so that they were frequently far in advance of all his competitors. His dispatches very often distanced the official reports of the War Department, and gave the first tidings of vital events to the government. Mr. Fulton accompanied the first iron-clad expedition against Fort Sumter and was on board the United States steamer "Bibb" when the attack was made. His controversy with the commander of the expedition and the Navy Department is part of the history of the war. His opinions regarding the premature withdrawal of the fleet were subsequently confirmed from southern sources. Mr. Fulton, amid all the excitement of that period, was remarkably successful in raising funds for the purpose of sending supplies of every kind to the Union prisoners at Richmond, who were reported to be starving and suffering from the want of clothing and other necessaries. The following resolution passed by the Maryland House of Delegates is evidence that his efforts were appreciated:

By the House of Delegates—

Resolved, That the thanks of the House be, and are hereby tendered to Charles Carroll Fulton of the City of Baltimore for his exertions for the relief of the soldiers of the Union now held by the so-called Confederate authorities; and especially for the aid afforded by him to the officers and enlisted men of the regiments of this State in Libby Prison, and Belle Isle, Richmond.

THOMAS H. KERN,
Speaker of the House of Delegates.
ALBERT V. R. COLE,
Chief Clerk of the House of Delegates.

Mr. Fulton did not confine his efforts to alleviating the miseries of the boys in blue in southern prisons, but in many cases the sons of Baltimoreans, who had donned the gray, were indebted to him for attentions while lying in northern prisons. Mr. Fulton's son (later associated in proprietorship of the "American") was an engineer aboard the "Hartford," Admiral Farragut's flag ship, and acted as correspondent, giving graphic descriptions of the great naval engagements in which the illustrious commander conquered.

The senior editor was present at the hoisting of the old flag over the ruins of Fort Sumter, when the country was in full time of rejoicing over the close of the war, unconscious of the impending calamity of President Lincoln's assassination. The setting sun that gilded the restored flag on the ruins rose the next morning on a nation mourning the martyrdom of its chief.

In 1871 Mr. Fulton accompanied the commissioners headed by Senator Wade, appointed by President Grant, to visit San Domingo and report on the advisability of annexing it to the United States. His letters gave glowing accounts of the delightful climate, prolific soil, attractive scenery, and its bountiful yield of tropical fruits. As editorial correspondent of the "American," he traversed all sections of the country, joined in excursion trips over new lines of railways, rambled through Texas, descended coal and iron mines, explored oil regions, and never failed to present the results of his observations in a manner attractive and interesting to his readers. His wanderings in foreign countries were also extensive. His work, entitled "Europe Seen Through American Spectacles," went through two editions and became a guide book, especially to Baltimoreans. As a politician, he occupied a prominent position in State affairs, and for many years represented his party in the National Executive Committee, and was a delegate to the National conventions of the Republican party. Modest, retiring in his manner, delighting in the eloquence of others, he was not an adept at speechmaking, though in social moments and in the committee room he expressed his opinions freely and to the point.

The public improvements of the city of Baltimore always received Mr. Fulton's ardent support. He advocated the purchase and improvement of Durid Hill Park, and the tax upon passenger railways to meet the outlay. Through his exertions the beautiful Centennial Fountain that adorns Eutaw Place was produced and erected, he being aided by other property owners fronting its site and the liberality of the city councils. He aided in a like manner all good causes, no man exceeding him in public spirit. His judgment was sound and true, his convictions deep, his sympathies broad as human nature itself, his fidelity to friendship and to a cause unfailing, his courage and fortitude not to be shaken, his energy exhaustless. His affections were warm and true and he was always accessible to the pleadings of humanity.

Mr. Fulton married (first) in Baltimore, Emily Jane Kimberly. They were the parents of four sons: Albert K. and three named Charles C., two of whom died in infancy, and three daughters: Annie E., Emma Ware and Dolly G. Annie E. married General Felix Agnus, who, at the close of the Civil War, was the youngest man in the Union Army holding the rank of general. After the death of his wife, Mr. Fulton married (second) Mrs. Caroline Driscoll. Shortly before Mr. Fulton's death he executed a deed of trust constituting General Agnus sole manager of the "American;" this in recognition of his long and faithful services to the paper and of his perfect fitness for so great a trust.

ARUNAH SHEPHERDSON ABELL

ARUNAH SHEPHERDSON ABELL, founder and owner of the "Baltimore Sun," was born in East Providence, Rhode Island, August 10, 1806, and died at his Baltimore residence, northwest corner Charles and Madison streets, April 19, 1888, in the eighty-second year of his age. Mr. Abell was of English descent, his paternal ancestors having been among the early settlers in the Massachusetts Bay Colony. He was sixth in descent from his colonial ancestor, Robert Abell, to whom a son was born during the voyage from the Old to the New World. The voyage was a long and stormy one, and, owing to the safety of mother and child during these perils by sea, the babe was christened Preserved.

Preserved Abell settled at Rehobeth (Seekonk), Rhode Island, and had a son, Joshua Abell, who had a son Robert, named for his colonial ancestor. Robert Abell, son of Joshua, had a son, Caleb Abell, who became the father of Arunah Shepherdson Abell.

Robert Abell, grandson of Preserved Abell and grandfather of Arunah Shepherdson Abell, served with distinction during the war of the American Revolution. Caleb Abell, son of Robert and father of Arunah Shepherdson Abell, was an officer during the war of 1812, and for more than thirty years after served his native town in various offices of public trust. He married Elona Shepherdson, daughter of Arunah Shepherdson, whose name has since been borne by three generations of the Abell family. She was a woman of high and noble character and of exceptional intelligence.

Arunah S. Abell was educated in his native town, and when fourteen years of age entered the business world as clerk in a firm dealing in West India commodities. His

inclinations turned strongly in literary directions. He resigned his clerkship in 1822, and became an apprentice in the
office of the "Providence Patriot," a Democratic journal,
published by Jones & Wheeler, printers to the State and
Federal governments. When he attained his majority, he
obtained employment in Boston, and was soon promoted to
the position of foreman of one of the best offices in that city.
He was offered a government position in the Boston postoffice, under Democratic administration, but having chosen
his career as journalist refused to consider any other vocation.
A little later he removed to New York, bearing flattering
letters of introduction to the foremost newspaper men of the
metropolis. His residence in New York quickly resulted in
his entering into partnership with two gentlemen, Azariah H.
Simmons and William M. Swain, also printers like himself,
to establish a daily penny paper. At this time New York
boasted several penny papers, while Philadelphia did not, and
it was decided to establish the new enterprise in the latter
city. Articles of association were drawn up February 29,
1836. The name first chosen for the new paper was "The
Times," but an ill fate had overtaken a preceding Philadelphia journal of that name, and the firm of Swain, Abell &
Simmons abandoned the name first chosen for that of "The
Public Ledger," under which title the paper entered upon
a long and prosperous career which continues to the present
time. The partners contributed an equal amount of money
and their united energies to the undertaking, and cast super-
stition to the wind when the first number of "The Public
Ledger" appeared, Friday, March 25, 1836.

Having seen the success of "The Ledger" fully established,
Mr. Abell, in April, 1837, visited Baltimore, where all the
newspapers published were known as "sixpennies." The year
was not a financially encouraging one, and here were five

newspaper competitors already established in the Baltimore field, yet Mr. Abell's business foresight incited him to make the venture of establishing a penny paper in Baltimore, and his partners agreed to supoprt him if he would personally undertake the control of the enterprise. This he agreed to do, and upon May 17, 1837, the first number of "The Sun" was issued, and the broad and wide policy outlined that has been the paper's inspiration through succeeding years.

While the paper was the property of the three partners, Mr. Abell was, from its inception, its sole manager, and the imprint of his strong intelligent and fearless character was manifest throughout his life in the conduct of the journal. It was designed to voice the sentiment of the people, while endeavoring their judgment aright, and, so far as possible, to carry out their will. The city and State, as well as neighboring States, soon realized that here was a newspaper which could neither be bought nor intimidated, with opinions based upon fact and judgment, with news collected by responsible workers, and the paper soon came to be relied upon as the voice of the people in the highest and best sense of the word. "The Sun" commenced its notable career with one reporter, but it was the pioneer in the field of giving local reports, and upon the first anniversary of its founding, May 17, 1838, "The Sun" had a circulation of 12,000 copies—a very large circulation for that day.

The first opportunity offered the paper for displaying the intense energy and initiative which characterized Mr. Abell's management, was President Van Buren's Message of December, 1838. Such messages usually reached Baltimore by mail, and appeared in leisurely fashion in supplementary newspaper issues. Mr. Abell had the message rushed to Baltimore from Washington by Canadian pony express, and brought with all possible speed to the office. In five minutes after its arrival, forty-nine compositors were at work upon it, and in two hours the first copy was printed in Baltimore and distributed to the public. The message thus appeared in "The Sun" two days in advance of its local newspaper competitors. "The Sun" was successful from its initial publication. In three months its circulation had outstripped that of "The Public Ledger" after nine months' publication, and in a year "The Sun" had more than twice the circulation of the oldest newspaper in Baltimore. The first printing office of the paper was at No. 21 Light street, near Mercer street, but this building became too contracted for the rapid development of the paper. On February 16, 1839, the office was removed to the southeast corner of Gay and Baltimore streets, and on December 22, 1850, Mr. Abell purchased the site upon which was erected the well-known "Sun Iron Building," the first iron-supported structure to be built in the United States. The structure had a front of fifty-six feet on Baltimore street and seventy-four feet on South street, with height of five well-pitched stories. The partnership between A. S. Abell, William M. Swain and Azariah H. Simmons was only dissolved by the death of the latter in 1855. "The Sun" property was sold December 22, 1860, to divide Mr. Simmons's estate, and was purchased by Mr. A. S. Abell.

In 1864 Mr. Abell sold out his interest in "The Public Ledger." He was now the sole proprietor of "The Sun," to the development and success of which he bent his undivided interest, and to which he contributed with enthusiasm his truly remarkable gifts as organizer and manager. It was a life-work which, for unswerving purpose and successful fulfillment, has no parallel in the journalism of the South. Initiative and conservatism were equally characteristic of Mr. Abell's personality, and this was shown, both in his development of "The Sun" and his relation to the city of his adoption. His conception of the mission of journalism was far above the ordinary plane of mere news circulation, although his initiative of obtaining reliable news quickly, immediately placed his paper in the lead of other sources of news supply, both official and journalistic. He always cherished a high conception of his personal responsibility as newspaper editor and proprietor, and his influence was always directed against sensationalism, scandal and idle gossip. To make "The Sun" what he aspired it should be, was Mr. A. S. Abell's life-work, and his reward was his paper's acceptance by the people of the South as a political guide and a paper that uplifted and enlightened every home which it entered.

An open mind made Mr. Abell a ready and earnest patron and promoter of mechanical enterprises and inventions. His firm was the first to purchase the rotary printing machine, the invention of Richard M. Hoe, of New York, which worked a revolution in the art of printing, and which invention had previously been rejected as impracticable by New York publishers. He gave substantial support to that marvel of modern times, the electric telegraph, and Mr. Abell was one of the incorporators of the first telegraph company organized. "The Sun" was one of the most enthusiastic advocates of the practicability of the new invention, and the first document of any length transmitted over the experimental line between Washington and Baltimore was President Tyler's message of May 11, 1846, which was telegraphed to and published in "The Sun," with a degree of accuracy that excited general astonishment. "The Sun's" telegraphic copy of this Message of May 11, 1846, which was telegraphed to and pubside by side with an authenticated transcript of the original.

The art of stereotyping, electric light, and many other

mechanical improvements were immediately recognized by Mr. Abell as important achievements, and promptly applied to the conduct of his business. The submarine cable received his vigorous support, and it was largely due to his efforts in the successful establishment of pony expresses for obtaining news promptly by European steamers and from the seat of war in Mexico that the Associated Press service was established, which now supplies the leading papers throughout the country with news. He was also the first to introduce in Baltimore the carrier system of delivering newspapers which has proved of such great convenience to city readers.

Mr. A. S. Abell, in conjunction with Mr. Craig, afterwards agent of the Associated Press of New York, organized an effective carrier pigeon express for the transmission of news between New York, Philadelphia, Baltimore and Washington, and the birds were also carefully trained to carry news from incoming ships. From four hundred to five hundred pigeons were kept in a house on Hampstead Hill, near the old Maryland Hospital for the Insane, and this carrier service was regularly conducted until the rapid flight of birds was superseded by the still more rapid transmission of news by telegraph. Even the short-lived Atlantic cable of 1858 was pressed into service by this indefatigable gleaner of news, and transmitted a special dispatch to "The Sun," this being the first news telegram from London over the Atlantic cable received and made public in Baltimore.

In order to obtain the earliest foreign news, "The Sun" established relays of horses from Halifax to Annapolis, on the Bay of Fundy, Nova Scotia, a distance of one hundred and fifty miles. Thence the news was carried by steamer to Portland, Maine, from there by rail to Boston, and via New York and Philadelphia to Baltimore, the distance of about one thousand miles being covered in fifty hours. "The Sun" published news of the ships "Liberty" and "Cambria" twenty-four hours ahead of other sources of information, and was the only Baltimore paper that joined in the charter of the pilot boat "Romer" to run to Liverpool, and return with foreign news.

During the war with Mexico, when all interests were centered in that section, "The Sun" organized, exclusively for its own department, an overland express by means of ponies from New Orleans, independent of any co-operation with other papers. The trip from New Orleans to Baltimore was made in six days by these carriers of war dispatches, and cost "The Sun" a thousand dollars a month; but it enabled the paper to publish pictures of Monterey and the army and the battlefied of Buena Vista, both before and after the battle, which would have been impossible under any other circumstances than those afforded by this extraordinary service from Pensacola. Throughout the Mexican War "The Sun" supplied not only the public with news, but kept the government advised as well.

These expresses became a public necessity, after their advantage over other means of communication was proven, and several northern papers then joined in profiting by the facilities thus afforded. "The Sun" was the first to announce, April 10, 1847, to President Polk and his Cabinet at Washington, the unconditional capitulation of Vera Cruz and the Castle of San Juan d'Ulloa. Even before the publication of this important news in the columns of "The Sun," Mr. Abell's patriotism inspired him to send to the President a private telegraphic communication of the surrender of the Mexican city and castle. "The Sun's" pony express brought news of the victories at Contreras and Cherubusco fully twenty-four hours ahead of steamboats, railways, and even telegraphs.

Another proof of the enterprise of the management of "The Sun" was given in 1876, when the paper united with the "New York Herald" and sent copies of the daily and weekly issues to the Pacific coast by Jarrett and Palmer's transcontinental train in eighty-four hours. Mr. Abell was an enthusiastic friend of Professor Morse when the latter was endeavoring to establish the telegraph. He used both his personal and journalistic influence to promote and develop this invention, and was instrumental in securing from Congress an appropriation of $30,000 for the construction of a line between Washington and Baltimore, and supplied part of the money to build between Baltimore and Philadelphia the first line of the Magnetic Telegraph Company, which was organized March 15, 1845.

The "Weekly Sun" was first issued April 14, 1838, and continued an important adjunct to the daily edition, especially in rural districts, until 1904. On Saturday, February 6, 1904, the day preceding the great conflagration of February 7-8, 1904, that enveloped the business portion of the city of Baltimore in a mantle of flame and wiped the "Sun Iron Building" out of existence, the last issue of the "Weekly Sun" was published. It had been an important household paper in the annals of Baltimore journalism, and through it, on numerous occasions, prizes ranging from $300 to $1,200 had been won for stories entered in competition.

In the year 1838, Mr. Abell married Mrs. Mary Fox Campbell, a young widow, daughter of John Fox, of Peekskill, New York. She was a lady greatly beloved by all who knew her, for her amiable and gracious womanliness and the wide charity of her nature. She bore her husband twelve children, nine of whom lived to reach man's and woman's estate. The children were: 1. Edwin Franklin Abell; married (first) Margaret Curley; (second) Elizabeth M. Laurenson. 2. George William Abell; married Jane Francis Webb, daughter of the late George Webb. 3. Walter Robert Abell; married (first) Sallie Sisson, daughter of the late Hugh Sisson; (second) Philomena, daughter of Henry Bogue. 4. Charles S. Abell; died unmarried, December 3, 1891. 5. Marie L. Abell; became a nun, and assumed the name of Mary Joseph. 6. Agnes Frances Abell; unmarried. 7. Annie F. Abell; married J. W. S. Brady. 8. Helen M. Abell; married L. Victor Baughman. 9. Margaret Abell; married John Irving Griffiss. 10. Arunah S. Abell; died in childhood. 11. Harry Abell; died in childhood. 12. Mary Abell; died in childhood. Mrs. Arunah S. Abell died in 1859.

Mr. Abell's personal appearance suggested dignity and reserve force. His height was medium, and his face in repose a trifle stern. His nature, however, was by no means stern, and his manners were genial, free from all affectation, and his personal friendship of the warmest character. He possessed a keen sense of humor, a vein of interesting reminiscence, and was a congenial companion for young or old. A man wholly without arrogance over his great achievements, he was regarded with ardent and reverential but also cheerful and companionable love, by every member of his household. Arunah S. Abell lived to celebrate the semi-centennial of the paper he had founded, upon which occasion announcement was made that upon that date the senior proprietor had associated with himself as co-partners his sons, Edwin F. Abell, George W. Abell and Walter R. Abell. Grover Cleveland, then President of the United States, was among the notable people who sent personal telegrams of congratulations to Mr. Abell upon this happy occasion.

Mr. Abell's death, which occurred April 19, 1888, was regarded as a municipal calamity by the people of Baltimore. The flag upon the City Hall was placed at half-mast by Mayor Ferdinand C. Latrobe, an unusual tribute to one not occupying an official position, and fifteen thousand persons congregated at Greenmount Cemetery upon the day of his interment, as a final tribute to his honored memory. The pallbearers were: Messrs. Hugh Sisson, Charles Webb, Professor Alan P. Smith, Robert Moore, Lewis M. Cole, Charles J. M. Gwinn, R. Q. Taylor, Meyer Stein, Colonel John Carroll Walsh, Robert Lawson, Enoch Pratt, Dr. John Morris, James M. Anderson and William H. Carpenter.

THOMAS HARRISON GARRETT

THOMAS HARRISON GARRETT, second son of John Work and Rachel Ann (Harrison) Garrett, was born in Baltimore, February 11, 1849. After attending private schools in Baltimore he entered Princeton. He was a member of the class of 1868, and later Princeton conferred upon him the degree of Master of Arts. He was deeply devoted to the interests of his *alma mater* and served as one of its trustees.

He was nineteen years of age when he left Princeton and entered the Baltimore banking house of his father, which was conducted under the firm name of Robert Garrett & Sons, and which had been founded by his grandfather in 1839. The sterling business traits which had characterized generations of the Garrett family found in him an apt and progressive representative, and his success was so marked that in 1871, although his father and brother remained members of the firm, he was placed in charge of the banking interests. His brother Robert was engrossed in the service of the Baltimore & Ohio railroad, and the duties of the bank devolved upon Thomas Harrison Garrett. It was a time of large operations, and the firm, in associations with great banking houses of Europe and America, negotiated most of the Baltimore & Ohio loans and did a large part of the vast business of the Baltimore & Ohio Company. He was a director of the Baltimore & Ohio, and, after Mr. Samuel Spencer became president of the road, was appointed chairman of the finance committee. His work in finance made him an active factor in the enterprise and development of Baltimore, and he was prominent in the most important movements of the day. He was a member of the Baltimore Stock Exchange, a director in the Western National Bank, and one of the incorporators of the company that built the Academy of Music. These are but few of his connections, but they show the wide range of his business activities.

Mr. Garrett occupied a unique place in the social and cultural life of the city. He was a man of many benefactions about which nothing was printed, most of them being made on the condition that his name should not be divulged. He accumulated the largest private library in Maryland, and among its treasures was one of the most complete bibliographies of the first railroad, the Baltimore & Ohio. His collection of autographs was comprehensive, containing letters from many prominent historical personages of America from the time of Washington. His numismatic collection was noted. But his best known possession was his collection of prints, including the famous Claghorn etchings, and many of these he allowed to be placed on exhibition at the Peabody Institute and several of the social clubs of the city. He was a member of the Maryland Historical Society, and contributed liberally to its needs, taking especial interest in the recovery of the old Calvert papers found on the estate of Colonel Henry Harford, near Windsor, England. He belonged to the leading social clubs, but his main devotion was to his home and to outdoor life, which he enjoyed at "Evergreen," in the uplands of Baltimore.

In 1870 Mr. Garrett married Alice, daughter of the late Horatio L. Whitridge, and they had five children: John W., Horatio W. and Robert, and a son and daughter who died in infancy. Horatio W. graduated from Princeton in 1895 near the head of his class, and in the same year married Charlotte D., daughter of Henry L., and Mrs. Pierson, of Summit, New Jersey; died in early manhood.

Mr. Garrett was a great traveler and was very fond of the water. His yacht "Gleam" was one of the swiftest boats on the Chesapeake, and it was while Mr. Garrett was on a cruise with friends that a collision occurred with the steamer "Joppa," on June 7, 1888, and he lost his life, he being the only one who was not saved. His death cast a gloom over the whole city. The mayor of Baltimore said: "Mr. Garrett's death is a municipal loss, and few citizens who will come after him will possess his liberality and public-spiritedness." The City Council paid the unusual tribute of spreading upon the journals of both its branches the following resolution: "Resolved, by the Mayor and City Council of Baltimore: That it is the duty of the City Council to record the sense of loss the city has sustained in the death of Thomas Harrison Garrett. He sought no public office and held none, but the example of his character and activities in every work tending to promote the interests of this city ought to be borne in perpetual remembrance."

Mr. Garrett was connected with the Associate Reformed Church, of which the Rev. Dr. Leyburn was for many years pastor. Rev. Mr. Ball, successor to Dr. Leyburn, conducted the funeral; it was attended by two thousand representative people of the city. The services were simple, as had been the life of Mr. Garrett, and Mr. Ball made no address, but in his Sunday sermon he said this: "Some of you may not know, but there are some of us who do, how substantial and persistent and benevolent were the offices performed by him whose loss we mourn. We have suffered a great loss."

WILSON BURNS TRUNDLE

SCION of one of the best known families of Maryland, and in his own right one of the foremost citizens of Baltimore, and an eminent member of the Baltimore bar at which he practiced for forty-three years, the career of Wilson Burns Trundle was one to excite interest and admiration. His English and Scotch ancestors came to this country early in the seventeenth century, and, as one of them was an uncle of the poet Burns, he came rightfully by his name Burns, and his inheritance of admiration for that great poet, Robert Burns, whom all Scotchmen love. In his numerous speeches and writings, not of a legal character, he quoted freely that poet's gems, many of which he could give in full. In addition to the cares of a large practice, and his many social obligations, Mr. Trundle gave freely of his time to church work, his interest in both church and Sunday school being life-long and intense.

Paternally he descended from David Trundle, of England, born in 1671, and maternally from John White, of Hulcote, England, who died in 1501. The Whites were seated in Hulcote, Bedfordshire, over four centuries ago; were of the Shire gentry and bore arms:

Arms—On a chevron between three wolves' heads erased sable a leopard's face or.

The first of the Trundle name, of which there is definite information, was David Trundle, of Suffolk, England, born in 1574, and died in 1671, aged ninety-seven years. His son, John Trundle, the founder of the family in America, came about 1640 or 1649. He was born in Suffolk County, England, about 1624, and died in Maryland, August 3, 1699. He settled in Anne Arundel County, Maryland, and owned

considerable land there, as, according to his will dated January 7, 1698, he bequeathed to his only son, John, his plantation of two hundred and fifty acres located in that county. His wife, Mary (Ross) Trundle, survived. She is spoken of in her husband's will as "my beloved wife, Mary." Their children were four daughters, who married, respectively, Benjamin Thorley, John Thorley, Samuel Thorley and Edward Thorley; and one son John.

John (2) Trundle, son of John (1) and Mary Trundle, was born December 26, 1687, and died April 15, 1771. Though he inherited his father's plantation in Anne Arundel County (according to his father's will) he must have later removed to Frederick County, Maryland, as his death and will are recorded in that county. He married, in 1717, Ann ————, and by her had three sons and one daughter, who were: Thomas, who married Rachel Lewis; John (see forward); Josiah and Joanna.

John (3) Trundle, second son of John (2) and Ann Trundle, was born in 1724, and was married in 1750. His wife died May 10, 1809.

John (4) Trundle, son of John (3) Trundle, was born March 6, 1753, and died March 1, 1797. He married, in 1775, Ruth Lewis, born 1753, and died May, 1810. John Trundle served in the War of the Revolution, was commissioned ensign in Maryland Militia, August 11, 1779, and promoted lieutenant, August 4, 1780 (see Militia officers of the State of Maryland, 1776-1779, and Original Commissions Maryland Historical Society). Children of John and Ruth (Lewis) Trundle: 1. David, born 1776, married, 1797, Drusilla Lewis. 2. James, married Eleanor Burns, moved to Tennessee in 1810. 3. Daniel, married, 1800, Esther Belt. 4. Ann, married Dr. Stephen Newton Chiswell White. 5. Mary, married Colonel Benjamin Shreve. 6. John L., married a Miss Veach, and had three sons and four daughters. 7. Hezekiah, married Christiana Whittaker, and they had five children. 8. Otho, see forward. 9. Charlotte, married Alfred Belt, had three sons and three daughters. 10. Eleanor, married Henry Jones, and had three sons and three daughters.

Otho Trundle, son of John (4) and Ruth (Lewis) Trundle, was born in 1781, and died in 1819. He married, January 27, 1804, Elizabeth Burns, daughter of William and Mary (Wilson) Burns. William Burns, son of Robert Burns, was born in 1759, came to this country in 1778, and married, February 27, 1781, Mary Wilson, daughter of Wadsworth and Eleanor (Walker) Wilson. William Burns and Robert Burns, the poet, were first cousins. They were sons of two brothers, namely, William Burns and Robert Burns. Each brother named his son respectively for the other, hence William Burns' son was named Robert (the poet), and Robert Burns' son was named William Burns (ancestor of Wilson Burns Trundle).

Otho Wilson Trundle, son of Otho and Elizabeth (Burns) Trundle, was born August 30, 1816, and died February, 1891. He married, December, 1838, Sarah White, daughter of Benjamin and Rachel White. Children: 1. Rachel, married Americus Dawson, no issue. 2. Benjamin Otho, died in infancy. 3. Elizabeth Ellen, married W. H. Dickerson; children: William Harrie, Edwin Trundle, C. Milton, Edith and Lillian. 4. Joseph Henry, married Emily R. Thomas; children: Emily Maude, Harry Burns and Bertha Thomas. 5. Wilson Burns, see forward. 6. Sarah Virginia, married Charles W. Baggarly. 7. William Edwin, died unmarried, aged twenty-seven years. 8. Margaret Ann, married John Owens, no issue. 9. John Wallace, died aged thirteen years. 10. Milton, married Margaret Corbin, of Missouri, and has two daughters, Ola Ray and Mabel May.

(The White Line).

John White, of Pocomoke, Somerset county, province of Maryland, was the American ancestor of Sarah (White) Trundle. He was a justice of the peace, member of the assembly of Maryland, from Somerset county, Captain of Horse, and Sheriff of Somerset county, in 1678 (Maryland Archives). He was the son of Thomas and Elizabeth (Fisher) White, of Bedfordshire, England, and was born August, 1624 (White book records). He emigrated to America between 1644 and 1650. He was named in the will of his brother, Thomas White, in 1670, as "living beyond the seas" (Maryland). He was descended from John White, of Hulcote, England, who died December 20, 1501.

John White was the son of Thomas White, who died 1661, son of Lawrence White, died 1599, son of Thomas White, died 1586, son of John White, died 1572, son of John White, of Hulcote, England, who died 1501.

John White, the founder in America, died in Somerset county, Maryland, October 3, 1685. He begins his will: "I, John White, of Pocomoke, Somerset county, Gentleman, Etc." He was a large landowner, willing several thousand acres of land to his family. He married, in 1652, Sarah Stevens, daughter of Colonel William Stevens. They had six children: William Stevens, John, Elizabeth, Sarah, Priscilla and Tabitha.

William Stevens White, son of John and Sarah (Stevens) White, was born in 1654, and died in 1708. He married Catherine White, and had four children: John, see forward; Rose, Sarah and Katherine.

John White, son of William Stevens and Catherine (White) White, died in 1672. He married Elizabeth ———, and had two sons and two daughters: John, William, see forward; Ann, married a Mr. Jones; and Margaret, married John Neal.

William White, second son of John and Elizabeth White, married Elizabeth Smith, daughter of Nathan and Elizabeth (Cole) Smith, died 1783. They had four sons and six daughters: 1. William, married Mary Whitehead. 2. Benjamin, married Rebecca Odell Chiswell, 1786. 3. Nathan Smith, see forward. 4. John, married Elizabeth Gott. 5. Sarah, married Edward Jones. 6. Eleanor, married Joseph Newton Chiswell, 1779. 7. Jane, married Hezekiah Thomas, 1780. 8. Elizabeth, married Mr. Allen. 9. Hester, married Mr. Whittaker. 10. Mary.

Nathan Smith White, son of William and Elizabeth (Smith) White, married, in 1787, Margaret Presbury Chiswell, daughter of Stephen Newton, son of Mary Newton, sister of Sir Isaac Newton, and Sarah (Newton) Chiswell; children: Benjamin, see forward; Nathan Smith; Stephen Newton Chiswell; Sarah, married John Waters and moved to Kentucky; Eleanor, married Lawrence Allnutt.

Benjamin White, son of Nathan Smith and Margaret Presbury (Chiswell) White, married, 1815, Rachel Chiswell, daughter of Joseph Newton and Eleanor (White) Chiswell. They had four sons and seven daughters, who were: 1. Nathan Smith, married Frederika McGuire, of Virginia. 2. John, married Tollie Wailes. 3. Joseph, married Anne Viers. 4. Benjamin Franklin, married Margaret Allnutt. 5. Eleanor, married Joseph Chiswell. 6. Sarah, married Otho Wilson Trundle. 7. Rachel Ann. 8. Mary Elizabeth, married Edward McGill. 9. Virginia Catherine, married Joseph Chiswell. 10. Hester Chiswell, married Walter Williams. 11. Rachel, married B. Allnutt.

Sarah White, daughter of Benjamin and Rachel (Chiswell) White, married Otho Wilson Trundle. They were the parents of Wilson Burns Trundle, to whose memory this tribute of respect is dedicated.

Wilson Burns Trundle, son of Otho Wilson and Sarah (White) Trundle, was born at Mount Auburn, Frederick county, Maryland, December 2, 1847, and died April 19, 1914. He received his early education with private tutors and in the public schools of that county, and later entered Calvert College at New Windsor, Maryland, completing the four years' course in two years, receiving his degree of Bachelor of Arts. He studied law with his uncle, Nathan White, at Charlestown, Jefferson county, West Virginia, and then entered the law office of the late Judge John Ritchie, of Frederick, who presented him for admission to the Maryland bar.

Mr. Trundle began his career as a lawyer in October, 1870, when he passed the State examination held at Frederick, Maryland. One month later he located in Baltimore with which city he was to become so actively identified in later years. For forty-three years he was a very successful member of the bar of Maryland, and one of the foremost workers for the advancement of the city of his adoption. In these many years of active professional life he became known to the leading members of the legal profession throughout Maryland, and numbered among his friends nearly all the judges who have sat in the courts of the State for many years.

Learned in the law, and skillful in its application, Mr. Trundle was recognized as an authority on equity and was widely consulted on that department of the law. He was a man of wide and varied information, legal and otherwise, and from the rich store-house of his mind his associates drew largely. His practice extended to all state and federal courts of the district, a large and influential one. He was a member of the city, county, State and national bar associations, and in 1911 was elected president of the Maryland State Bar Association. He was a director of the Western

National Bank, counsel for that institution for seventeen years, and counsel for the Baltimore Stock Exchange for a number of years.

Soon after taking up his work in Baltimore, Mr. Trundle became interested in politics. He was a staunch Democrat, but did not care for political offices, although he served on the Board of Fire Commissioners under Mayor Hayes, who reorganized the fire department by introducing civil service, the laws of which Mr. Trundle wrote. He was one of the most ardent advocates of civil service reform, and always argued that the State could best be served in its purposes by having men in a position who owed their office not to political friendship, but to intellectual superiority and mental equipment.

Mr. Trundle was a devoted churchman, senior warden and member of the vestry of St. Bartholomew's Episcopal Church, their treasurer for thirty-six years, and for twenty years superintendent of the Sunday school of the church. He was a member of the Sons of the American Revolution and St. Andrew's Society, his Scotch and patriotic ancestry entitling him to membership in both. He was a member of the Country Club and thoroughly enjoyed its social features; member of the United States Reform Association; Baltimore Bar Association; Maryland Bar Association, and Sons of the American Revolution.

In 1873 Mr. Trundle married Anne Maria Dryden, daughter of Joshua and Cordelia Elizabeth (Owings) Dryden, a descendant of Richard Owings in the following line Richard Owings married Rachel Beall, daughter of Ninian Beall; their son, Samuel Owings, married Urith Randall daughter of Thomas Randall and Hannah Beale; their son Thomas Owings, married Ruth Lawrence, daughter of Levin Lawrence, son of Benjamin and Rachel (Mariartee) Lawrence, and grandson of Benjamin and Elizabeth (Talbot) Lawrence, and Susanna Dorsey; their son, Dr. Thomas Beale Owings, married Cordelia Harris, daughter of Nathan Harris, and Rachel Lawrence, widow of Captain Philamon Dorsey; their daughter, Cordelia Elizabeth Owings, married Joshua R. Dryden, son of Major Joshua Dryden, of the War of 1812, and Anne Maria (Roberts) Dryden, descendant from Hugh Roberts, friend of William Penn; their daughter, Anne Maria Dryden, married Wilson Burns Trundle. Children of Wilson Burns and Anne Marie (Dryden) Trundle: Harris White, born 1873; Cordelia Elizabeth, born 1875, died 1892; Albert Burns, born 1877, died 1895; Eldon, born 1883, died 1896. Mrs. Trundle survives her husband, and continues her residence at No. 2414 Madison avenue, Baltimore.

CHARLES D. FISHER

PROBABLY the greatest compliment that can be paid a man is that he has made himself an honor to his Nation in the great commercial world, as well as a credit to the mercantile community in which he has lived, and this can be said in the truest sense of Charles D. Fisher, whose sudden and untimely death removed from Baltimore a man of fine natural endowments, spotless probity of character and useful influence.

David Fisher, grandfather of Charles D. Fisher, was born in 1754, and died October 15, 1815. His family had been residents of Carroll county, Maryland, for a number of generations. He married Elizabeth Galt, born in 1769, died April 16, 1849.

William Fisher, son of David and Elizabeth (Galt) Fisher, was born in 1808, and died in 1867. Shortly after his marriage he removed to Baltimore, where he was engaged as a merchant in the wholesale dry goods business for a number of years. Later he became the senior partner of the widely known banking house of William Fisher & Sons, which he had organized, and as his sons arrived at maturity, they were admitted to partnership. He married Jane Alricks Boggs, who was born January 15, 1814, and died July 26, 1862. Among their children were: 1. Charles D., see forward. 2. William Alexander, who served as Senator and Judge, and in a number of other responsible public offices. 3. J. Harmanus. 4. Parks.

Charles D. Fisher, son of William and Jane Alricks (Boggs) Fisher, was born at Westminster, Maryland, January 20, 1848, and was killed on Thanksgiving Day, November 29, 1906, in a wreck on the Southern railway, in which the president of that line, Samuel Spencer, was also killed. Mr.

Fisher was a very young lad when his parents removed to Baltimore, and he was educated under excellent masters in a well known private school. When he had attained the age of eighteen he entered the banking business of his father as clerk. Scarcely more than a child at the time of the outbreak of the Civil War, yet he volunteered his services and bore his share with honor in the ranks of the Confederate Army.

After the death of his father, Mr. Fisher embarked that portion of the fortune which he had inherited in the grain business in association with E. W. Barker, forming the firm of Barker & Fisher. While this undertaking did not increase the capital of Mr. Fisher very greatly, it gave him a thorough insight into the methods and details of the grain business, and laid the foundation of his future success in this line of commerce. The partnership was dissolved in 1873, and in July of the same year, he associated himself with General John Gill, who had been identified with the grain business for a period of seven years, forming the firm of Gill & Fisher, brokers and grain merchants. Both partners had had an unusual amount of experience and were men of sound judgment, and success attended their efforts from the inception of the business. They made a specialty of the exportation of grain in large quantities, purchasing their supplies of breadstuffs in the West, mainly for exportation purposes. Although the financial panic of 1873, the year in which they started, overthrew many old-fashioned firms, it speaks well for the capable management of this concern that it was able to weather the financial storm and come off with flying colors. Mr. Fisher derived great and personal pleasure from the management of his large interests. It was due to his foresight and representations to John W. Garrett, president of the Baltimore & Ohio railroad, that the first grain elevator in Baltimore, the first at the seaboard, was constructed, and the methods of handling grain which had hitherto been in vogue were completely revolutionized. Baltimore immediately pushed her way into the foreground as a grain market, and was enabled to compete with New York, and other elevators being erected in other cities, the exportation of grain was enormously increased, and the entire country reaped the benefit of the idea which had emanated from the brain of Mr. Fisher. Two years after the organization of this firm, the business world commenced to realize the value of the mind of Mr. Fisher as a leader in commercial and financial affairs and he was elected president of the Corn and Flour Exchange, was re-elected the following year, and served as president of the Board of Trade from 1885 to 1889, in all of these offices being the youngest man who had ever held these responsible positions. The firm had immense dealings with western concerns and was recognized as one of the most important in its line in the country. The partnership was in existence until General Gill withdrew and accepted the presidency of the Mercantile Trust Company, and Mr. Fisher withdrew from the active management of affairs in 1905, leaving the conduct of the business in the hands of Blanchard Randall and George W. Jackson.

Naturally Mr. Fisher desired success, and rejoiced in the benefits and opportunities which wealth brings, but he was too broadminded a man to rate it above its true value, and in all of his mammoth business ventures he found that enjoyment which comes in mastering a situation—the joy of doing what he had undertaken. Among the other financial enterprises with which Mr. Fisher was connected may be mentioned the following: He was one of the original directors of the Baltimore Chamber of Commerce Building Company, which erected the first Chamber of Commerce Building in 1880, which was completely destroyed in the disastrous fire of 1904. He was a valued member of the finance committee of the Mercantile Trust Company, and served for a long time as one of the directors of the Seaboard Air Line railroad. As president of the American District Telegraph Company he rendered excellent service. He never took any active part in political controversies or sought public office, but so universal was the esteem in which he was held by all classes, that a few years ago the nomination for mayor was offered him by the Citizens' Committee of One Hundred, at a time when nomination was practically equivalent to election, but the honor was declined by Mr. Fisher. While he took an intelligent interest in public policies and his advice was frequently sought, the responsibilities of business engrossed his entire attention, and he felt that he could not, with justice to either, serve two masters.

Mr. Fisher married, April 15, 1868, Nannie Poultney, daughter of the late Dr. Septimus Dorsey, a physician of note in Baltimore county; and the home presided over by this gracious and refined woman, in unison with her home-loving husband, was indeed a charming and most hospitable one.

Both Mr. and Mrs. Fisher were fond of travel and Mr. Fisher made annual hunting trips to the South and to Scotland. His social affiliations were with the Maryland, Merchants, Elkridge Hunt, Bachelors and Junior Cotillon clubs, in which his genial disposition and fine nature won for him innumerable friends. His plans were always formed with a due amount of deliberation and while he was a money-maker, his benefactions in the name of charity were generous in the extreme. As president of the Home for Incurables he gave not only of his money, but of his time and personal service— contributions not to be valued lightly. As vestryman of Christ

Protestant Episcopal Church, he was personally active in the good works connected with that institution. In the matter of recreation, he found his chief pleasures in such sports as brought him in close communion with nature, and he truly appreciated the joy of living. Hunting was one of his chief forms of outdoor sport, and resulted in the excellent health and robust constitution of which he was possessed.

Evenness and poise were among his characteristics, and he was a dependable man in any relation and in any emergency; a man ready to meet any obligation of life with the confidence and courage which come of conscious personal ability, proper conception of relative values, and an habitual regard for what is best in the exercise of human activities. All in all, he was a splendid type of the American citizen whose interests are broad and whose labors manifest a recognition of the responsibilities of wealth as well as ability in the successful control of commercial affairs.

EDWIN FRANKLIN ABELL

IT IS the custom in monarchical countries to bestow upon great rulers some name, independent of august titles, which is indicative of the people's estimate of their characters. Were such an ancient custom followed in Democratic America, Edwin Franklin Abell would bear among his fellow citizens of Baltimore the name bestowed upon Christ's favorite disciple—that of "Well Beloved."

Edwin Franklin Abell, from May 1, 1894, president of the A. S. Abell Company, publishers of "The Sun," and eldest of the twelve children of Arunah Shepherdson and Mary Fox-Campbell) Abell, was born in Baltimore, Maryland, May 15, 1840, and died in the same city, February 28, 1904, at his residence, northeast corner of Charles and Preston streets. He was the eldest of the twelve children of the founder of "The Sun," and his parents resided at the time of his birth on Lee street, at that time one of the prominent residential sections of the city. He was in the sixty-fourth year of his age, and with his decease passed the last of the sons of A. S. Abell.

Edwin F. Abell was educated in the public schools of Baltimore and of Harford county, near Jerusalem Mills, and also attended Dalrymple's Old University School of Maryland, on the south side of Mulberry street, at what is now the head of Cathedral street, and which has since been cut through to Saratoga street. His classmates in this school were many who afterwards became prominent men of Baltimore. When sixteen years of age Mr. Abell entered the counting room of "The Sun," and from that time continued almost uninterruptedly his business association with the paper. Although always identified with the publishing of "The Sun," he gave his attention more closely to the management of his father's extensive estate, and not until the death of his brother,

George W. Abell, May 11, 1894, did he assume the direct control of the paper. With duties and responsibilities almost doubled by reason of his brother's death, he became the directing head of the paper's policies in national questions and local affairs. With what success his efforts were rewarded by the entire State is best indicated by the respect and confidence with which "The Sun" is regarded in the thousands of homes it enters every day.

There has probably never lived a man occupying so commanding a position as did Mr. Abell, whose personal identity was so carefully kept from the public gaze as Mr. Abell studiously kept his own. On public questions he was absolutely fearless in matters he thought right, and having with calmness and judgment arrived at his own conclusions, he made his ideas felt and respected by reason of their force and common sense. With no personal wishes to be gratified in the political world, with no friends to reward nor enemies to punish politically, he directed the columns of "The Sun" for what he felt to be the best interests of the community, irrespective of party or men. His only wish was to serve the State as he honestly thought it should be served, by proper recommendations in legislation and in the conduct of public service. Apart from the public welfare but three interests engaged Edwin F. Abell's attention—the affairs of "The Sun," his father's estate, and his home circle. Although a member of the Athenaeum, the Maryland and Country clubs, he cared little for club or even social life beyond the environment of his hearthstone, preferring to entertain friends in his home, free from conventionality, and in accordance with the hospitality inspired by a warm and generous heart.

As he loved all that was beautiful in nature and his fellow-men, so Mr. Abell loved instinctively the inspiring creations of man's brains and hands. In art his taste was keenly discriminating and his judgment remarkably correct for one who had received no professional training along artistic lines. He studied works of art through eyes that instinctively eliminated the gross or rude, and turned only to that which was beautiful in character and where true artistic merit was revealed.

As a judge of real estate, Edwin F. Abell had few equals. His long experience in the management of his father's property gave him opportunity to exercise his excellent judgment in purchases and improvements. Foreseeing that Baltimore, like other cities, might be visited by a great conflagration, he erected "The Sun's" emergency building at the southwest corner of Calvert and Saratoga streets, which proved a timely refuge when the Great Fire of February 7th and 8th, 1904, swept the "Sun Iron Building" out of existence and destroyed the most valuable portion of the commercial section of Baltimore. Mr. Abell was confined to his residence by illness when the fire occurred, and the shock occasioned by the calamity, and especially the destruction of the "Sun Iron Building," is considered to have hastened his death. The ruin of so large a portion of the business properties of Baltimore was a deep grief to him, aside from his personal losses, as many of the improvements that other real estate owners had made in years gone by were the result of his suggestion and practical advice.

Edwin F. Abell's death, occurring, as it did, as an almost immediate consequence of the conflagration of 1904, was regarded by his fellow-citizens as one of the first and most lamentable results of that tragic event. The general Assembly of Maryland ordered resolutions to be spread on its journal to the effect that Mr. Abell, through his management of "The Sun," had labored effectively for the uplift of the State, while the House of Delegates declared that in losing Mr. Edwin

F. Abell the State had lost one of its foremost citizens. Both branches of the City Council passed resolutions of respect and honor and deplored his death as a distinct loss to the city, and doubly a loss at a time when his clear judgment, ripe experience and distinguished patriotism were peculiarly needed for the restoration of Baltimore.

Edwin Franklin Abell was twice married; (first) to Margaret Curley, a daughter of the late Henry R. Curley, and (second) to Elizabeth M. Laurenson, daughter of the late Francis B. Laurenson. His children by his first marriage were two sons: Arunah S. Abell, and W. W. Abell; and one daughter, Mary Abell. Arunah S. Abell and W. W. Abell were associated with their father in the conduct of "The Sun" for a number of years, and, upon the death of Edwin F. Abell, his second son, W. W. Abell, was elected president of the A. S. Abell Company, and manager of the paper. The Sunday edition of "The Sun" was inaugurated under Mr. Edwin F. Abell's administration, the first edition being issued October 6, 1901.

Mr. Abell's death was announced in all the Baltimore churches Sunday morning, February 28th, and his funeral took place from the Cathedral, Wednesday, March 2nd, and was attended by the chief dignitaries of State and city. The great building was thronged to its fullest capacity with a multitude of sorrowing people that included rich and poor, high and low. Cardinal James Gibbons delivered an impressive memorial address, and a pontifical high mass of requiem was celebrated by Bishop A. A. Curtis. The interment was made at Bonnie Brae Cemetery, and the honorary pallbearers were chosen from those who had been the longest in the service of "The Sun," and from the heads of the departments of the paper.

Charles S. Lane

CHARLES SETH LANE

WITH truth it may be written of Charles Seth Lane that he was an important factor in the business life of his city and State, that his ability as a financier was of the highest order, statements proven, if proof were necessary, by the fact that he was a vice-president of the American Bankers' Association, prominent in the Maryland Bankers' Association, and president of Trust Company, Water Company and Insurance Company in his own city of Hagerstown. To this more is to be added of activity in the business world, of public service and general usefulness, but his highest eulogy was pronounced by an editorial friend: "He stood by his friends and was kind to every one." Loyalty and kindness were his dominant traits, and in accumulating for himself he gave generous aid and opportunity to others. Not only was his advice and counsel freely sought and as freely given in shaping the course of enterprises and concerns of great moment to his city, but individuals leaned on him and in his strength they relied, their trust never being misplaced. Many men of fine judgment and great business foresight were equally strong in handling their own affairs, but without the human sympathy and love of fellow-man which marked Mr. Lane as a truly great man who "in honor preferreth not himself."

Members of the class of 1872, Princeton University, recall the three Lane brothers whose college days were a period of close brotherly intercourse, mutual help and incentive, and of these Charles Seth Lane was the eldest, Colonel William P. Lane and John Clarence Lane the others of the three Lane brothers who made class history at Princeton. They were sons of John C. and Elizabeth (Horine) Lane, of Washington county, Maryland.

Charles Seth Lane was born in Frederick county, Maryland, October 27, 1848, and died in Hagerstown, Maryland, November 19, 1916. Left a widow in 1855, Mrs. Lane removed with her sons to Washington county, Maryland, locating in Boonsboro, and there Charles S. began his education in a private school. Later he attended St. Timothy's School at Catonsville, Maryland, then with his brothers, John Clarence and William P., became students at Edgehill Academy, Princeton, New Jersey, a school which prepared young men for the University. All entered Princeton, class of 1872, and all graduated A. B. John Clarence was the first of the brothers to finish his earthly course, Charles Seth next, the last brother, Colonel William P. Lane, yet a resident of Hagerstown, Maryland.

Charles S. Lane, after college years were over, became a clerk in the banking house of Johnston Brothers & Company, of Baltimore, but in the autumn of 1874 transferred his service to the then youthful banking firm, Hoffman, Eavey & Company, of Hagerstown. His banking genius must have deeply impressed the house, for not long afterward he was admitted a member. Upon the death of Mr. Hoffman, the house reorganized as Eavey, Lane & Company, and upon Mr. Eavey's death in December, 1903, Mr. Lane succeeded him as a senior member. The life of this highly successful private banking house terminated on May 31, 1908, and upon its broad, sound and secure foundation arose the Maryland Surety and Trust Company, Charles Seth Lane, president from its organization until his death. Sound in judgment, broad of vision, strong in position and high ability, and in many particulars the most important man of his city, he won public trust and confidence to a most surprising degree, as the tendency of the general public is to view a banker with caution at least and with a certain amount of distrust. But Mr. Lane in his intercourse with the public broke down all barriers, and in a generous, helpful spirit co-operated, encouraged and advised men to their financial betterment. He was a citizen and a neighbor, entirely independent and self-reliant, acting for the good of all and for that which he believed best for all regardless of who or what might oppose.

He was long interested in public utilities, having been one of the incorporators of the Hagerstown Street Railway Company, serving as director and vice-president until the merger as the Hagerstown & Frederick Railway Company. Prior to 1911 he had been a director and vice-president of the Washington County Water Company, succeeding Edward W. Mealey as president of that corporation, May 1, 1911. He was also president of the Washington County Mutual Insurance Company, and otherwise interested in the business enterprises of Hagerstown and Washington county. He was elected vice-president of the American Bankers' Association in 1896, was an active influential member of the Maryland Bankers' Association, served on many of its important commissions, and in Maryland financial circles rated one of the ablest bankers of Western Maryland. He was a Democrat in politics, served a term as street commissioner, that being his sole public office, public life having no attraction for him. He was one of the original members of the Conococheague Club, and interested in everything which interested his neighbors, friends or fellow-citizens.

Mr. Lane married Hetty McGill, daughter of Rev. Alexander H. McGill, D.D., LL.D., of Princeton Theological Seminary, sister of Alexander T. (2) McGill, Chancellor of the State of New Jersey until his death, and sister of Dr. John Dale McGill, Surgeon General of the State of New Jersey at the time of his death. Mrs. Hetty (McGill) Lane survives her husband, a resident of Hagerstown. The three sons of Charles S. and Hettty Lane are: Alexander M., Charles Seth, Jr., and John McGill; the three Lane brothers were graduates of Princeton University.

JOHN CLARENCE LANE

ASSOCIATED with the business life of Hagerstown in a most attractive manner, a lawyer of great ability, a man of the highest and best type, J. Clarence Lane was a man his fellow-men delighted to honor. He was an exemplar of the highest ethics of his profession, a profound student, a traveled, cultured gentleman, and both in private and public life all that was admirable. As a Democrat he was consistent in measures and independent in action, his best years of public party action being as the energetic lieutenant of William T. Hamilton, they devoting their ability and strength to the causes then prevailing for the betterment of the party and State. Single-hearted and true in his attitude toward all public questions, without devious interpretation of men or measures, he was honestly warm-hearted in the support of a cause he espoused and its strong advocate. Highly regarded professionally and as a business man he was not less popular socially, of jovial disposition and pleasing personality, he was welcome in every circle and many warm friends mourn their fallen comrade.

J. Clarence Lane, second son of John C. and Elizabeth (Horine) Lane, was born near Middletown, Frederick county, Maryland, March 13, 1850, and died in Hagerstown May 6, 1914. He was but five years old when his father died and his mother removed to Boonsboro. Here he grew up and received his early education in the public and private schools. Later he studied at the Cumberland Valley Institute, Mechanicsburg, Pennsylvania, and at the Princeton University, where he graduated with his two brothers, class of 1872. He at once began the study of law in the office of his brother-in-law, Henry H. Keedy, of Hagerstown, later entered the law department of the University of Maryland and was graduated LL.B. in the spring of 1874. After graduation he was admitted to the bar of Washington county, located in Hagerstown, and henceforth until his death was engaged in the practice of his profession, member of the law firm of Lane & Keedy. The senior partner, who was also his preceptor and brother-in-law, died, and his place in the firm was taken by his son, also Henry H. Keedy, the firm name continuing as before, uncle and nephew practicing together until death dissolved the bond.

Mr. Lane was an attorney for and a director of the Hagerstown Street Railway Company and its allied interests; attorney for the Baltimore and Ohio Railway Company from 1884 until his death; director of the Washington County National Bank of Williamsport; director of the Hagerstown Heat and Lighting Company; attorney for Eavey, Lane and Company, a private banking house of which his brother, Charles Seth Lane, was senior partner; attorney for the Cumberland Valley Railroad Company; the Moller Organ Company and for the Hagerstown Spoke and Bending Company.

In politics Mr. Lane was an independent Democrat, and was honored by his party, although during his later years he withdrew from active participation in public affairs, but he was long a conspicuous figure in Washington county politics and a strong advocate of all forward movements. In 1884 he was elected State Senator, and during his term in committee and on the floor was eloquent and energetic in forwarding routine work and eloquent in his advocacy or opposition to the measures presented to the Senate by the regular organization. He was a member of the Board of Visitors to Maryland Asylum and Training School for Feeble Minded Children, an institution incorporated by the Legislature in 1888. As a member of the Conococheague Club he was active and popular, his social nature there unfolding and expanding. He was a member of and from 1875 a vestryman of St. John's Protestant Episcopal Church. Mr. Lane never married.

THOMAS EMERSON BOND, M.D.

THE entire history of the Bond family is unusually interesting, including, as it does, the annals of numerous men famous in the various walks of life. The family is of Norman origin, and may easily be traced to John le Bonnd, of Hatch Beauchamp, Somersetshire, England, who was assessed as an inhabitant of that parish as early as 1327, during the reign of Edward III, and again in 1332 as John Bonde. His grandson, Robert Bond, of Hatch Beauchamp, married Mary, daughter of Sir John Hody, Knight, Chief Justice of England in 1440, and sister of Sir William Hody, Knight, Chief Baron of the Exchequer. A descendant, Roger Bond, was a priest, rector of Kingston Russell, and died in 1559. Giles Bond, another descendant, baptized in 1571, was captain of the ship "Dragon," of Weymouth, and his son, John Bond, of London, was appointed captain-general to command an expedition for the "discovery" and occupation of Madagascar during the reign of Charles I, and he was also in the East Indies. A cousin of Captain-General John Bond, "fair Alice" Bond, who was baptized in 1617, married, in 1636, John Lisle, one of the judges of Charles I. He was a Lord Commissioner of the Great Seal of Oliver Cromwell, a member of the House of Lords, and was assassinated at Lausanne, Switzerland, 1664, and his wife, Alice (Bond) Lisle, after being tried and condemned for high treason by Lord Jeffreys, was beheaded at Winchester in 1685. Dennis Bond, born in 1588, was a member of Parliament in 1648, was named one of the commission to try Charles I, but appears not to have taken any part in that proceeding.

(I) Peter Bond, the American progenitor of this family, came to America and for a time was in Virginia, from whence he came to Maryland in 1660. He received large grants of land on both sides of the Patapsco River about the mouth of Gwynn's Falls, which became known as Bond's Pleasant Hills, and now included within the limits of Baltimore. He also patented Harris' Trust, and purchased the adjacent tract called Prosperity, in 1691, this lying on both sides of the Bush River. It is said that two brothers came with Peter Bond to America, but nothing further is known of them, and it may be only tradition. He was twice married, and died in 1705. He left a number of children, among them being: Peter and Thomas, of whom further; William and John.

(II) Peter, son of Peter Bond, succeeded to all the estate of his father except Prosperity and Harris' Trust, which were divided by will among his three younger brothers, Thomas, William and John. He was a member of the General Assembly of Maryland in 1716-17, and died in 1718.

(II) Thomas, son of Peter Bond and his first wife, died in 1755. He established himself in what was afterward Harford county, and patented in 1703 Knave's Misfortune, adjacent to the tracts mentioned above, where he built a substantial brick dwelling in which he lived and which was in excellent preservation within recent years. In 1714 he received from Lord Baltimore the grants of Bond's Forest, 3,100 acres, lying between Bynam's Run and Little Falls of the Gunpowder; and in 1731 a manor of 5,000 acres lying in Baltimore county, on the west side of the Susquehanna River, called Bond's Manor, which was near York, Pennsylvania, on the debatable land between Maryland and that State. He sold a portion of this land in 1739 to Captain Thomas Cresap, who thus became involved in the boundary dispute. Thomas Bond in 1735 patented Poplar Neck, which comprised 1,000 acres on Bush River, and in 1749 made a deed to his sons, Thomas and John, as trustees, conveying a lot, part of the tract known as Bond's Forest, to be laid out

conveniently near the main road, including a house intended
for a meeting house for "the people called Quakers" to wor-
ship God, and also a schoolhouse already built. The records
of Gunpowder Meeting show acceptance of this deed in 1753,
and this was the commencement of the Little Falls Meeting
at Fallston. In 1710 Thomas Bond was a member of the celebrated grand jury which protested against the removal of the
county seat from Forks of Gunpowder to Joppa, denouncing
it as "a palpable, notorious grievance to this county. The
land records of Baltimore contain many conveyances signed
by Thomas Bond, and also many signed by his wife. He
married, in 1700, Anne Robertson (or Richardson), of Anne
Arundel county, Maryland.

(III) John, son of Thomas and Anne (Robertson or
Richardson) Bond, was born in 1712. He resided in winter
on Fell's Point, and was known as "John Bond, Gentleman,"
of Baltimore Town. As a record of his residence there we
have Aliceana and Bond streets. He was a large land owner
and merchant, shipping tobacco from Joppa and Baltimore to
England, until he became involved in financial difficulties connected with the Bush River Company, which he and his
father-in-law had organized, and for which the first iron fur-
nace in the colonies had been erected. He was among those
who purchased in 1746 lots in Joppa, which was the county
seat from 1708 until 1768. Bills of lading, etc., from the
"Port of Joppa" are still to be found among his papers. He
was one of the foremost men of his time, served as justice
of the peace, coroner, judge of the Orphans' Court, 1769-73,
and was dealt with by Gunpowder Meeting for taking the
oath of office "contrary to the testimony," finally being read
out of meeting for his contumacy. The family of Bonds
seem to have been found "unruly members" by the Quakers,
for from 1759 until 1776 the sons and daughters, including

the two trustees of the meeting house, were dealt with twelve times for serious offenses, such as "lent a man a gun," "took oath as magistrate," "purchased a negro," "married out of meeting," etc. It was probably owing to his earlier affiliation with meeting, although he had been read out of it, that John Bond declined to serve Harford county as a member of the "Committee on Correspondence" to which he had been called. His brother Jacob was prominent as a member of Revolutionary committees and was a member of the legislature from Harford county in 1776. A nephew, Thomas Bond, was one of the signers of the Maryland Declaration. John Bond married, 1732, Alice Anna Webster, and among their descendants we find such names as Fell, Kell, Lee, Wilson, Bradford, Johnson, Gibbs, Walsh, Carrington and Augustus W. Bradford, Governor of Maryland.

(IV) Thomas, son of John and Alice Anna (Webster) Bond, served as a justice of the peace and as a judge of the Orphans' Court. He was one of the earliest adherents of the Methodist denomination, and his house became the rallying place of the society. He married (first) 1771, Rebecca, daughter of Captain Tobias Stansbury, (second) Sarah Chew.

(V) Dr. Thomas Emerson Bond, second son of Thomas Bond, studied medicine at the University of Pennsylvania, where his kinsmen, Dr. Thomas Bond and Dr. Phineas Bond, were members of the faculty. He was one of the founders of the Medical School of the University of Maryland, and it is said that when the bill for its incorporation was presented to the legislature one of the members observed that but one of the names signed was followed by the letters "M.D." He expressed surprise that not more of the signers had been honored with a medical degree, and it was explained to him that this degree had been conferred by an English university, and that American colleges could not legally confer it. The legislature then formulated a resolution to the effect that American physicians were entitled to degrees with as much right as English ones, and decided that these letters be inserted after each name, the degree being conferred by statute. Dr. Bond was engaged in the practice of medicine in Baltimore for many years after his marriage, his residence being in Lombard street, near Sharpe street, at that time one of the most desirable residential districts of the city, but now given over to whole-sale warehouses, and he retained the Harford homestead as a summer residence. He retired from medical practice in 1844, and accepted the office of editor for "The Christian Advocate," the official organ of the Methodist Episcopal church. This necessitated his removal to New York City, where he resided until his death in 1856.

Dr. Bond married Christiana, daughter of Dr. Solomon and Jane (McCulloch) Birckhead, the latter a brother of James McCulloch, collector of the Port of Baltimore. Dr. Solomon Birckhead, who was one of the most eminent physicians of his day in Baltimore, was the son of Colonel Christopher Birckhead, of Talbot county, Maryland.

ANDREW CROSS TRIPPE

ANDREW CROSS TRIPPE, noted as a lawyer, distinguished as a statesman, and deservedly honored as a brave soldier, amply displayed his possession of the traits which came to him by right of direct inheritance, and which rendered many of his ancestors distinguished in the various walks of life. The Trippe family is an old one in England, dating back to the time of William the Conqueror, and the family seat was in Kent county. The name is to be found on record in the Domesday Booke in the title of lands. In 1234 Nicholas Tryppe gave Lamplands, County Kent, to Elham Church. The first record we have of the family in Maryland is in 1663. Thomas Trippe, brother of the Lieutenant Colonel Henry Trippe mentioned below, is mentioned by James, Duke of York, afterwards James II., in his autobiography (Nairn papers), as aiding him to escape from St. James' Palace after the beheading of Charles I.

(I) Lieutenant Colonel Henry Trippe, the immigrant ancestor, was born in Canterbury, England, 1632, and died in Dorchester county, Maryland, March, 1698. He had fought in Flanders under the Prince of Orange, afterwards William III of England, and came to America in 1663, bringing with him to the Province three of his troopers, and took up land in Dorchester county, where he attained a prominent position in the management of affairs. He was a representative in the Maryland Assembly, 1671-75, 1681-82, 1692-93; one of the Committee of Twenty for regulating affairs in Maryland, 1690; justice and county commissioner, 1669-81, 1685-94; captain of foot of Dorchester county, 1676; major of horse, 1689. He married (first), 1665, Frances, widow of Michael Brooke, of St. Leonard's Creek, Calvert county, Maryland; married (second) Elizabeth ———, who died in April, 1698, by whom he had five children.

(II) William, son of Lieutenant Colonel Henry Trippe, was born in Dorchester county, Maryland, and died April 24, 1770. He married Jean Tate, and had children.

(III) Edward, son of William and Jean (Tate) Trippe, was born in Dorchester county, Maryland. He married Sarah, daughter of Edward Noel, of Castle Haven, Dorchester county, and widow of Joseph Byus.

(IV) James, son of Edward and Sarah (Noel) (Byus) Trippe, died in Cambridge, Maryland, September, 1812. He married (first) Elizabeth Purnell, who died without leaving children; married (second) Mary Purnell, of Worcester county, Maryland, who died in Cambridge, Maryland, in September, 1812. Child: Joseph Everitt, see forward.

(V) Joseph Everitt, son of James and Mary (Purnell) Trippe, was born at Cambridge, Maryland, July 18, 1805, and died at Baltimore, December 28, 1882. He married May 30, 1837, Sarah Patterson Cross, born November 11, 1813, died October 8, 1853. Children: 1. Andrew Cross, see forward. 2. Mary Purnell, married William Belt, and died September 11, 1904, without leaving children. 3. Rachel Elizabeth, unmarried. 4. Joseph Everitt, born May 6, 1845; married Frances, daughter of Daniel Holliday.

John Cross, immigrant ancestor, and grandfather of Mrs. Sarah P. Trippe, was born in County Antrim, Ireland, 1730, and died in Baltimore, Maryland, September 29, 1807. He settled in Cecil county, Maryland, 1772. He married Jane Young, also an immigrant, born in County Monaghan, Ireland, 1743, died in Baltimore, Maryland, March 6, 1826. Andrew, son of John and Jane (Young) Cross, and father of Mrs. Trippe, was born in Cecil county, Maryland, October 4, 1772, and died in Baltimore, September 23, 1815. He married Rachel, born December 15, 1780, died March 12, 1843, daughter of Thomas and Esther (Patterson) Wallace

(VI) Andrew Cross, son of Joseph Everitt and Sarah Patterson (Cross) Trippe, was born in Baltimore, Maryland, November 29, 1839. He was educated at private schools, and at Newton University, Baltimore, later becoming a student at Lafayette College, Easton, Pennsylvania, from which he was graduated in 1857 with the degree of Bachelor of Arts, and the same institution conferred upon him the degree of Master of Arts in 1860. Having studied law under J. Mason Campbell, of Baltimore, son-in-law of Chief Justice Taney, for three years, he was admitted to the bar at the age of twenty-one years, in 1861.

Very shortly afterward he went to Virginia, there joining the famous Maryland company of Captain William H. Murray, Confederate States Army. His military record from the very outset was an honorable, gallant and distinguished one. He was advanced to the rank of lieutenant of artillery and ordnance officer in May, 1863, but entered into the battle of Gettysburg with his old company. On the third day of this struggle, at Culp's Hill, he was severely wounded in the right shoulder, and, with Colonel Herbert, Major William W. Goldsborough and Lieutenant Barber, carried to a vacant house nearby, where they were left for dead. When he returned to Richmond he found that all of his clothes and his equipment had been given away, as he was reported among the dead. He was also an active participant in the second battle of Winchester, and at Fredericksburg, being permanently disabled by the severe wound received at Gettysburg, which was caused by a bursting shell, which tore away a part of his right shoulder, from which he took with his own hands a piece of shell three inches in length. He returned to Baltimore, where he resumed the law practice in which he had been engaged before the commencement of the Civil War. He served as colonel and aide-de-camp to Gov-

ernor Robert M. McLane, of Maryland, 1804; colonel and
aide-de-camp to Governor Henry Lloyd of Maryland, 1885-
88; major-general commanding Maryland Division of United
Confederate Veterans, 1898. His political affiliations were
with the Democratic party, but he entertained independent
opinions.

In addition to his private legal practice he was counsel
for a number of organizations, among which may be mentioned the following, in which he also held official position:
Director of the Hospital for Consumptives and the Lynch-
burg Orphanage; member of advisory board of the Young
Women's Christian Association; and member of the executive
committee of the Merchants' and Manufacturers' Association and was its legal counsel. He was a member of the Greek
letter fraternity Delta Kappa Epsilon; past supreme regent
of the Royal Arcanum; member of University and Baltimore
clubs, Maryland Historical Society, Society of Colonial
Wars, United Confederate Veterans, Baltimore Bar Association, and Maryland Bar Association.

Mr. Trippe married, at Baltimore, November 7, 1872,
Caroline Augusta, daughter of James and Mary Dawes (Grafton) McConky. Children: 1. James McConky, born March
4, 1874; judge and president of the Appeal Tax Court; married, December 4, 1906, Mary Hanson Kirby, and has one
daughter, Mary Ringgold. 2. Grafton Wallace, born October
13, 1875, died in infancy. 3. Sarah Patterson, born July 17,
1877; died September 10, 1898. 4. Andrew Noel, born
November 19, 1878; is engaged in mercantile business.

Mr. Trippe was thoroughly conversant with every detail
of his profession, and threw into the conduct of the cases he
undertook the same energy and vital force which distinguished
him so signally on the field of battle, when he and his com-
panions struggled against adverse circumstances and condi-

tions.   A high sense of honor and an innate nobility were among his most noticeable characteristics.   He occupied an enviable position among his fellow-citizens, who willingly accorded to him a place in their first ranks, not alone for his many professional and business qualities, but for every trait that marks the true Christian gentleman and the man of honor. His heart was ever in sympathy with the sorrows of the unfortunate, and his hand ever ready to contribute to the alleviation of distress.   But, perhaps, the richest traits of his character were his strong domestic sentiments and habits, which impelled him to seek his highest happiness in the family circle. He was the last surviving member of the Baltimore bar to be admitted before the Civil War.   He died at Baltimore, Maryland, July 17, 1918.

THOMAS GORDON HAYES

IN TRACING the life history of Thomas Gordon Hayes there are many titles found to which he held just claim; student, lawyer, Assemblyman, State Senator, Mayor, but nowhere is he referred to as a politician; for, although he was the storm centre of many a political battle, it was the very fact that he was not a politician which caused those battles. He had political ambitions, it is true, and it is still truer that the people wanted him, but he was of that "old school" citizen and official, believing with Henry Clay that it was better to be right than to be President, and with Grover Cleveland that a public office was a public trust. Such sentiments and such independence did not please the "powers that rule," and after an experience in attempting to usurp his power as Mayor, they let him severely alone, a more pliable man suiting their purpose better. But his term as Mayor of Baltimore is one of the bright spots in the city's history, and the fact that he was not renominated and allowed to carry his plans through to completion was Baltimore's loss and no discredit to Mayor Hayes.

Contemporaries who have survived him, and are themselves men of eminence and high in public life, have freely expressed themselves and branded Mr. Hayes as one of the strongest men the State of Maryland has produced and the best Mayor Baltimore ever had. "A great lawyer, public spirited and patriotic, a factor for good, a man of sterling honor, gifted with intellectual powers and high ideals, splendidly able, a learned and successful lawyer." To a man possessing such a character and reputation, and his party naturally dominant in city and State, there was every temptation to so trim his sails that he might follow a course pleasing to party rulers, State and local, but as the first Mayor of Baltimore,

Thomas G. Hays

under the new charter, which was practically his own child, he placed the city's interest above his own and cast all consideration of personal preferment aside.

In the course he pursued as Mayor he knowingly faced the alienation of friends and the desertion of political allies, but he took the "bit in his teeth," grimly carried out his own ideas of his duty to the taxpayers, and walked out of the City Hall at the end of his term with but a remnant of the throng who acclaimed him at his inauguration.

But the fact that he had signed his own political "death warrant" brought him no regrets. Stubbornly and inflexibly honest, his sufficient reward was the knowledge of duty well performed, and the certain knowledge that the future welfare of his city would result and that history would write his administration as wise, patriotic and just. The tangible results of that administration are many and enduring, while its influence is still felt in the City Hall, as standards were set that enlightened public opinion has indicated to those who have followed him it would be wise to maintain.

Brusque, unyielding and combatative, full of prejudices, brainy and indomitably courageous, with none of the arts and artifices of the man who seeks popularity, he was cordially hated by the professional politician, but as the fine "old school" lawyer, he bore the good will of all. Like all really big lawyers, Mr. Hayes made no pretentious appearance either in his office or in the trial of cases in court. His offices were modest rooms on the second floor of No. 202 North Calvert street, and his nearest approach to an office assistant was a boy to run errands and remain in the office when he was out. He would not tolerate either typewriter or telephone in office or home, and while clients might complain of difficulty in reading his manuscript or extol the virtues of the telephone, he would not employ the aid of

modern conveniences, but pursued the even tenor of his way.
He was very methodical. On his office door was painted
"office hours from 10 A. M. until 1 P. M.," and that sign
meant what it said. He always took an early morning ride
in his automobile, took regularly an afternoon nap, and before
the advent of the automobile, the bicycle was his favorite
recreation, a daily ride following the afternoon nap. Prior
to either, horseback riding was his favorite exercise. He
loved his profession deeply, was eminent in its practice, and
was counsel in some of the most remarkable cases in the legal
annals of his State.

When the Governor of Maryland made his memorable
attack upon the Baltimore police board, he was counsel for
the board. As counsel for the defense, he secured the acquittal of the four alleged dynamite conspirators, defended ex-
Mayor Hooper, when as a member of the school board he
was held to answer charges made by the president of the
school board, and the record might be indefinitely continued,
as the list of celebrated cases is a very long one. He seldom
lost a case, and was held in veneration by the legal profession. Frequently he would carry a Bible into the court
room, and from its pages read to the jurymen a portion of
scripture he deemed appropriate. He was a son of the Rev.
Thomas C. and Julia (Gordon) Hayes, of Northumberland
county, Virginia.

Thomas Gordon Hayes was born in Anne Arundel
county, Maryland, January 5, 1844, died at Mountain Lake
Park, while on his summer vacation, August 27, 1915. He
was trained under the influences of a Christian home by
devout, cultured Christian parents, an influence reflected
throughout his entire life. After preparation in private
schools, he entered Virginia Military Institute, Lexington,
Virginia, leaving to enter the Conferedate Army. After the

war ended, he returned to the Institute and was graduated in the class of 1867. After graduation he was appointed assistant professor of mathematics and continued at the institute in that capacity until offered the chair of natural science at Kentucky Military Institute, when he resigned. He filled that chair at Kentucky Military Institute, located near Frankfort, for four years, during which period he studied law under Attorney General Rodman, and was admitted to the Kentucky bar.

In 1872 Mr. Hayes located in Baltimore, the scene of his legal and political activities for more than forty years. He was then twenty-eight years of age, thoroughly furnished intellectually, and fully equipped for the profession he would follow. He soon demonstrated his ability and in course of time gathered around him a strong, influential clientele. He was an ardent Democrat, and soon made his influence felt in city affairs, receiving his first official recognition in 1880, when elected to the Maryland House of Delegates. In 1886 he was appointed by President Cleveland, United States district attorney for the Baltimore district, and in 1893-94 was city solicitor under Mayor Latrobe. These purely legal offices added greatly to his professional reputation, and when Baltimore was found in need of a new city charter, Mr. Hayes was one of the men selected to draft it. He is often called the "father" of the new charter, and, in fact, many of the vital features of that document were prepared by him. He knew the charter word by word, and when called to the mayor's chair as the first executive under the new law, he was continually finding in it authority for all the things he wanted to do for the city, no one else seeming to be aware of the clauses he could refer to by chapter and page.

After retiring from the executive chair, Mayor Hayes resumed the practice of law, appearing in several notable cases. As a criminal lawyer he was without a peer, and in general practice was very successful, ranking with the best in legal learning. Gifted with intellectual powers of a high order, this great lawyer did not use them basely, but splendid in his upright Christian manhood, used them to promote a higher ideal of citizenship, a more enlightened public spirit, a higher standard of civic righteousness. His own honor as a lawyer and as a citizen he held inviolate, and from his entrance to the city in 1872 until his death was a factor for good in city and state affairs. His political career, so far as the public is concerned, began in 1880 with his election to the House of Delegates, followed by his choice as State Senator in 1884, 1886, 1892 and 1894. In the House he was chairman of the committee on militia and chairman of the special committee, insolvent laws. In this latter capacity, in connection with Judge William A. Fisher, chairman of a Senate committee of like importance, he drafted and pressed to final passage the present insolvent laws of the State. His Senate term was interrupted by his appointment by President Cleveland as United States District Attorney, June 1, 1886, but he was again State Senator in 1892 and the father of the "Hayes" bill for the reassessment of Maryland property, which he vigorously pressed. That bill passed both houses of the Legislature, but was vetoed by Governor Brown. His term expired in 1895 and so valuable had been his public service that he was a prominent candidate for Governor in that year, an office which he had a laudable ambition to fill. He had the promised support of United States Senator Arthur P. Gorman and a banner was prominently displayed across Baltimore street declaring his candidacy. But he was defeated by the edict sent forth by an organization leader who was not in sympathy with the attitude Senator Hayes had taken in the Senate nor with his spirit of independence. The fiat went

GENEALOGICAL AND MEMORIAL

forth that John E. Hurst should be nominated and he was, only to be defeated at the polls by Lloyd Lowndes. He served as city solicitor under Mayors Latrobe and Hooper, then was out of public office until 1899.

In that year the party leaders saw a great light. They had beaten Senator Hayes for Governor in 1895 and had seen their nominees go down in defeat in that year and in 1897. While ex-Governor Brown was opposed to Mr. Hayes on account of the differences which had arisen between them over the "Hayes" reassessment bill which Governor Brown had vetoed, he withdrew his opposition when the wisdom of nominating a Democrat for Mayor of Baltimore who was not in sympathy with the State machine was shown him. He also had the support of Senator Gorman and the city leader, not for the love they bore him, but that they might return to power in the city through his popularity with the voters.

He was elected Mayor and during his three years as chief executive of the city, 1899-1903, there was never any doubt as to who was Mayor. The new charter of which he was the acknowledged father was adopted, and with vim and enthusiasm Mayor Hayes began reforming the city government under its provisions. Old departments, rusty with disuse and misuse were abolished; other departments were merged, and new ones established. Mayor Hayes took the leadership rightfully attached to the office he held, worked early and late, met the many difficulties, solved the unexpected problems, found a way around the many troubles that beset him and in time, to the surprise of those who opposed, had the new governmental machinery smoothly running and doing splendid service. One of the most apparent features of this reorganization was the uplifting of the standard of efficiency in the public schools. J. H. Van Sickle was brought from the West, his appointment resulting in changes most beneficial.

But the crowning achievement of Mayor Hayes' administration was the sale of the Western Maryland Railway, a
property long a burden on the taxpayers of Baltimore, a burden steadily increasing year after year with no prospect of
relief. The Mayor, with characteristic energy and directness,
set about to effect a sale, but not until speculative offers had
been swept away did a bona fide bid appear. Then an ordi-
nance authorizing the sale of the road was introduced by
Harry F. Linderman in the second branch of the City Council
and passed. And finally, after a period of widest discussion,
public meetings and public excitement, a sale was effected
giving Baltimore a net profit of nearly four and one-half
million dollars out of its dealings with the Western Maryland
Various uses for this amount were suggested, but Mayor
Hayes determined it should be dedicated to a system of sani
tary sewers. He had a committee of the city's engineers make
an exhaustive survey and estimate of cost for a complete sewerage system for the city, but before action could be taken his
term expired. At that time Mayor Hayes issued a statement
stating he wished a second term in order that he might carry his
policies through to successful conclusion. He was opposed
by I. Freeman Raisin, the leader of the regular city Demo
cratic organization, who at the primary election elected his
delegates, although Mayor Hayes was supported by the Cres
cent Club, led by influential Democrats. This was the ven
geance promised the Mayor by the organization for his loyal
to the people's interest and his refusal to take orders from the
"machine" in his government of the city.

After his retirement from office and the laying aside of
public duty, Mr. Hayes did not again appear in public affairs
although in 1911 he was urged for nomination for attorney
general, and in 1914 flattering offers of support were made
him for United States Senator, but he declined. His last year

were spent in law practice and in greater activity in religious work. In 1909 he became leader of a Bible class, connected with the Central Methodist Episcopal Church, which class became very dear to his heart. The original class of forty men grew to over a hundred, and to its conduct Mr. Hayes devoted himself with all his characteristic force. Every Saturday he published in the Baltimore "Sun" an exposition of the lesson to be taught the next day, these attracting widespread interest as evidenced by the many complimentary letters he received from Bible teachers and students. He possessed a fine library of legal and theological books at his home, No. 2901 St. Paul street, where he resided with his sister, Miss Julia Hayes, the only relative to survive him.

ARUNAH SHEPHERDSON ABELL

ARUNAH SHEPHERDSON ABELL, the second to bear this honored name, was born at Pikesville, Baltimore county, Maryland, eldest son of Edwin Franklin and Margaret (Curley) Abell. From his earliest youth he was of a robust constitution, and exceedingly fond of athletic sports and country life in general. He enjoyed the advantages of an excellent education, being first a student at St. Mary's College at Emmitsburg, Maryland, and then at Georgetown University, Washington, D. C.

Mental activity has always been a distinguishing trait of the members of the Abell family, and Mr. Abell was no exception to the rule. He immediately sought and found occupation in the business department of "The Baltimore Sun," and when this was incorporated as the A. S. Abell Company, he was elected a director, holding the offices of secretary and treasurer, in both of which positions his executive ability is still beneficially felt.

Mr. Abell married, June 22, 1892, Anna T. Schley, and had seven children. He was devoted to his home and family, finding there the greatest pleasures of his life, and the greater part of the year was spent in the country in the vicinity of his city home, as he wished his children to have the benefit of the country life he so richly enjoyed in his own youth. While Mr. Abell took no active part in the political affairs of his country, he was by no means indifferent to the outcome of affairs, and gave his staunch support to the principles of the Democratic party. His religious affiliations were with the Roman Catholic church, of which he was a member. Mr. Abell evinced a decided love of nature and natural objects, but the beauties of art also appealed to him in a very strong manner, as is amply testified by the collection of pictures and other works of art which was to be found in his home. Of a high standard of intellectuality, it was but natural that he should have acquired in the course of time an extensive library of the choicest and best selected literature, this being one of the charms that made his home such an attractive one. In the midst of these refined surroundings, the home was an almost ideal one and one which is not frequently found. Mr. Abell was a contributor to numerous benevolent undertakings, and his charity was always bestowed in an unostentatious manner. His death occurred July 27, 1914.

WILLIAM GRAHAM BOWDOIN

IN presenting to the public the representative men of the State of Maryland who have by superior force of character and energy, together with a combination of ripe qualities of ability and excellency, made themselves conspicuous and commanding in private and public life, we have no example more fit to present and none more worthy a place in this volume than the late William Graham Bowdoin. Not only did he rise above the standard of his line of business, but he possessed in a high degree the excellencies of human nature that makes men worthy of regard among their fellows. He was a high-minded and liberal man, one who was keenly alive to all the varying requirements of business. In an extended search it would be difficult to find one who better than Mr. Bowdoin gave substantial proof of the wisdom of Lincoln when he said, "There is something better than making a living—making a life." With a realization of this truth, Mr. Bowdoin labored persistently and energetically not only to win success, but to make his life a source of benefit to his fellow men.

William Graham Bowdoin was born in Baltimore county, Maryland, July 28, 1842, son of George E. and Mary Ann (Graham) Bowdoin, grandson on the maternal side of Captain William Graham, and a descendant of Huguenot ancestry on the paternal side, the progenitors of the American branch having emigrated from Rochelle, France. George E. Bowdoin was a Virginia planter of Northampton county before his removal to Baltimore.

William Graham Bowdoin received his early education from private tutors, and later attended the Dalrymple School, the knowledge thus obtained being supplemented by attendance at the University of Virginia. At once thereafter he commenced the active business career which only terminated at his death. He entered the banking house of Alexander Brown & Sons, in Baltimore, of which his uncle, William H. Graham, was a member, and in 1872 he was admitted to partnership, George S. Brown, since deceased, being then the executive head of the concern. Later Alexander Brown and Mr. Bowdoin constituted the firm. This concern is the parent house of Brown Brothers & Company, of Philadelphia, New York and Boston, and of Brown, Shipley & Company, London, with all of whom they were most intimately connected in business transactions. In many financial matters of great moment this firm was an important factor. The arduous and exacting duties attached to the affairs of his firm did not deter Mr. Bowdoin from assuming other responsibilities. He was a director of the Merchants' National Bank, the Eutaw Savings Bank, and was treasurer of the Baltimore and Annapolis Short Line Railroad Company. He was a vestryman of St. Paul's Protestant Episcopal Church, and one of the trustees of the Church Charities, one of the organizations of the Diocese of Maryland. He was also a trustee of the Johns Hopkins University.

By his own honorable exertions and moral attributes, Mr. Bowdoin carved out for himself friends, affluence and position. By the strength of his own character he overcame obstacles which to others less hopeful and less courageous would seem unsurmountable. He was a business man and a gentleman of the best type, and no man ranked higher than he in qualities of character. He was justly regarded in Baltimore as one of the leading, most representative and public-spirited citizens of that great city. Scrupulous and honorable in all his dealings with mankind, he bore a reputation for public and private integrity of which any man might be proud, and he left to his family a heritage of a good name which is more to be desired than great wealth.

Mr. Bowdoin married, in April, 1878, Katherine Gordon, daughter of James E. Price, a highly esteemed citizen of Wilmington, Delaware. Children: Marion Gordon, married Dr. J. H. Mason Knox, of Baltimore; Katherine Gordon, married Dr. John Staige Davis, of Baltimore; and William Graham, Jr., a lawyer by profession. Mr. Bowdoin died in Baltimore, on November 12, 1904.

John T. Morris

COLONEL JOHN T. MORRIS

A MAN of great versatility, Colonel John T. Morris divided his talents between two great professions, law and journalism, practicing at the Baltimore bar, and rising in journalism to the city editor's desk on the Baltimore "Sun." The honors of both professions came to him, and in addition to these civic and political honors were his also. His military title was gained as a member of the staff of Governor Jackson, and during the Golden Jubilee of Pope Leo XIII, Colonel Morris was appointed to convey, as a gift to His Holiness, a volume containing a copy of the Constitution of the United States in exquisitely bound form. The foregoing but indicates the versatility of the genius of Colonel Morris and does not at all indicate his popularity in the city in which his years, fifty-seven, were spent, years of ceaseless activity and usefulness.

Colonel John T. Morris was born in Baltimore, Maryland, June 20, 1859, and died at his home in Catonsville, Maryland, August 3, 1917, following an illness of nearly a year. He prepared for college at the various institutions conducted by the Catholic Order of Christian Brothers, and later entered Manhattan College, New York City, receiving from that institution the degree of Doctor of Philosophy at graduation. He then returned to Baltimore and entered the employ of the Baltimore "Sun," his first service being as reporter. His worth was soon recognized, and he was promoted to the position of news editor and was later transferred to the city editor's desk, occupying that important position until the year 1900. During his connection with the "Sun" he was adjudged to be in contempt of court through his refusal to divulge to the Grand Jury the source of the informa-on which a study of the presentation of Sheriff Fledderman, of attempted bribery, was based. Colonel Morris held that as a newspaper man he could not be compelled to give his source of information, and was punished for his refusal by a week's imprisonment. He was upheld by the late George M. Abell, then the managing director of the "Sun" and by the public generally. His courageous conduct furnished an example which has been followed by newspaper reporters throughout the country in their refusal to divulge sources of information. Colonel Morris reported the Sullivan-Kilrain prize fight in Louisiana, which took place nearly thirty years ago, and he also reported some of the greatest events of his day during his years as active reporter, and it is a well-known fact that no reporter was ever on better terms with the police department than Colonel Morris. It was during his newspaper career that he made the journey to Rome, Italy, as President Cleveland's personal representative to present to Pope Leo XIII the gift of a magnificent volume containing a copy of the Constitution of the United States, the occasion being the fiftieth anniversary of the Holy Father's ordination as a priest. He wrote letters to the "Sun" describing the celebration, and letters analyzing political and economic conditions as then existing in Europe, these being both instructive and interesting.

In February, 1900, after his retirement from journalism, he was appointed a member of the Board of Police Commissioners of the City of Baltimore, the appointment being made by Governor John W. Smith. Colonel Morris, while performing the duties of his office, read law, a long cherished desire, completed a course in the law department of the University of Maryland, was graduated with the degree of Bachelor of Laws in 1903, and in that year was admitted to the Baltimore bar. After his retirement as police commissioner, Colonel Morris began the practice of law with his son, John T. Morris, Jr., this connection continuing until the death of the son, August 23, 1916, they meeting with well-merited success. Upon his admission to the bar, Colonel Morris was presented with a handsome leather library couch by the United Irish League of Baltimore, of which he was formerly president. The couch bore a suitably inscribed silver plate. This action was taken pursuant to a resolution adopted by the league expressing the pride which its members felt upon the admission of Colonel Morris to the bar. The presentation was made through James T. O'Neill, chairman.

Colonel Morris married, October 30, 1884, Virginia C. Maguire, who died April 17, 1916. They were the parents of two children: John T., Jr., born August 18, 1885, a member of the Baltimore bar, associated with his father in the practice of law, died August 23, 1916; and Virginia C., born November 1, 1889, a resident of Baltimore.

While Colonel Morris had been in poor health for a year, the final breakdown was caused by the death of his wife in April, 1916, followed a few months later by that his son. When the death of Colonel Morris was announced only the Superior Court was in session; the motion that the court adjourn out of respect to his memory was made by Eugene J. Cronin and seconded by Chapin A. Ferguson, and the motion was granted by Judge Dobler in suitable words of regret and respect. The funeral services were held at St. Martin's Roman Catholic Church. The church was filled with friends from various circles, principally political and professional, among them being a number of Chinese merchants whom he had served as counsel in their legal difficulties and as their friend. The Christian Brothers, under whom he studied, were largely represented, as were Eccleston Council, Catholic Benevolent Legion, and the Ancient Order of Hibernians, institutions of which he had long been a member. The pallbearers were friends of the Baltimore bar. A high mass of requiem was celebrated, and at the conclusion of the last, absolution was pronounced by the Rt. Rev. Owen B. Corrigan, Auxiliary Bishop of Baltimore. His remains were interred in Bonnie Brae Cemetery.

NICHOLAS RUFUS GILL

PROMINENT among those in the city of Baltimore who rose to eminence at the bar was Nicholas Rufus Gill, who was a man of marked capacity and decided character, and of the most undoubted integrity. He was modest and unassuming in his deportment, and retiring in his habits, with no disposition to put himself forward, but in whatever position he was placed he was emphatic and decided. He went further than the mere requirements of the ethical code. He was always anxious, not merely to act honorably to a professional brother, but also to serve him, if he could, by advancing his interests, and increasing his claims to public estimation and confidence. In the language of the lamented Lane, "He was so constituted, that it was impossible for him to be guilty of dishonorable rivalry towards his fellow practitioners." He scorned the tricks of the profession and those who practiced them. To the junior members of the faculty, he was particularly kind and generous. They were at once made to feel that he was one in whom they could place their confidence.

Nicholas Rufus Gill was born in Western Run Valley, Baltimore county, Maryland, March 12, 1838. He received his early education in Lamb's School and Milton Academy. When twenty-one years of age he entered the law offices of the late David Stewart and read law for one year, after which he matriculated at Harvard, graduating from the law department of that institution in the class of 1859. Immediately after his graduation he returned to Baltimore and opened an office for the general practice of his profession. His skill and ability were soon recognized and he enjoyed a lucrative patronage, practicing alone until such time as his sons were able to assist him, when he formed the firm of N. Rufus Gill

& Sons. His connection with the firm of which he was the founder had been of late years as adviser to his sons, owing to the fact of impaired hearing, which affliction had greatly interfered with his law practice. Mr. Gill was not a politician, although a consistent Democrat. He was a member of the first branch of the city council three terms and twice served in the capacity of president of that body. At the expiration of his last term his fellow councilmen passed resolutions recognizing his faithful services. He declined to allow his name to be used for any other elective office. His last public position was as president of the water board, about 1890. Thus it will be seen that his life has been an active one, being widely extended, and will be felt and recognized for many years to come, although he has passed from the scene of his earthly labors.

Mr. Gill, who was injured October 27, 1905, in a driving accident on St. Paul Street Bridge, died October 30, 1905, at the sanitarium of Dr. Miller, whither he was taken immediately after the accident. He and his daughter, Miss Agnes Gill, were thrown from a buggy, the accident being due to a high-spirited horse. The funeral services were conducted by the Rev. John G. Murray, rector of St. Michael's and All Angels Protestant Episcopal Church, and the Rev. William H. Falkner, rector of St. Peter's Protestant Episcopal Church. Fifty members of Crusade Commandery, Knights Templar, attended the services, their members acting as active pallbearers. At the grave in the family lot at Greenmount Cemetery the Masonic rites were observed.

PHILEMON HALLAM TUCK

THE Tuck family is one which has held a prominent position in the highest circles of Maryland for a long period, and the subject of this narrative, Philemon Hallam Tuck, inherited in full the measure the charms of intellect, nobility and courtliness which have characterized his ancestors. He was a direct descendant of several of the most distinguished families of the State, among them being the Brookes, Chews, Bowies and Spriggs. Personally he made a name for himself in the legal profession, and especially in real estate matters his business acumen and foresight were of the greatest benefit to his many clients. His paternal line is as follows:

William Tuck, an honored resident of Annapolis, Maryland, possessed a widespread reputation as one of the most progressive men of his day. His active and conscientious public spirit identified him with the majority of the public and social enterprises of importance in his community, and he was honored with positions of trust and responsibility. From his earliest years his literary ability was recognized as being of a high order and the most accomplished men of the day were his intimate associates.

William Hallam, son of William Tuck, was born in Annapolis, Maryland, November 20, 1808, and died there March 17, 1884. The Legislature adjourned in respect to his memory, and preceded by the sergeant-at-arms bearing the mace, attended the funeral in a body, which was an unprecedented honor. His education was acquired under the most favorable auspices, and he received in 1827 the degree of Master of Arts from St. John's College. The consistency and uprightness which characterized his performance of all duties which fell to his share naturally attracted the attention of those high in office, and although Mr. Tuck rarely sought public office, it was repeatedly tendered him, and he accepted these trusts, deeming it for the best interests of the people that he should do so. For many years he was a member of the Court of Appeals, and subsequently Governor Bradford appointed him Judge of the Circuit Court of Anne Arundel and Calvert counties. At the time of his death he was president of the Board of County Commissioners, having been appointed to this office by Governor Hamilton. As a member of the House of Delegates of Maryland, he served a number of terms, and during one term was speaker of the House. He also served as a member of the Constitutional Convention in 1851, and later as a Senator. In financial matters he was also in the foremost rank, having held office as president of the First National Bank of Annapolis, the Citizens' Bank of Annapolis and the Traders' National Bank of Baltimore; was a director of the Baltimore & Ohio Railroad, representing the State of Maryland stock in that corporation. He was a member of the board of governors and visitors of St. John's College, being succeeded in this office by his son, Philemon H. Judge Tuck married Margaret Sprigg Bowie Chew, born January 3, 1818, died March 12, 1885.

Philemon Hallam, son of William Hallam and Margaret Sprigg Bowie (Chew) Tuck, was born in Prince George county, Maryland, July 22, 1852. Endowed by nature with a mentality of unusual caliber, his scholastic course from the outset was one of honor. His elementary education was obtained in private schools and by the invitation of Governor Bradford he shared the instruction of the Governor's sons in the Government House in Annapolis, and he then attended the preparatory school connected with St. John's College. He matriculated at St. John's College, from which he graduated with high honors, obtaining the degree of Bachelor of Arts, then from the post-graduate course with the degree of Master of Arts. Becoming a student at the Law School of the University of Maryland he was graduated from this institution with the degree of Bachelor of Laws.

Engaging in the practice of law in Baltimore in 1875, he achieved success, his power of concentration making this an assured fact. He was, however, a man of action, rather than of words, and his untiring energy and undoubted business talents decided him to attempt another field of industry. He accordingly gave considerable attention to real estate matters, in connection with his legal practice, and undoubtedly had more experience and accomplished as good results in this branch as any other lawyer in Maryland. His broad, comprehensive grasp of all questions arising in his practice gave him an unquestionable ability to cope with large matters. He never cared to hold public office, but as a private citizen had done his full share in upholding the principles of civic cleanliness and progress, by casting his vote for those who were best able to further these ends. He was a member of the Reform League, and had served for many years as a member of the executive committee of the Civil Service Reform Association. He was one of the board of visitors and governors of St. John's College and vice-provost of the board of regents of the University of Maryland. His professional affiliations were with the State Bar Association and the Baltimore City Bar Association. He was an honored member of numerous social organizations, among them being: Sons of the Colonial Wars, Churchman's Club of Maryland, Sons of the Revolution, Society of Colonial Lords of Manors in America, Bachelors' Cotillon and the following clubs: University, Baltimore Country. He was a vestryman of Christ Episcopal Church of Baltimore, and was appointed by Bishop John G. Murray, chairman of the committee whose duty was to seat the invited guests on the occasion of Cardinal Gibbons' Jubilee when possibly twenty thousand persons were in the audience, and many of the chief dignitaries of the nation on the stage. He was a liberal giver to all charitable objects. He was especially interested in assisting young men of ambition and ability, and was quick to notice unusual qualities of mind or heart in any one.

Mr. Tuck married (first) Grace G., daughter of William Devries, founder of the firm of William Devries & Company, in its day one of the leading dry goods houses of the South. Mr. Tuck married (second) Dorcas V., daughter of Philip Jamieson, a prominent merchant of Toronto, who was considered one of the most astute business men of the city. Mr. Tuck traveled extensively in the United States, Canada, Europe, Egypt and other parts of Africa, but he considered it his duty, as well as his pleasure, to study his own country above all others. He inherited the patriotism, courage and courtly bearing which distinguished his ancestors, and his fine presence and youthful glance and ardor made him in all respects worthy of the traditions of his well-known family. His death occurred August 5, 1917.

JORDAN STABLER

JORDAN STABLER, who was a leader in the commercial circles of Baltimore and head of the firm of Jordan Stabler Company, one of the largest grocery houses in the South, was descended on both sides from colonial Quaker families of English origin.

The earliest notice found of the Stabler family in the London records dates back to the time of King Edward I, about 1274. In the history of York, England, we find the marriage of George and Ann Stabler in 1680; one son is mentioned as Ishmael Stabler, Gentleman.

Edward, the son of Ishmael, was lord mayor of York from 1774 to 1779. At the time of his death in 1786 he was one of the aldermen of that corporation. A record published on that date reads:

> Edward Stabler, who served the office of Lord Mayor, 1774 to 1779. A gentleman who discharged the duties of public and private life with the most conscientious integrity, and in whom were happily blended all the amiable virtues that could dignify human nature and constitute the character of a truly good man. His loss will be long and severely felt and deplored.

Another Edward Stabler, born in Yorkshire in 1732, a close relative of the lord mayor, emigrated to America in 1753; married Mary Robinson, of Chester, Pennsylvania; settled in Petersburg, Virginia, and was a prominent shipping and importing merchant during the Revolution. An interesting story of courage and devotion to principles was given us by Rev. Moncure D. Conway, formerly of Virginia, who mentions Edward Stabler, of Petersburg, Virginia, the great-grandfather of Jordan Stabler, in his "Memoirs of the Long Island Historical Society." Mr. Conway's story is as follows:

During the French and Indian War, about 1756, Governor Dinwiddie of Virginia issued an order that all Quakers who were drafted for the army, and refused to take up arms, or pay ten pounds sterling for a substitute, should be put in jail and lashed every day until they complied. Edward Stabler of Petersburg, Virginia, then twenty-four years of age, realizing the injustice of this order, because it was against the principles of members of the Society of Friends to aid or abet in war, volunteered to make the trip on horseback, through the forests and over the mountains (infested with savage Indians) to Fort Duquesne, two hundred and fifty miles, to obtain a letter from his friend General Washington requesting Governor Dinwiddie to rescind that order.

General Washington gave him the desired letter to the Governor and after another two hundred and fifty miles' ride back to Virginia he secured the release of the "Quakers" from jail. The stone horseblock, dated 1756 and weighing over a ton, from which he mounted to take this long and perilous journey, is now used by one of his descendants at Harewood, Sandy Spring, Montgomery county, Maryland.

Dr. William Stabler, son of Edward Stabler, of Petersburg, Virginia, married Deborah Pleasants, of Goochland county, Virginia, and settled in Leesburg, Virginia. In 1793 they moved to Harewood, Sandy Spring, Montgomery county, Maryland, where the doctor continued to practice medicine until his death from hemorrhages in 1806. His wife, Deborah (Pleasants) Stabler, was a recommended minister of the Society of Friends, well known and beloved by a large circle of friends throughout Maryland and Virginia. During the War of 1812, her son Edward, the father of Jordan Stabler, was a clerk in the drug house of his uncle, Edward Stabler, in Alexandria, Virginia. He was drafted for service in the militia. Refusing to serve, he was arrested and placed in jail. His mother, who had been a schoolmate and friend of Dolly Madison, learning of her son's arrest wrote to the lady of the White House:

DEAR DOLLY: My son Edward has been arrested and lodged in jail

in Alexandria because he refused to take up arms. I want thee to tell James
to have him released at once.

Thy respected friend,
DEBORAH.

It is needless to say, through Dolly's influence, the request
was granted.

Edward, son of Dr. William and Deborah (Pleasants)
Stabler, was born September 26, 1794; married Ann R.,
daughter of Bernard Gilpin, Sr., of Mount Airy, Sandy
Spring, Montgomery county, Maryland. Mr. Stabler died
September 3, 1883, on the old Harewood estate, where he
was born, passing away, by a singular coincidence, in the same
room in which he had first seen the light eighty-nine years
before. The Harewood estate was part of the original
"Charlie Forest" grant from Lord Baltimore, and is one of
the three farms in Montgomery county which up to the present
time, have never passed out of the families of their original
owners.

Jordan, son of Edward and Ann R. (Gilpin) Stabler,
was born January 16, 1840, on the Harewood estate. He
received his preparatory education at the neighboring country
schools, afterward attending Springdale Academy, Loudoun
county, Virginia. He acquired, meanwhile, so thorough a
knowledge of agriculture, that he was able, as a fifteen-year-
old boy, to manage the farm for two winters, during which
time his father was absent in Washington, assisting Obed
Hussey to secure an extension to his patent for the first successful mowing and reaping machine ever built, called the
Hussey Mowing and Reaping Machine.

Mr. Stabler's inclinations, however, were for a commercial rather than an agricultural career, and in 1857, after
completing his course of study, he came in the autumn to
Baltimore, where he secured a position as clerk in the old

grocery house of G. H. Reese & Brothers. The natural aptitude for his new duties which he immediately displayed
proved that in his choice of a lifework he had been guided
by a true instinct, that he possessed the qualifications of the
genuine business man. To such good use did he put his
capabilities and so faithfully did he discharge the obligations
devolving upon him, that in July, 1862, he went into the
grocery business on his own account, opening a store on Lombard street which he conducted until 1866, when he sold out
and recommenced business in a store on Madison avenue,
which had been built expressly for him. In 1875 he bought
out the firm of Charles Reese & Company, whose place of
business adjoined his own, and into this he moved, retaining
the old building for storage purposes. In 1892 he purchased
a third building. His trade extended throughout the country,
and he also sold large orders to the United States government.
He imported extensively, dealing in none but the finest goods,
both foreign and domestic. A stock company was formed in
1900, by taking in four clerks whom he had trained from the
beginning and another who had been with him for some years,
Mr. Stabler selling them stock in the business. He was president of the company from its organization until his death. In
1906, he however, relinquished the detail work, but still gave
his attention to the important branches of the business. He
was a man of strong will, inflexible purpose and sound judgment, quick to see an emergency and equally quick in devising
a plan to meet it, and these characteristics were the foundation of his successful career.

Mr. Stabler's thorough business qualifications and his
well-known executive ability were in demand on boards of
directors of different organizations, and his public spirit led
him to accept many such trusts. He was a director in the
Commonwealth Bank, and for thirty years he was the president of the Grocers' Exchange. He was vice-president of the

E. Stabler, Jr., Coal Company and was interested in several large building propositions. For many years he was a director in the Crown Cork and Seal Company. He was a member of the Board of Trade and the Merchants' and Manufacturers' Association. His devotion to his friends and his strict business probity were well known to every merchant of Baltimore and met with a rich return of personal regard and some measure of financial success. A vigilant and attentive observer of men and measures, his opinions were recognized as sound and his views as broad, his ideas therefore carried weight among those with whom he discussed public problems. In the national elections he voted the Republican ticket and in local elections supported the best man. He was active in the Good Government Club when that organization was in its prime, and was ever ready to lend his aid to any project for the welfare and improvement of his native city. He was a member of Emanuel Protestant Episcopal Church.

Mr. Stabler married, February 14, 1877, Carrie E., daughter of Dr. Robert Semple, of Philadelphia, and three children were born to them. The mother of these children died in 1886, and Mr. Stabler married, March 21, 1894, Ellen W., daughter of Rev. Horace Dean Walker, of New York. Of this marriage there was no issue.

Mr. Jordan Stabler, the subject of this narrative, was a representative of the prominent merchant to whom business is but one phase of existence, not excluding active participation in other vital interests which go to make up human existence. He was a type of the Baltimore merchant of whom his city is justly proud, whose enterprise and integrity not only develop its commerce, but give it an enviable reputation for fair dealing and honorable methods. It is such men who lay, deep and strong, the foundation on which is reared the fair structure of a great city's financial prosperity. He died in his native city, June 20, 1916.

GEORGE FREDERICK PATTERSON

THE American career of George F. Patterson, extending over a period of thirty-four years, 1880-1914, was passed in the city of Baltimore, in connection with the shipping interests of the city. He came to Baltimore the matured man of forty, his boyhood, youth and early manhood all having been spent in an atmosphere of ship building and the shipping business. In fact, his coming to the United States was in the interest of a shipping firm, and the firm he founded in Baltimore became one of the most important and best known along the Atlantic seaboard. The name Patterson was a very prominent one in marine circles in England, and it is interesting to note in connection with the life of George F. Patterson, of Baltimore, that he was a son of William Patterson, of Bristol, England, who may be called the "father" of steam navigation on the Atlantic.

William Patterson was president of the Great Western Steamship Company of Bristol, the company which among others built the paddle steamer "Great Western," designed by Brunel, one of the greatest architects of that time, and which proved to be a historic ship, the first Atlantic steamer, of 1340 tons measurement, 120 feet long and 35 feet beam. She was launched July 19, 1837, and sailed from Kingroad for New York, April 8, 1838, which port she reached after an uneventful voyage of fifteen days ten hours. The Bristol ship exceeded the most sanguine expectations. She easily made her ten miles an hour, as Brunel proposed, and instead of burning 1480 tons of coal, as savants had calculated, she went home at a cost of 392 tons. Great excitement prevailed on both sides of the Atlantic, and a crowd of one hundred thousand cheered the ship as she left New York. The "Great Britain," another celebrated ship designed by Brunel and

The American Historical Society.

George F. Patterson

built by the Great Western Steamship Company, was of 3,000 tons and launched by His Royal Highness the Prince Consort, July 19, 1843. She was the first screw steamer built for the Atlantic. The "Great Britain" is today still doing service, being used as a wool storage warehouse in the Falkland Islands. After building several other well-known merchant ships, Mr. Patterson built many gun boats for the British government, which proved valuable additions to the navy.

George Frederick Patterson, son of William Patterson, was born in Bristol, England, May 24, 1840, died in Baltimore, Maryland, February 13, 1914. He was well educated in Bristol schools, and in his early life gained a familiarity with ships and the shipping business, through association with his father, who was heavily interested in ship building and operation. When still a young man he entered the shipping firm of Gibbs, Bright & Son, of Liverpool, later transferring his services to William Johnston & Company, Ltd., continuing with the latter firm of ship owners and shipping merchants until the year 1880. He had, during the years which had passed, gained complete and comprehensive knowledge of the details of the business as conducted by William Johnston & Company, and in 1880 he was sent with Robert Ramsay to act as representative of the Johnston line of Atlantic steamers in Baltimore. The firm of Patterson, Ramsay & Company, steamship agents and brokers, was formed in Baltimore, and through that house, which became widely and favorably known, steamers were loaded at Baltimore, not only for the Johnston line, but for other lines trading with the principal ports of Great Britain and the Continent. The offices of the company became the center of the foreign shipping business of Baltimore, and the tonnage shipped through their agency was enormous. Mr. Patterson continued at the head of the company he founded until 1907, when he retired, having reached the age of sixty-seven years, and won the right by an unintermitted business career covering nearly half a century.

His business in Baltimore brought him into intimate relation with financiers and leading mercantile men of the city, and in such circles he was regarded as a man of highest ability, while his every business transaction was marked by the strictest observance of the principles of honor and fair dealing. He was one of the best known business men of the city, and was universally respected. Broad in his sympathy, genial and courteous in manner, he attracted both young and old. He was a member of the Maryland, Merchants and Baltimore Country clubs. After his retirement from business he resided in Roland Park.

ALBERT RITCHIE

THE State of Maryland has been happy in the services of many able and upright men upon the bench, and none have been more dearly beloved, respected and esteemed, or more faithful and efficient, than Albert Ritchie, who was born September 7, 1834, in Frederick, Maryland, the son of Albert Ritchie, a prominent physician of that place.

Albert Ritchie was educated at Dickinson College, Carlisle, Pennsylvania, and the University of Virginia, from whose law school he was graduated in 1856. He was immediately admitted to the bar at Frederick, and two years later settled at Baltimore, where he was admitted May 9, 1859. For nearly half a century his home was in Baltimore, and for a quarter of a century he was one of the most active members of the bar of that city. Mr. Ritchie lived without reproach, and at his death left to his family and friends the greatest legacy possible in his personal character and high standing. It has been said of him that he was "without fear and without reproach." "No man can have a higher ambition than that, and to achieve such an aim, to have it recognized by his fellow men, forms an imperishable heritage." His legal attainments quickly won for him a place which was strengthened and advanced by the passing years. To the principles of law he gave earnest and patient study, and he never undertook a case until he was satisfied of its inherent justice. When satisfied upon that point, to the conduct of the case he gave most careful and painstaking preparation, and entered upon its conduct with zeal and energy, regardless of any emoluments which it might bring to him. "His time, his learning and his strength were as earnestly given to one from whom no reward but gratitude could be expected as to his wealthiest client." In 1888 he was chosen president of

the Bar Association of Baltimore, testifying to the regard
in which he was held by his contemporaries.

Very early in life he began to give attention to political
matters, and he was much in the public service. In 1867
Mr. Ritchie took a prominent part in the proceedings of the
State Constitutional Convention, and from 1872 to 1876 he
was city solicitor. In 1880 and 1881 he was president of the
board of supervisors of elections, and was again at the head
of the city's law department during the terms of Mayors
Davidson and Latrobe. He was still in this office when he
was appointed by Governor Brown to fill out the unexpired
term of Judge William A. Stewart, an associate judge of the
supreme bench of Baltimore. This service began September
24, 1892, and at the election in the following November he
was elected for a full term of fifteen years. In 1888 he was
a delegate to the Democratic national convention in St. Louis,
at which President Cleveland was nominated.

For several years preceding Judge Ritchie's death, which
occurred September 14, 1903, at Narragansett Pier, Rhode
Island, he was president of the Maryland Historical Society.
In this he felt a deep interest and contributed many essays
and articles on the early history of the State, the first buildings of Baltimore, and other kindred subjects. At the expiration of the term of Chief Judge William Brown, of the
supreme bench, he was urged by his friends to accept an
appointment as Judge Brown's successor, but declined. The
Baltimore "Sun" said: "Judge Ritchie was distinguished not
only for his great ability as a lawyer and his zeal as a student,
but for the dignity which he believed should pertain to the
high office he held, and for the kind and courteous manner
in which he treated all with whom he came in contact." To
the public service he gave the same faithful care that his
private business received. "His deep conviction and sense

of civic obligations would not permit him to stand idly by, or shirk when there was need of voice or pen or brain upon the part of the city or the State. As a private citizen, or in public station, he ever bore the 'full and manly part' and contributed much to the general weal. When first tendered a position on the bench he declined it, but four years later, when it was again offered, accepted, and the last decade of his life was devoted to that work. Already have the bench and bar paid a tribute to his worth as a jurist, when the eloquence of the advocate had been succeeded by the impartiality and industry of the judge. His work during this period of his life is so recent, so well known of all men, that it needs only to be said, that on the bench, Albert Ritchie perpetuated in his own person, not one, but all of the best traditions of the bar and bench of this State, which have made the annals of the legal profession one of the brightest pages in Maryland's history."

To him official position of any sort was not an idle honor, and was viewed in the light of an extended opportunity for work. In 1896 and again in 1900 he read before the Maryland Historical Society papers on "The Early County Seats and Court Houses of Baltimore County," a most valuable addition to the annals of the community. "His was a rounded manhood, in which the best qualities of brain and heart were developed in equable proportion to each other. Having almost reached the allotted span of life, it was his fortune to fall ere decay had shown itself in any of the traits which evoked the admiration and affection of those who knew him." The following resolutions were adopted by the Maryland Historical Society:

1. Resolved, That in the death of Judge Albert Ritchie, President of this Society, we recognize the loss of one who has long and faithfully labored for the advancement of learning, and the promotion of the best interests

of our State, and who, by his gentle courtesy, had endeared himself to each one of us.

2. Resolved, That we regard his demise as a misfortune to this community, in which he had so long and unselfishly toiled for high ideals and the uplifting of humanity.

3. Resolved, That we, by this means, express to his bereaved family our profound and heartfelt sympathy with them in their affliction, that their sorrow may be lightened by the sharing of it.

4. Resolved, That a copy of the memorial minute reported by the committee and of these resolutions be sent to his family, and that they be recorded among the proceedings of this meeting.

Speaking of Judge Ritchie's death, the late John P. Poe, one of Baltimore's most prominent lawyers, said:

In Judge Ritchie, Baltimore has lost one of her ablest legal lights. Gifted with great legal learning, he was an admirable justice. He was a man of deliberation, most careful in reaching conclusions, and capable of arriving at and of expressing his opinions clearly. His manner on the bench would be indeed hard to improve upon. Always courteous and patient, he was firm in his desire to have the questions before him fully argued. Judge Ritchie was well versed in practice and procedure. He was an admirable lawyer. Before going to the bench he was an excellent speaker, and was always thoroughly prepared when a case he was interested in came up. He also was a frequent contributor to the press on political affairs. Judge Ritchie's connection with the Law School of the University of Maryland was pleasant and his talents were appreciated by the students. His commercial law lectures there are remembered well by many of the young lawyers of the city and State. We of the University especially deplore his loss. I knew Judge Ritchie intimately for about forty-five years, and I know him always to have been strong and dignified.

The late William S. Bryan said of him:

Judge Ritchie was one of the strongest pillars of the Baltimore courts. In many ways he was the strongest. His knowledge of practice and procedure was greater than many jurists often acquire and he was better versed on precedents and analogous cases than is usual in men of his position. Judge Ritchie was a patient listener and always grasped the point of argument. Perhaps there are some who grasped the point more quickly, but certainly there was none who took more care to absorb the full import of the case in hand and to have both sides thrashed out well before decision was rendered.

The late Edgar H. Gans said of him:

One of the best judges the city ever had was Judge Ritchie. His professional life was characterized by an infinite amount of patience. He never decided a case against anyone without first having a full hearing on both sides. He was levelheaded, of strong common sense, and possessed a great learning of law. Many judges are inclined to be impatient at times. Judge Ritchie was never impatient. I have never argued a case before a judge more willing and more anxious to listen and to have brought out absolutely all the evidence in any case which might at the time be in hand. He was very approachable. Although ever dignified, he was affable and sociable when approaching upon matters relating to cases in law. It will be very hard to supply the place he has vacated.

Extracts from Baltimore "American":

Hon. Albert Ritchie was a native of Frederick county, Maryland, a son of Dr. Albert Ritchie, a distinguished physician and was born in 1834. He studied law with his brother, • Hon. John Ritchie, chief judge of the Sixth Judicial Circuit, and also at the Law School of the University of Virginia, from which he graduated in 1856. He was shortly afterward admitted to the Frederick bar, and in 1858 came to Baltimore, where he was also admitted to practice on May 9, 1859. On the expiration of Chief Judge George Brown's term Mr. Ritchie was asked to accept the appointment as chief judge, but he declined the honor, and the Hon. Henry D. Hatlan was appointed, being subsequently elected to fill that office. * * * Judge Ritchie was a lawyer of distinguished ability, a hard student, methodical and painstaking in securing the fullest information concerning the cases which came before him for judicial determination both as regards the law and the facts, and having once arrived at an adjudication, was rarely reversed by the appellate tribunal. As a judge he was the personification of the dignity which he believed should always attach to that office, a gentleman at all times and under all circumstances, courteous to the extreme and, withal, social and gracious in his manner to each and everyone with whom he came in contact.

Judge Ritchie married, October 27, 1875, at St. Paul's Church, Richmond, Virginia, Elizabeth Caskie Cabell, born

May 1, 1851, in Richmond, daughter of Robert Gamble and Margaret Sophia (Caskie) Cabell, of that city. Judge and Mrs. Ritchie were the parents of a son, Albert Cabell Ritchie, born August 29, 1876, now a prominent attorney at the bar of Baltimore, and attorney general of Maryland.

Mrs. Ritchie is descended from Nicholas and Rachel Cabell, who lived in Warminster, near Bristol, England. Their son, Dr. William Cabell, born March 9, 1699, in Warminster, graduated from the Royal College of Medicine and Surgery in London, and engaged in practice there. Entering the British navy as surgeon, the vessel on which he sailed landed at Norfolk, Virginia, and was detained there some days, during which time he made an excursion into the interior of the State. Being very much pleased with the country, he decided to settle there, returned to England, resigned his position in the navy, and came to Virginia about 1723. For some time he resided in St. James' Parish, of Henrico county, where he is found of record as early as 1726, and where he served as deputy sheriff. He removed to Licking Hole Creek in the upper part of the present Goochland county, and in 1728-29 was justice of the county court, member of the grand jury in 1728, and coroner in 1729. It is interesting to note that nearly all financial transactions in that day were reckoned in pounds of tobacco. He was the first Englishman to remove west of the mouth of Rockfish river, where he entered a great deal of land, and on September 12, 1738, received from Governor Gooch a patent of forty-eight hundred acres, and ten days later four hundred and forty acres additional. The completing of this patent was managed by his wife during his absence in England. His father died in 1730, and because of his extensive interests in England he was obliged to return to that country, whither he went in 1735, and remained to 1741. His mother died in 1737, and other relatives about the same time, and he was thus detained five years in England to settle up his affairs. Soon after his return he received a patent of seven thousand nine hundred and fifty-two acres, and in 1743 an additional twelve hundred acres, and settled at the mouth of Swan creek, where he built a house, mill and warehouse, and established a settlement which he called Warminster, in honor of his native place in England.

Col. Nicholas Cabell, youngest son of Dr. William and Elizabeth (Burks) Cabell, was born October 29, 1750, and baptized December 15, following. He was kept at school from the age of four years and three months, finishing his studies at William and Mary College. He resided with his father until the latter's death, and owned a plantation below the paternal property, extending five miles along the James river, now known as Liberty Hall. He was a captain of militia in the Revolutionary service in 1776, and on June 25, 1778, was commissioned lieutenant-colonel. He was appointed colonel of Amherst county militia in 1780, and saw service in 1781. He was one of the first vestrymen of the parish in 1779, and was a member of the Virginia Society of the Cincinnati. He was justice of the peace of Amherst county, and representative in the State Legislature in 1783-84-85. In 1785 he was elected to the State Senate, and continued a member of that body until his death in 1803, affiliating with what was then known as the Republican party. He was a trustee of the College of Washington, of Virginia, in 1796-97; was active in establishing George Lodge, Free and Accepted Masons, and prominent in the Grand Lodge of Free Masons, in which he held various offices.

He married, April 16, 1772, Hannah, daughter of George and Anne (Mayo) Carrington, born March 28, 1751, died August 7, 1817. William H. Cabell, eldest child of Colonel Nicholas Cabell, married Agnes S. B. Gamble, and they were the parents of Robert Gamble Cabell, above mentioned.

LAWRENCE BUCKLEY THOMAS, D.D.

THE Thomas family, of which Rev. Lawrence Buckley Thomas was descended, is of Welsh origin, and was early established in Maryland. Philip Thomas, son of Evan Thomas, of Swansea, Glamorganshire, Wales, removed to America in the year 1651, and settled in the Province of Maryland. On February 19 of that year he received a patent of five hundred acres of land, called Beakely or Beckly, on the west side of Chesapeake bay, in consideration of which "he hath in the year 1651 transplanted himself, Sarah, his wife, Philip, Sarah and Elizabeth, his children, into our province." He was appointed one of the six high commissioners of the Provincial Court, and was very active in promoting the affairs of the colony. He married, in England, Sarah Harrison, and besides the children previously mentioned had Martha and Samuel. The last named was born about 1655, and was a minister of the Society of Friends, probably as early as August 4, 1686, when Herring Creek quarterly meetings approved his proposal to attend the yearly meeting at Philadelphia. On April 13, 1688, he was appointed a committee on "drowsiness" by the West River meeting. In 1674 a tract of seventy-two acres was surveyed for him on Talbot's Ridge, north side of West river. He married, May 15, 1688, Mary Hutchins, of Calvert county, Maryland, who died in July, 1751, having survived him more than eight years. He was deceased at the time she made her will, February 10, 1743. Children: Sarah, born March 31, 1689; Samuel, February 1, 1691; Samuel, March 11, 1693; Philip, mentioned below; John, April 15, 1697; Elizabeth, December 28, 1698; Mary, November 6, 1700; Samuel, November 12, 1702; Ann, October 8, 1703; Margaret, 1710.

Philip Thomas, third son of Samuel and Mary (Hutchins) Thomas, was born March 1, 1694, and was a prominent man in the community and in the province, nearly always engaged in public service. He was a member of a committee appointed November 24, 1732, on the part of the West River meeting to prepare an address of welcome to Lord Baltimore, and was a member of the Governor's Council as early as May 20, 1742. On March 13, 1744, he was commissioned judge and register of the land office, and represented Maryland in a treaty with the Indians at Lancaster, Pennsylvania, to settle the western bounds of the province. He married (first) in March, 1721, Frances Holland, who was the mother of a son, William, born about 1722. He married (second) August 11, 1724, Ann Chew, who died May 20, 1777, having survived her husband more than fifteen years. He died November 23, 1762. Children: Samuel, mentioned below; Philip, born July 3, 1727; Mary, January 1, 1731; Elizabeth, March 8, 1733; Richard, July 17, 1736; John, August 26, 1743.

The eldest son of Philip and Ann (Chew) Thomas was Samuel Thomas, born June 12, 1725. He resided at Perry Point, Havre de Grace, on the Susquehanna river, and was proprietor of ferry rights on both sides of the stream. He married, October 23, 1750, his cousin, Mary Thomas, daughter of Samuel and Mary (Snowden) Thomas, who died March 4, 1770. He survived her more than fourteen years, and died July 17, 1784. Children: Ann, born October 2, 1751; Philip, August 12, 1753; Samuel, July 20, 1757; Richard Snowden, February 25, 1762; John Chew, mentioned below; Samuel, February 2, 1766; Evan William, February 6, 1769.

John Chew Thomas, fourth son of Samuel and Mary (Thomas) Thomas, was born October 15, 1764, and in his sixteenth year entered the University of Pennsylvania, from which he was graduated A.M. in 1783, in his nineteenth year. His home was at "Fairland" in Anne Arundel county, Maryland, which place he sold for fifty thousand dollars. He was an active member of the Society of Friends, a man of very high character, a lawyer by profession, admitted to the bar at Philadelphia, Pennsylvania, December 15, 1787. In early life he was much interested in political matters, and was elected by the Federal party in Maryland as representative to the Congress of 1799-1801. While in that body in the last named year he took part in the election of President, which was consummated after three days of intensive excitement with thirty-five ballots, resulting in the election of Thomas Jefferson, and the transfer of the government to the Republican party. He declined a re-election to Congress, and gave his attention to the active practice of his profession. He appears to have lost his membership in the Friends Society because of marrying out of meeting and to a slaveholder. His wife and five children were admitted as members of the Society, September 20, 1811, and on February 12 following he manumitted his slaves and applied for a reinstatement. Before August 7 of that year he was again received into membership, and was appointed clerk of the Indian meeting, February 21, 1817. He died at his residence in Ridley, Pennsylvania, May 10, 1836. He married, September 18, 1788, Mary Snowden, daughter and heiress of Richard and Eliza (Rutland) Snowden, of Fairland, Anne Arundel county. She survived him more than eight years, and died November 13, 1844. Children: Mary Ann, born January 23, 1790; Ann Snowden, March 13, 1791; Eliza Snowden, August 8, 1792; Samuel, March 28, 1794; Thomas Snowden, February 19, 1796; John Chew, August 21, 1797, died young; Henrietta Maria, July 30, 1799; Mary Snowden, September 22, 1801; John Chew, mentioned below; Dr. Richard Henry, June 20,

1805; Samuel Evan, March 12, 1807; Julia, August 16, 1808; Harriet, March 20, 1811; Maria Russell, August 29, 1812; Charles, August 18, 1816.

Dr. John Chew Thomas, son of John Chew and Mary (Snowden) Thomas, was born September 22, 1803, at Fairland, and entered the University of Pennsylvania in his fifteenth year, graduating in 1821, before he was eighteen years old. He subsequently pursued the medical course of the same university, from which he received the degree of M.D. in April, 1824. While a student he was a member of the Philomathian Society, For some years after graduation he was in the service of the United States, as clerk, during the construction of the New Castle breakwater. Subsequently he settled in Baltimore, Maryland, and there practiced his profession, with great success. He was a man of many social gifts, of considerable inventive genius and some artistic talents, painting quite well in oils. He died August 29, 1862. He married, March 2, 1848, Jane Lawrence, daughter of Thomas and Anna (Lawrence) Buckley, a member of the Society of Friends, afterward baptized and confirmed in the Protestant Episcopal church. Children: 1. Lawrence Buckley, mentioned below. 2. Julia, born March 9, 1850; married, October 14, 1879, James Valentine Wagner, former cashier of the National Marine Bank, of Baltimore, and United States Consul to Nicaragua; children: Effingham Buckley, Edgar and Julia T. 3. Walter Wood, born June 11, 1852; married Mary Ellicott, who died June 9, 1889.

Rev. Lawrence Buckley Thomas, eldest child of Dr. John Chew and Jane L. (Buckley) Thomas, was born December 6, 1848, on Lombard street, Baltimore, Maryland, was baptized June 8, 1851, by Rev. H. V. D. Johns, D.D., pastor of an Episcopal church of that city. He was a student at the public schools of Baltimore and at Topping and Carey's academies, and became an active lay worker in Emmanuel Protestant Episcopal Church, of Baltimore. He was a clerk, assistant librarian at the Mercantile Library, and an antiquarian bookseller. On January 15, 1876, he was elected secretary and treasurer of the Baltimore Book Trade Association, and in 1878-79 was librarian of Bishop Whittingham's Library. He entered the General Theological Seminary at New York, in September, 1879, and was graduated May 31, 1882, and ordained deacon by Bishop Horatio Potter, of New York, at St. John's Church in that city, June 4 following. He was ordained to the priesthood, May 18, 1883, by Bishop John M. Clark, of Rhode Island, at Grace Church, Providence. On the following day he received from the General Theological Seminary of New York the degree of B.D. St. John's College, Annapolis, Maryland, conferred upon him the degree of D.D., June 20, 1894. In 1882, immediately after his ordination, he became minister at Pontiac, Rhode Island. There he established a public library in 1884, and began a building fund for a church. Subsequently he became assistant minister of the Church of the Redeemer at Bryn Mawr, Pennsylvania. Soon after, on April 10, 1885, he organized the parish of St. Mary, at Ardmore, Pennsylvania, gathered the congregation and built a church, becoming its first rector, May 1, 1887. During the summer of 1888 he was in temporary charge of Christ Church at Pottstown, Pennsylvania, and under his auspices a fund was started which resulted in the erection of a town hospital there. On September 1, 1888, he accepted a call to become rector of St. Stephen's Church, Beverly, New Jersey. Under his charge the church debt was paid off and an endownment for a parish building fund was begun. In the summer of 1892 he was in charge of St. Andrew's Parish, West Philadelphia, and on December 1 of that year became rector of Trinity Church,

Antrim, Pennsylvania. He became senior curate of St. Peter's Church, Philadelphia, October 1, 1893, and in November of the following year returned to Antrim, assuming also charge of St. Andrew's Church, Tioga. During the last fifteen years of his life he was in charge of a church in Nevis, West Indies, looking after both the temporal and spiritual welfare of the people, and was largely instrumental in the establishment of water works by the British government. He died, December 28, 1914, at the age of sixty-six years.

In speaking of Dr. Thomas, the Baltimore "Sun" said: "Born in Baltimore, Mr. Thomas spent much of his life elsewhere. He was a member of the old Thomas family of West River, Maryland, and was among the first eminent researchers in a genealogical line. Among his prominent works is the history of the Thomas and Allied families of Colonial times. The branches take in Snowdens, the Chews, Ellicotts, Careys and other names well known in Maryland." He was a member of the Society of Colonial Wars in the State of New York, of the New York Shakespeare Society, of the Conservative Club, Philadelphia, the Elmira Theological and Literary Society, a corresponding member of the Wisconsin Historical Society, elected in 1879 in recognition of his genealogical labors, and member of the Maryland Historical Society.

Dr. Thomas was married, October 11, 1882, at the Church of the Reformation, Brooklyn, New York, by Rev. D. V. M. Johnson, D.D., Mary Berry, youngest daughter of Thomas Farrell and Marion L. (Berry) McCobb, originally of Baltimore, Maryland, who died November 16, 1884, and is buried in St. John's Churchyard, Waverly, Maryland.

SNOWDEN FAMILY

FROM the coming of Richard Snowden to the province of Maryland, the Snowdens of Maryland, like those of Pennsylvania, have occupied high place in public life and have been extensive land owners. There seems to be no connection between the Pennsylvania and Maryland families, the former tracing to William Snowden, of Yorkshire, England, whose son, John Snowden, the American ancestor, owned land in Delaware county, Pennsylvania, as early as 1677, prior to the coming of William Penn.

Captain Richard Snowden, the first of the name in Maryland, was commissioned officer of the province at the period when King William and Mary of England were represented here by Royal Governors, Lord Baltimore's power having been overthrown. In 1688 he was captain of a company of militia whose activities were against the Indians when uprisings amongst the unfriendly tribes endangered the lives of the inhabitants of the province. Captain Richard Snowden was of high social standing and influence in the colony, and family tradition claims that he was born in Wales and served as major in Oliver Cromwell's army.

Snowden arms—Argent on a fesse azure, between three escallops, gules: three mullets azure, pierced of the first.

Crest—A peacock in his pride.

Motto—*Dum spiro, spero.*

The earliest records found relative to the first of the Snowdens in Maryland is in Anne Arundel County Court House, Annapolis, where it is recorded that: "January 11, 1669, George Yates of Anne Arundel county, 'gent,' sold to Richard Snowden and Thomas Linthicombe of the same county, for 11,000 lbs. of tobacco a parcel of land called 'Iron

Mine' in Anne Arundel county at the head of South River in said county on the west side of the south branch of the said river;" the records also show on June 8, 1675, Thomas Linthicombe sold his part of the "Iron Mine" to Richard Snowden, the extent of the tract being 500 acres. This was the beginning of the iron industry in the province of Maryland, which grew to great proportions during the life of his grandson. Nothing further is found of him until 1681, when on August 13, he is mentioned in a report to Lord Baltimore's Council regarding the Indians, who then menaced the houses and plantations owned by him and Mr. Duvall. On February 26, 1685, a tract of land was granted by Lord Baltimore to Richard Snowden containing 1976 acres of land, which was named "Robin Hood Forest." It was situated on the forks of the Patuxent river, Anne Arundel county. Another tract of land called "Godwell," containing 805 acres, was purchased by Richard Snowden from William Parker on August 14, 1688, situated at the head of South river.

The first mention of Captain Snowden in the records by his military title was on October 9, 1695, when he was named as one of the commissioners "to adjust the accounts of John Duvall, late administrator of Henry Ridgely." A year later we find him mentioned in the Maryland archives as one of the military officers in Anne Arundel county, who signed an address to King William and Queen Mary of England. Although originally a member of the Society of Friends, Captain Snowden forsook for a time the teachings of his faith in accepting a military commission. Later his conscience so troubled him that he appeared before the West River Monthly Meeting asking forgiveness, acknowledging his fault and requesting reinstatement in the Meeting 21st day, 1st month, 1704.

Captain Richard Snowden married Elizabeth Grosse,

daughter of Roger Grosse, and sister of John Grosse, of Anne
Arundel county, who, in his will, dated December 4, 1675,
bequeathed to his sister, Elizabeth, wife of Richard Snowden,
400 acres of land on the Wye river, Talbot county, Maryland.
Roger Grosse, an early official under Lord Baltimore, appeared in the province as early as 1652. He was one of the
gentlemen justices and commissioners of peace for Anne
Arundel county, being first named by Lord Baltimore's Council on July 12, 1658, and again in 1661-65.

Captain Richard Snowden died May 20, 1711. The
record of his death on All Hallows Church Record, page 86,
reads literally as follows: "May 20, 1711, was buried Richard Snowden, the elder of the three of the name and family."
Other entries regarding the Snowdens are in All Hallows
Register, proving that some of the family must have been
identified with this church. Captain Richard and Elizabeth
(Grosse) Snowden had two sons, Captain Richard, Jr., and
Samuel Snowden. His eldest son, Richard (2), by the law
of primogeniture, inherited his large estates and personal
property, the latter, according to the inventory, amounting
to £2,020.

Captain Richard (2) Snowden, son of Captain Richard
(1) and Elizabeth (Grosse) Snowden, is first mentioned in
public records in connection with military affairs, July 22,
1695, as having signed a receipt for a barrel of gunpowder
from one Michael Greenberry by the order of the governor.
He also signed as a military officer the address to their Majes-
ties, King William and Mary of England, as recorded in the
Maryland archives under date of 1696. He built about the
year 1690 the famous Birmingham Manor House, in which
mansion for two centuries generations of the Snowden family
entertained their friends, true Southern hospitality.

A description of this colonial mansion preserved in the

family reads as follows: "Situated on the beautiful Patuxent River, in Anne Arundel county, Birmingham Manor House stood on a site overlooking the river on one side and a lordly estate of rolling fields and wooded park on the other side. Modelled after the old English half-shingled brick mansions, it was quaintly interesting with its deep recessed windows reaching to the second floor." This ancestral seat was destroyed by fire, August 20, 1891. To his already large holdings, Captain Richard (2) Snowden added another estate of one thousand acres called "Snowden's Manor," receiving a grant from Lord Baltimore, May 24, 1715, his property in all aggregating nearly thirty thousand acres. There is no record of the death of Captain Richard Snowden, Jr., and he seems to have left no will.

He married, about 1709, Mary Linthicum, daughter of Thomas Linthicum. They are known to have had two sons, Thomas and Richard Snowden (3), the former died young, the latter survived and became sole possessor of his father's and grandfather's vast estates.

Richard (3) Snowden, son of Captain Richard (2) and Mary (Linthicum) Snowden, besides inheriting the large estates of his father, received additional grants from Lord Baltimore, which increased his holdings to such an extent that he became one of the greatest landed proprietors in Maryland, exceeded only by the Carrolls of Carrollton. The colonial records shows him to have owned twenty-six thousand acres of the finest land on the Western Shore, including Snowden's Manor, Snowden's Manor Enlarged, New Birmingham, Montpelier, Snowden's Hall, Fairland, Oakland, Avondale, Woodland Hill, Alnwick, Elmwood, Brightwood, Maple Grove, and other tracts. The iron industry inaugurated by his grandfather on the land granted him as "Iron Mine" prior to the year 1700, Richard Snowden continued. He formed a company in 1726 called the Patuxent Iron Works Company (among the first ever operated in Maryland), Edmund Jennings, Judge and Register of the Land Office, Annapolis, becoming one of the chief stockholders, Richard Snowden being the largest, and at the time of his death he was sole owner of the works.

Richard (3) Snowden married (first) May 19, 1709, Elizabeth Coale, daughter of William and Elizabeth (Sparrow) Coale, who died about 1716. Children: 1. Deborah, married, June 21, 1725, James, son of Roger and Eliza (Hutchins) Brooke. 2. Eliza, married, April, 1727, John, son of Samuel and Mary (Hutchins) Thomas. 3. Mary, born in 1712, married, August 11, 1730, Samuel, son of Samuel and Mary (Hutchins) Thomas. Richard (3) Snowden married (second) December 19, 1717, Elizabeth, who died 1775, daughter of Samuel and Mary (Hutchins) Thomas. Samuel Thomas was a minister of the Society of Friends and son of Judge and High Commissioner Philip Thomas, settled in the province of Maryland in 1651. Children: 4. Richard, of Prince George's county, Maryland, born in 1719-20, died without issue, March 18, 1753; he married, before October 30, 1748, Elizabeth, daughter of John and Miriam Crowley, of Prince George's county. 5. Thomas, of Prince George's county, born in 1722, died in 1750-51; he married, before 1744, Mary, daughter of Henry and Elizabeth (Sprigg) Wright, of Prince George's county. 6. Ann, married Henry Wright Crabb. 7. Margaret, married John Contee. 8. Samuel, see forward. 9. Elizabeth, married Joseph Cowman. 10. John, married Rachel, daughter of Richard Hopkins.

Samuel Snowden, third son and fifth child of Richard (3) and Elizabeth (Thomas) Snowden, was born November 2, 1727. He inherited a large estate from his father, including six thousand acres in Anne Arundel county and Prince

George's county, as well as a third of Richard Snowden's great iron works, making him one of the richest men of his day. He attained considerable influence in the State, and in the stirring times that preceded the Revolution he served on the Committee of Safety (in 1774). He married his cousin, Elizabeth, who died January 30, 1790, daughter of Philip and Ann (Chew) Thomas, of "Lebanon," West River. He died June 27, 1801, leaving his vast acreage to be divided among his children: 1. Richard, married, August 2, 1782, Hannah Moore, daughter of William and Rachel (Orrick) Hopkins. 2. Ann, married, December 23, 1774, Richard, son of Gerard and Mary (Hall) Hopkins. 3. Elizabeth, born 1758, died August 25, 1793. 4. Philip, see forward. 5. Mary, died August 15, 1834; married, February 3, 1786, Joseph, son of John and Sarah (Hopkins) Cowman. 6. Samuel, born in 1766, died May 26, 1823; married, December 1, 1796, Elizabeth, daughter of John Cowman. 7. Henrietta, married, October 14, 1804, Gerard, son of Joseph and Elizabeth (Howell) Hopkins. 8. Sarah, married, November 24, 1769, Elisha Hopkins, M.D., son of Gerard and Margaret (Johns) Hopkins. 9. John, born in 1774, died January 26, 1790.

Philip Snowden, son of Samuel and Elizabeth (Thomas) Snowden, was born in Prince George's county, Maryland, about 1760. He inherited from his father an estate in Anne Arundel county called "Duvall's Delight," and like his ancestors he was a member of the Society of Friends. He married, December 1, 1791, Patience, born November 5, 1771, died October 16, 1822, daughter of Joseph and Elizabeth (Howell) Hopkins. She was also a member of the Society of Friends. Children: 1. Elizabeth, born October 8, 1792, died November 7, 1795. 2. Samuel, see forward. 3. Mary Ann, born May 28, 1796, died August 10, 1824. 4. Joseph

Hopkins, born April 26, 1798, died October 14, 1801. 5. Richard, born March 19, 1800, married, June 17, 1829, Mary, daughter of Isaac and Letitia West. 6. Elizabeth, born May 13, 1802, died April 24, 1804. 7. Philip Thomas, born June 26, 1803. 8. Caroline, born January 4, 1807. 9. John P., born February 25, 1809, died August 20, 1819. 10. James, born October 6, 1811. 11. Isaac, born September 9, 1813. 12. William, born May 20, 1815.

Samuel Philip Snowden, son of Philip and Patience (Hopkins) Snowden, was born January 13, 1794, at Indian Spring, Maryland. He married in Anne Arundel county, January 18, 1822, Mary Richardson, daughter of John T. and Jemima (Sheckells) Richardson. Children: 1. John Thomas, for a number of years clerk in Supreme Court. 2. Marcellus P., born June 16, 1824. 3. Richard Hopkins, see forward. 4. Philip M., born June 14, 1831, sheriff of Baltimore City in 1876; married, November 18, 1851, Sallie E. Knighton; children: i. Florence May, born October 22, 1856, married, April 14, 1880, Frank Ehlen. ii. Ella, born in October, 1859; married Henry Norment. 5. Samuel, born October 13, 1833, died November 9, 1894; married, May 14, 1863, S. Emma Hoff; children: 1. Corinne Adelaide, born in March, 1864. ii. Mary Ida, born in June, 1865. iii. Samuel Guy, born in September, 1868. iv. Margaret Elizabeth, born in August, 1875.

Richard Hopkins Snowden, third son of Samuel Philip and Mary (Richardson) Snowden, was born November 19, 1827. He was a prominent and successful member of the legal profession. True to the faith of his forefathers he remained a member of the Baltimore Friends Meeting. He married, January 18, 1853, Martha A. Sells, of Columbus, Ohio. He spent all his active life in the city of Baltimore, where he became a highly respected and influential citizen.

He died December 15, 1877. Martha A. (Sells) Snowden was a daughter of Ephraim Sells, born near Columbus, Ohio, son of William Henry and Elizabeth (Ebbey) Sells, grandson of Ludwick and Catherine (Deardorff) Sells, and great-grandson of John Sells, who came from Holland to Pennsylvania in 1723. Ludwick Sells served in the Revolutionary army and William Henry Sells in the War of 1812. Children of Richard Hopkins and Martha A. (Sells) Snowden: 1. Wilbur Lee, born December 7, 1854, married in 1875, Mary Reilly; children: i. Francis R., born October 4, 1876. ii. Mattie Sells, born June 26, 1877, died August 19, 1878. 2. Annie Richardson, see forward. 3. Kate, born December 27, 1857. 4. Harris, born September 16, 1860. 5. Louis, twin of Harris. 6. Richard Hopkins, born May 8, 1864. 7. Ray Cooper, born July 16, 1870.

Annie Richardson Snowden, daughter of Richard Hopkins and Martha A. (Sells) Snowden, was born May 25, 1856. She married, April 4, 1877, Charles M. Lanahan, a prominent merchant and banker of Baltimore and son of William and Mary (Jackson) Lanahan. Charles M. Lanahan received his education in the schools of Baltimore and at Chester Military Academy, Chester, Pennsylvania. Shortly after graduation from the latter institution he became associated with his brothers, William Lanahan, Jr., and Samuel J., in the business founded many years before by their father. Inheriting the progressive ideas that brought wealth and fame to his father, he largely increased the scope of the firm's business. As a business man he was noted for his aptitude in grappling with details and for his accurate and keen perception, but his strongest points, perhaps, were his executive ability, his power to analyze any business proposition and his fertility of resources. He was a tireless worker, a man of strong and steady purposes, rare judgment, and those admirable qualities which have given high character to the commercial life of Baltimore. Quick and decisive in his methods he was keenly alive to any proposition and its possibilities, and found that pleasure in the solution of a difficult business problem without which there can be no real success. His death, which occurred February 7, 1901, was keenly felt by all who knew him, and was an irreparable loss to the business world of Baltimore. Children: 1. Mary Sells, born June 4, 1878; married, January 6, 1904, Charles Warren Leland, son of Warren and Mary (Cobb) Leland; children: Helen May, born May 29, 1905, died January 18, 1907. 2. Helen Snowden, born February 9, 1880; married, October 21, 1903, Wilson Miles Cary, son of John Brune and Frances (Daniels) Cary; children: Anne Snowden, born July 26, 1904, and Wilson Miles, born January 22, 1906. 3. Josephine Reeder, born August 20, 1882; married, June 10, 1903, James Clarke Dulany, son of James Clarke and Caroline (Dickey) Dulany; one child: Josephine Clarke, born January 23, 1906. 4. Adelaide Daniels, born May 30, 1885; married, November 15, 1905, Henry Duranquet Brennan, son of Thomas and Catherine Brennan; children: Catherine, born October 15, 1906; Josephine, born November 6, 1907; Margaret, born December 19, 1908; Anne Snowden, born September 12, 1915. 5. Charles M., born January 18, 1894.

Michael Jenkins.

MICHAEL JENKINS

CONSPICUOUS in his civic virtues, deeply interested in any enterprise affecting the moral, material or civic improvements of Baltimore, generous in his contributions and benefactions, yet most unostentatious, Michael Jenkins did not need the prestige of his high position in the business world to endear him to his fellow-men.

Although a leader financially, and possessed of a large fortune, accumulated through wise investment, and far-sighted business judgment, he was never a lover of money for the sake of possession, but valued his wealth for the opportunity it gave him to help his fellow-men, and to aid the cause of christianity, education, philanthropy and charity. Although he was ranked among the great "Captains of Industry" he was a constructive captain, not a wrecker; a builder, not a destroyer. He dealt in a big broad way, was scrupulously just, and never took a business advantage of anyone. Nothing was so repugnant to his nature as the thought of wrecking a property to secure control of it, or for driving a man to the wall for profit to himself. His theory of business was that any transaction could be carried through on terms absolutely fair to all concerned, and would not lend his aid to any transaction requiring a departure from that theory, but subordinated business to equity, his personal relations and his friendships.

Mr. Jenkins walked in the footsteps of his honored father, his public and official life marked by a high sense of justice, commercial honor and integrity. His public services were many. His great activity in the reconstruction of Baltimore after the fire of 1904 was one of them, and to him, primarily, belongs the credit of the city's acquisition of a large part of its present water front property under favorable conditions, for when litigation threatened to delay indefinitely the purchase of the property, he avoided the clashes between rival property interests by purchasing the front needed for piers, and deeded it to the city at the price paid. Difficult indeed would it be to enumerate all the material benefits which have accrued to Baltimore through the life and service of Mr. Jenkins; difficult to put into words the power of his example, and the force of his inspiration in leading others to emulate that example. For half a century, Michael Jenkins and his father, Thomas C. Jenkins, were closely associated in the management of the Baltimore Safe Deposit and Trust Company, and with the Merchants and Miners Transportation Company, both institutions potent in the upbuilding of Baltimore.

The charities of Mr. Jenkins were unbounded, but he dispensed without ostentation, trying not to let his left hand know what his right hand was doing. They could not, however, be concealed, his reputation for generosity becoming widespread. Appeals were made to him from all quarters without distinction of race or religion. His desk, in the office of the Safe Deposit and Trust Company was often stacked with petitions for relief, which, with great patience and good humor, he would investigate, assistance being granted to those found deserving.

Mr. Jenkins was a devoted member of the Catholic church, and a warm personal friend of Cardinal Gibbons, who relied implicitly upon the judgment of his friend, the financier, when any sum of appreciable size was to be invested for church institutions. No one will ever know the great number of gifts that Mr. Jenkins made through the Cardinal, and other clergy of the arch-diocese, to charity. Practically every charitable institution, orphanage, and hospital, under the patronage of the church, enjoyed his beneficences. For his splendid work for the Catholic University of America, and for his other activities in behalf of the cause of Catholicism, Mr. Jenkins and his wife were ennobled by Pope Pius X, in May, 1905, and created Duke and Duchess of the Holy Roman Empire. When interviewed by a reporter concerning the honor, Mr. Jenkins said: "All you can say for me is that I am an American citizen, and will never be anything else."

Michael Jenkins, youngest child of Charles Courtney and Louisa (Carrell) Jenkins, was born in Baltimore, Maryland, December 27, 1842, died there September 7, 1915. He prepared in Baltimore schools, then entered Mount St. Mary's College, whence he was graduated, class of 1862. In 1865, he succeeded with his brother to the leather business established by his father, and as a member of the firm, Jenkins Brothers, began his business career. As his father withdrew from his other enterprises, he succeeded him, and upon the death of B. F. Newcomer, succeeded to the presidency of the Merchants' and Miners' Transportation Company. That office he held from 1896 until 1907, when he resigned, but retained his interest in the company, and its management, as chairman of the board of directors.

Mr. Jenkins became also heavily interested in railroad enterprises, especially in the Atlantic Coast Line Railway, and its subsidiaries; controlled with his brother, George C., and Joseph W. Jenkins, and Alexander Brown, the United Railways of Baltimore; the Baltimore Electric Company; was one of the largest individual stockholders of the United Railways; of the Merchants' and Miners' Transportation Company; of the Atlantic Coast Line Company; the Louisville and Nashville Railroad Company; was a large holder of the securities of the Consolidation Coal Company; the Consolidated Gas, Electric and Power Company; the Northern Central Railroad Company; and interested in many enterprises in Baltimore, and elsewhere. He was officially connected with the Atlantic Coast Line from early manhood, and was always consulted by Henry Waters, its official head, upon any matter of policy or expansion. He and Mr. Waters were close personal friends, as well as business friends, and it was in this spirit of warm personal regard that they consulted, not as two business men planning from a selfish standpoint.

Mr. Jenkins became president of the Atlantic Coast Line Company of Connecticut, which was the holding company for the stock of the railroad company, the Atlantic Coast Line, of which he was a director. He was also vice-president of the Northern Central Railway, and a director of the Metropolitan Savings Bank. He rarely missed a meeting of the board of directors of the railroad company, or of the holding company; was exceedingly alert as to the physical condition of the property, it being his custom to make tours of inspection over the lines with the other officials at least once, and frequently twice each year. In the local enterprises in which he was interested, he never sought official representation, his brother, George C. Jenkins, who was also connected in practically all the enterprises named, being particularly in charge of such affairs. An exception was the Safe Deposit and Trust Company, of which Michael Jenkins was president. He grew to the position of one of Baltimore's foremost citizens, his influence great, probably greater and broader than any other citizen enjoyed. This influence was not gained by his wealth, but because of his personality, his keenness of financial judgment, his understanding of the human side of investment, and his absolute willingness to give every party to a transaction his just due. He was of Baltimore, he believed in Baltimore, and was one of the not numerous body of men who appreciated the value of industrial development to the extent of standing sponsor financially.

Mr. Jenkins was never a public character; was a Democrat, rarely missed voting, but never took active part in politics. He was deeply interested in bringing the National Democratic Convention to Baltimore in 1912; contributed largely to the movement to obtain that convention; escorted his friend, Cardinal Gibbons, to the armory to deliver the opening prayer, and was constant in his attendance upon the sessions. He was not a clubman in the accepted sense, but held membership in many clubs, including the Maryland, Merchants, Elk Ridge, Green Spring Valley, Baltimore University, Baltimore Country, and the Bachelors' Cotillion.

It was for his philanthropies that he was best known to the community at large. He was deeply interested in educational affairs generally, especially friendly toward Peabody Institute, and the Maryland Institute. He was a trustee of Peabody, and, with Andrew Carnegie, gave the present lot and building now occupied by the institute. When the big fire in Baltimore left the Maryland Institute homeless, Andrew Carnegie promised to give $263,000 toward the erection of a new building, provided Baltimore would give the site. The lot adjoining Corpus Christi Church, erected by the family of Thomas Courtney Jenkins, was chosen as a suitable location. This vacant lot had been bought by Michael Jenkins with the sole purpose of protecting the surroundings of the church, and when he was approached by the committee, and asked to sell, he told them he would donate the valuable lot, provided a suitable building was erected, one that would harmonize architecturally with the church. His offer was accepted, and when Mr. Carnegie was notified that the lot was secured he wrote: "I congratulate the Maryland Institute upon receiving such a splendid gift, and I also congratulate Baltimore upon having such a citizen as Mr. Jenkins."

A member of the Roman Catholic church, as were his parents, he gave to that church the devotion of a lifetime. He was one of the founders of the Catholic University of America, was its treasurer and member of the board of trustees, and one of the largest subscribers to its building fund. As trustee, he worked in association with Cardinal Gibbons, and was largely instrumental in clearing up the affairs of the university after the Wagaman difficulties of 1904. He was also a trustee of the Baltimore Cathedral, and with his brothers and sisters caused Corpus Christi Church—Jenkins Memorial Church—to be erected as a memorial to their parents, an edifice regarded as the most beautiful church building in Baltimore. It was for such activity as a layman that the title previously referred to was conferred by Pope Pius X, in May, 1905. Mr. Jenkins' charities were bestowed from a high sense of religious obligation. He regarded himself, not as the absolute owner, but as the steward of those goods which were placed in his hands, and he experienced the truth, that the greatest happiness in life is the contributing to the happiness of others, and to bring relief to the suffering, to bring sunshine to hearts heretofore dark and desolate.

Mr. Jenkins married, October 2, 1866, Mary Isabel Plowden Jenkins, born October 4, 1844; died in 1911; daughter of Austin Jenkins, of Baltimore, born May 10, 1806; died May 30, 1888. Austin Jenkins married, October 27, 1840, Margaret A. Jenkins, born December 15, 1816; died April 22, 1901, daughter of Judge John J. Jenkins, of Charles county, Maryland, and his wife, Mary (Plowden) Jenkins, of St. Mary county, Maryland, to whom he was married, February 22, 1822. The married life of Mr. Jenkins was most attractive, and in his home the domestic and religious virtues were cultivated in a marked degree. Mr. Jenkins often said that he regarded his wife under three aspects, as wife, as sweetheart, and as a companion. When she died in 1911, he received a blow from which he never recovered. So deep was his sorrow for her death that he never afterwards entered the city house, in which she died, nor even the country house, in which they spent the summers.

One of the last charitable acts of his life was the donation of a check, sent to the Pope through Cardinal Gibbons, that his Holiness was to use for the relief of war sufferers. The reply with an acknowledgement came but a few hours prior to his death.

WILLIAM REED

THE name of Reed, in various forms, is in use among many nations, the spelling being varied in many cases to suit individual taste. The mode of spelling in use by the Puritan ancestors was usually Reade, but in some cases Reede, and one of them called it Rede. The mode of spelling the name in this country has gradually assumed one of the three following forms: Read, Reed and Reid, and different members of the same family use all these methods. It was formerly combined with other words to form names with new signification as Ethelred, or Reed the Good; Conrad, or Reed the Powerful; Elred, or Reed the Elder; Alfred, or Reed the Shrewd; and it was found that when William the Conqueror took possession of the English throne in 1066, the legal heir to the throne was brother-in-law to the King of Scotland. It is to be seen from the earliest records of the Reed family that they were, as a rule, large in stature and of unusual strength, and these physical characteristics still distinguish the majority of the family at the present day. In 1400 the name Thomas Reed, of Redesdale, occurs in the county records, and in 1427 his name appears in the jury about Elsden Church. In 1400, Sir Huphrey Lisle Kent gave to William Reed, of Thoroughhend, the hamlet called Bromhope, in Redesdale, in exchange for lands in Rutland and Redsmith, and not long after the reign of Elizabeth, John Reede of the family is styled "chief" of his name. He kept up the habits of his family, and cultivated the martial spirit for which they had become justly celebrated.

A scion of this house was George Compton Reed, of Heathpool and Northumberland, and by his will he bequeathed money to the poor of Kirk-Newton parish. George Compton Reed succeeded his cousin as ninth baronet. William Reed, grandson of Edward Reed, of Berkshire, obtained from Henry VIII, Barton Court, which was part of the property of the abbey of Abingdon in 1536. He was buried in St. Helen's Church, of which he was a great benefactor. Thomas Reed, son of the preceding, married Ann Hoo, of the Hoo, County Hertford. They had a son Thomas, who married Mary Stonehouse, of Little Peckham. Their son, also named Thomas, was knighted by Queen Elizabeth, and married Mary, daughter of Sir John Brocket, in Hertfordshire. They had five children: Thomas, John, James, and two daughters. The sons were all knighted.

Thomas Reed, son of Thomas and Mary (Brocket) Reed, married Mary Cornwall, daughter of Thomas Cornwall, Lord of Stropshire, and they had children: Compton, who as the eldest son, secured the honor of knighthood; Edward, whose daughter, Elizabeth, married, February 12, 1635, John Winthrop, Jr., first Governor of Connecticut; Thomas and John, who came to this country in 1630; William, who came to America in the ship "Defense," in 1635, and settled in Woburn, Massachusetts. He is said to be the ancestor of the Reeds of Maine, and many others. Thomas settled in Salem, Massachusetts. He was a very prominent man in the colony, held the rank of colonel as early as 1643, and had several sons born in this country. He returned to England, was a colonel in the British army at the time of the restoration of Charles II, died, in England, in 1663, and his son, Abraham Palmer, settled his estate in America.

John Reed, fourth son of Thomas and Mary (Cornwall) Reed, was commonly called Major John Reed. He came to America, in 1630, with his brother Thomas. The land granted to him at Salem was forfeited for not being occupied. He was a resident of New London in 1650, removed to the Barbadoes, and had extensive mercantile interests in that place, which, after his death, was carried on by his son, Joseph. He had three sons: John, Joseph and Thomas.

Joseph Reed, son of John Reed, after accumulating considerable capital in the West India trade, decided to settle his sons upon what was then western land, and as early as 1700 was located with his sons at what is now Trenton, New Jersey. In 1734 a post office was established at his residence in Trenton, and his son, Andrew Reed, was made postmaster. He had other sons, John, Andrew, William, and probably Thomas. Andrew Reed was long an active and prominent citizen of Trenton. Besides being postmaster, he was chosen, September 1, 1744, commissioner of the loan office; in 1746, was made one of the burgesses of the newly created borough of Trenton, and its treasurer, and March 28, 1749, was commissioned one of the judges of the courts of Hunterdon county. He was engaged in mercantile pursuits, and in addition was considerably interested in the iron industry, in association with others. In 1743 Andrew Reed, and Joseph Peace, advertised for the recovery of a servant lad, twenty years old, who had run away. In 1748 the iron works near Bordentown was advertised for sale. This was an extensive plant for that day, located on Black Creek, about half a mile from "Burden's Town." The creek was navigable for boats up to the works, and these works included three fires, with hammers, anvils, bellows and all appliances, also a dwelling-house and two dwellings for workmen, stables, storehouses and various conveniences. The land covered twenty acres, or thereabouts, lying on both sides of the creek, with a small orchard of some forty well-grown apple trees. The owners, beside Mr. Reed, were Joseph Yard, David Davis and Francis Bowes, the latter, Mr. Reed's father-in-law, who was then residing in Philadelphia. This sale seems to have been accomplished, for in 1749 Andrew Reed removed to Philadelphia, accompanied by his neighbor, John Pettit, and there they engaged in general merchandising under the style of Reed & Pettit, with a store on Front street. Reed & Pettit were among the prominent underwriters of Philadelphia, for we find the firm subscribing to marine policies in considerable amounts as early as July, 1759, as shown by Walter Shee's books, and as late as November, 1762, we find them in Kidd's and Bradford's books. In 1749 Mr. Reed was manager of a lottery "set up" in Philadelphia for the benefit of the New Jersey College—the Princeton University of the present day. Andrew Reed is said to have resided in Philadelphia ten years, at the end of which period he removed back to Trenton, and later to Amwell township, Hunterdon county, where he died, December 16, 1759. He was thrice married (first) to Sarah Pearson; (second) to Theodosia Bowes; and (third) to Louise de Normandie, and was the father of ten children: Two by first wife: Elizabeth Reed, born 1736; married, 1767, Rev. Joseph Montgomery, and died two years later, in 1769; Sarah, married, April 5, 1758, Charles Pettit, son of John Pettit. Six by second wife: Bowes, married (first) Margaret Johnson, who died, December 6, 1786; (second) Caroline Moore, who died, November 6, 1789; Joseph, mentioned below; and Ann, Mary, Thomas and Francis, these last dying in infancy, or in early childhood. There were two children by the third wife: John and Andrew, the latter died in infancy, and the former in 1807, in Cecil county, Maryland.

Joseph Reed, son of Andrew and Theodosia (Bowes) was one of the most conspicuous figures of the Revolutionary period. He was born August 27, 1741, in Trenton, New Jersey, and received his early education at the old Philadelphia Academy, which institution, in due course of time, became the University of Pennsylvania. At the age of ten years he returned with his family to New Jersey, and was graduated from Princeton College, then the College of New Jersey, in 1757, at the age of sixteen years. Subsequently entering the office of Richard Stockton, the leading lawyer of New Jersey —afterwards one of the "Signers"—Mr. Reed prepared himself for the legal profession, and was admitted to the bar of that province, in 1763. Determining to acquire the best professional equipment obtainable, he went to London, entered himself at the Middle Temple, took a two years' course, and returned to America, in 1766. The period of his residence in England was one of great importance so far as concerned the relations between Great Britain and her colonies, involving, as it did, the stamp act agitation, and the discussion and consideration of the crown's colonial policy; and the young lawyer had ample opportunity to hear the exciting debates in parliament and catch the spirit of the day, as it swayed and swept the British capital, now for, and now against, the employment of coercive measures in the treatment of the sons of England across the seas.

Almost immediately after the return of Mr. Reed to America, and his arrival in Philadelphia, the annual commencement was held at the institution which he had attended in 1751, now become the College of Philadelphia. The Sargent medal was offered for the best essay on "The Reciprocal Advantages of a Perpetual Union Between Great Britain and Her Colonies." Mr. Reed, as a former student at the institution, determined to compete, though he had but a brief time at his disposal. The papers submitted were opened and read, May 8, 1766. While the young Jerseyman was not accorded the first honor—which went to Dr. John Margan, afterward a distinguished surgeon in the Continental Army —nor the second, which went to Stephen Watts—he won third place in the competition. Mr. Reed was at this time twenty-five years of age. The treatise written by him evidenced his interest in a subject which, a few years later, when it became a paramount issue between Great Britain and her offspring, engrossed his best thoughts and highest energies. He at once entered upon the practice of his profession with characteristic zeal, first, for two or three years, in Trenton, New Jersey, his native city, and then after his marriage, in Philadelphia. So rapid and pronounced was his progress that not many years elapsed before he had become the leader of the local bar. Writing, February 29, 1772, to her brother in England, his wife said:

Of the four greatest lawyers in the city, three have resigned from practice. Mr. Galloway being a good deal advanced in life, and having a very large fortune, cares very little about it. Mr. Dickinson also married a wife worth £30,000, is improving and building on his estate, and Mr. Wain, whom you may remember in the Temple with Mr. Reed, is on a sudden turned Quaker preacher. He had a very great business—they say nearly £2,000 a year, but he has resigned on principle, as he says no good man can practice law.

Writing in his diary, two years later—August 28, 1774 —upon his first visit to Philadelphia, as a delegate to the Continental Congress, John Adams said: "Jo Reed is at the head of his profession in Philadelphia; Fish is next. Wain and Dickinson have retired."

But, successful and distinguished as Mr. Reed became at the bar, the events which were about to happen, in the city of his adoption, were of such a character as to require his best abilities in a different direction, and the last decade of his short, but brilliant life, a period of great strenuosity for him, was almost entirely given over to public affairs. When the tension between Great Britain and the colonies reached a critical stage, and hostilities seemed imminent, Mr. Reed's sympathies and influence were all cast into the scale in favor of the American Revolutionary program, though almost without exception the other great lawyers, then at the local bar, pursued a contrary course. When John Adams arrived in Philadelphia at the close of August, 1774, to attend the first Continental Congress, he found Joseph Reed one of the leaders among the thinking men of the day, and took occasion to seek the Quaker City attorney's society as frequently as possible. He makes mention of Mr. Reed in his diary upon the very day of his arrival in the city—August 29, 1774—and there are frequent references to him in the subsequent pages. A few days thereafter he wrote: "This Mr. Reed is a very sensible and accomplished lawyer, and of an amiable disposition, soft, tender, friendly; he is a friend of this country and to liberty. Mr. Reed was so kind as to wait on us to Mr. Sproat's meeting where we heard Mr. Spence."

Writing February 10, 1775, to Lord Dartmouth, secretary of state for the colonies, whom he had known, in London, Mr. Reed thus expressed his sentiments upon the strained relations then existing between England and America: "I am very sensible that the disposition I have mentioned may by some be imputed to timidity and apprehension of division among ourselves. * * * But this country will be deluged with blood before it will submit to any other taxation than by their own Legislature."

Mr. Reed was appointed a member of the committee of correspondence for Philadelphia, in November, 1774; was a delegate to the provincial convention of July 15, 1774; also to that of January 23, 1775, of which body he was made president; served as a member of the committee of safety, October 20, 1775, to July 22, 1776; was chosen lieutenant colonel of the Pennsylvania Associators, or militia, organized after the battle of Lexington, and July 4, 1775, was commissioned lieutenant-colonel and military secretary to the commander-in-chief, General Washington. A year later, June

5, 1776, he was appointed adjutant general of the Continental Army with the rank of colonel. This he resigned January 2, 1777. Having served with Washington during the movements about New York, including the battle of Long Island, he was solicited by his chief in 1777 to accept a commission —which Congress had offered—as brigadier-general, with command of all the American cavalry. This he declined, as he did also an appointment, March 20, 1777, as the first chief justice of Pennsylvania under the constitution of 1776, preferring to remain attached to Washington's headquarters as a volunteer aide, without rank or pay. With Washington he participated in the battles of Brandywine, Germantown and Monmouth, though chosen a delegate to Congress, September 16, 1777, and again in December, of the same year. In October, 1777, he had also been elected a member of the assembly, but declined the office, though he had previously served in that body for a short time, having been chosen in January, 1776. He was elected a member of the Supreme Executive Council, July 21, 1778, which post he accepted, and December 22, 1778, he was made president of the council, a position equivalent to the governorship of the commonwealth. This latter office he held three years. The extravagance attendant upon the maladministration of Benedict Arnold during his command of the American forces in Philadelphia are well known. Upon charges brought by President Reed, and the council, Mr. Arnold was court-martialed, and thereafter he was aggressively hostile to President Reed. Writing, February 8, 1779, to Margaret Shippen, whom he married shortly afterward, he said: "I am treated with the greatest politeness by General Washington, and the officers of the Army, who bitterly execrate Mr. Reed and the council for their villainous attempt to injure me." A notable incident in Joseph Reed's Revolutionary career, and one with which

all students of American history are familiar, was the attempt
of a representative of the British government, Commissioner
George Johnstone, to bribe him with an offer of £10,000 in
cash, and an appointment to any office in the Colonies within
the gift of the crown. Mr. Reed's reply was: "I am not
worth purchasing, but such as I am, the King of Great Britain
is not rich enough to do it."

Leaving the presidential chair, in 1781, Joseph Reed
resumed the practice of his profession. In the year following
he was chosen one of the "councillors and agents" of Pennsylvania in the dispute between this State and Connecticut,
which had resulted in bloodshed not long previously. His
argument before the commission lasted two days. He was
later elected a delegate to Congress, but owing to ill health,
never took his seat. There was a sentimental side to Joseph
Reed's life which is more interesting to the reader than a
portrayal of his public career. In England, when a student
at the Temple, he had met and fallen in love with Esther de
Berdt, daughter of Dennis de Berdt, a London merchant, a
representative of an old Huguenot family which had removed for political and religious reasons from Ypres,
Flanders, to England, in the middle of the sixteenth century. When Joseph Reed returned to America, from London,
in 1766, he and Miss de Berdt—who was born in that city,
October 22, 1746—were practically engaged, but the prospect
for their union was altogether dubious. The de Berdts were
opposed to their daughter's removal to America, while Mr.
Reed could not see his way clear to locating permanently
in England. Moreover, Mr. Reed's father, now well advanced in years, was in no small degree dependent upon the
son for support. The love letters which passed between the
two, breathing of highest form of devotion and solicitude,
are found in the exquisite little volume, "Life of Esther

Reed," edited by their grandson, William B. Reed, and published in 1853. In 1769, came the death of the father, Andrew Reed, following which event, Joseph sailed for England, and May 22, 1770, the wedding took place. Shortly thereafter bride and groom sailed for America and established their home in Philadelphia, on Chestnut street, below Fourth. Like her husband, Mrs. Reed became a notable figure in the life of Philadelphia. In the spring of 1780, when the distress of the American army was at its height, money being scarce, and prices of all commodities having risen to a phenomenal height, the ladies of Philadelphia undertook the collection of money and clothing for the half-starved and poorly clad troops. Mrs. Reed assumed the lead in this movement, which was successful to a degree unanticipated, the collections in Philadelphia city and county alone amounting to $300,000, paper currency. In a letter of July 4, 1780, addressed to General Washington, Mrs. Reed acquainted him with the result of the collection, and added:

The ladies are anxious for the soldiers to receive the benefit of it, and await your directions how it can best be disposed of. We expect considerable additions from the country, and have also written to the other states in hopes the ladies there will adopt similar plans to render it more general and beneficial. With the utmost pleasure I offer any further attention and care in my power to complete the execution of the design, and shall be happy to accomplish it, agreeable to the intentions of the donors and your wishes on the subject. The ladies of my family join me in their respectful compliments and sincere prayer for your health, safety and success. I have the honor to be with the highest respect,

Your obedient humble servant,

E. REED.

Mrs. Reed did not long survive the writing of this letter. In the previous January she had been ill with smallpox, and her death occurred September 18, 1780. This notice of the event is found in the "Pennsylvania Gazette" of the 27th instant:

On Monday the 18th instant died after a few days illness, in the thirty-third year of her age, Mrs. Esther Reed, consort of his Excellency, the President of this State. Possessed of every female virtue which could adorn herself and station, this amiable lady lived beloved and died lamented by all who had the happiness of her friendship and acquaintance. On Tuesday her remains were interred in the Second Presbyterian burial ground in this city, with every mark of respect due to her merit and character, being attended by his Excellency, the President, and the members of Congress and their principal Boards, the General Assembly and Supreme Executive Council, officers of the Army and the State, and a great concourse of numerous friends and acquaintances

Her husband survived her less than five years, and died March 5, 1785, being not quite forty-four years of age. Joseph and Esther (de Berdt) Reed were the parents of six children: 1. Martha, born May 21, 1771, died unmarried. 2. Joseph, mentioned below. 3. Esther, born July 21, 1774, died May 22, 1847. 4. Theodosia, born October 2, 1776, died may 12, 1778. 5. Dennis de Berdt, born May 12, 1778, graduated from Princeton College, in 1797, and died at sea, February 5, 1805. 6. George Washington, born May 26, 1780, graduated from Princeton College, 1798, was commissioned midshipman, United States Navy, January 13, 1799, and lieutenant, March 10, 1803. In the early stages of the War of 1812, he commanded the brig "Vixen," which was captured by the British frigate "Southampton," commanded by Sir James Lucas Yeo. Shortly after the surrender of the "Vixen" both vessels ran ashore and were wrecked. The property was largely recovered through the generous and hazardous exertions of the captive American sailors. The British commandant publicly acknowledged his obligations to Lieutenant Reed for the services of his crew, and offered him a parole with permission to return to the United States. He declined, however, to leave his comrades. He died shortly afterward, January 4, 1813, at Kingston, Jamaica, while still a prisoner-of-war, of a fever induced by exposure and fatigue.

Joseph Reed, second child of Joseph and Esther (de Berdt) Reed, was born July 11,1772, in Philadelphia, and died March 4, 1845. Graduating from Princeton College in 1792, he was admitted to the Philadelphia bar, March 10, 1792, having studied law while still in college. At this time, it will be observed, he was not yet twenty years of age. He was appointed, January 2, 1800, prothonotary of the Supreme Court of Pennsylvania, and continued in that office until May 13, 1809. In the same month, January 22, 1800, he was likewise commissioned clerk of the Court of Quarter Sessions of the County of Philadelphia, and filled this post until November 9, 1805. In 1810-11 he filled the office of city solicitor of Philadelphia. For a portion of the period—October 2, 1810, to January 26, 1811—he also held the post of attorney general of the commonwealth. In the year first mentioned, 1810, he was likewise appointed to the position of recorder of the city, and performed the duties of this important judicial office until 1829. He was also named, in 1818, a member of the first board of control of the public schools. Mr. Reed was elected a member of the Hibernian Society in 1811. At a "war meeting," held August 25, 1814, when Philadelphia was threatened by the British, he acted as secretary, and was placed on the "Committee of Defense" at that time appointed. He had been elected a member of the First Troop, Philadelphia City Cavalry, May 12, 1798, but had resigned May 7, 1810. When, however, his native city seemed in peril, Mr. Reed, August 27, 1814, rejoined his old command, but a year later, August 4, 1815, all danger being past, he resigned a second time. January 19, 1816, he was chosen a member of the American Philosophical Society. In 1816, he was a candidate for Presidential elector on a combination ticket, supported by independent Democrats and by Federalists, but the regular Democratic ticket was successful. Joseph Reed married, June 15, 1805, Maria Ellis Watmough, daughter of James Horatio and Anna Christiana (Carmick) Watmough, born December 18, 1784; died January 22, 1865, nineteen years a widow. They had seven children: 1. William Bradford, mentioned below. 2. Henry Hope. 3. Anna, born June 3, 1811, died August 8, 1812. 4. Maria, born May 24, 1813, died at an advanced age. 5. Emily. 6. Margaret Sergeant. 7. Joseph, born November 28, 1825, spent a year at the University of Pennsylvania, 1841-42, received an appointment as an assistant in the United States Coast Survey Service, and lost his life by drowning at Annapolis, Maryland, in 1852.

William Bradford Reed, eldest son of Joseph and Maria Ellis (Watmough) Reed, was born June 30, 1806. He inherited the intellectual abilities of his progenitors, and attained a high degree of distinction in professional and public life. Graduating from the University of Pennsylvania in 1822, he studied law, and was admitted to the Philadelphia bar, November 26, 1826. So successful was he as a legal practitioner, that April 2, 1838, he was made attorney general of Pennsylvania. He was also solicitor for the County of Philadelphia, 1836-41. He was recognized not only as an able advocate, but was also renowned for his oratorical abilities. He was likewise noted for his scholarly attainments along other than merely professional lines, in 1850 was appointed professor of American History at the University of Pennsylvania, was the author or editor of a number of biographical and kindred works, among others: "Life and Correspondence of Joseph Reed," 1847; "Life of Esther de Berdt, afterward Esther Reed," 1853; "President Reed of Pennsylvania, a Reply to George Bancroft, and Others," 1867; "A Rejoinder to Mr. Bancroft's Historical Essay," 1867, and others. When a young man Mr. Reed had a brief experience in the diplomatic service, as private secretary of Joel R. Poinsett, who was appointed United States minister to Mexico, March 8, 1825. Thirty-two years afterward he re-entered the service, being commissioned, April 18, 1857, minister to China, where he remained nearly two years, during which time he negotiated the important treaty of June, 1858, "that secured to the United States all the advantages that had been acquired by the allies from the Chinese." Returning to America, Mr. Reed removed to New York City, where he re-engaged in the practice of his profession, and where his death occurred February 18, 1876. William B. Reed married (first) October 13, 1833, Louisa Whelan, daughter of Thomas and Eliza (Bickham) Whelan, of Baltimore, who died November 27, 1847. He married (second), January 15, 1850, Mary Love Ralston, daughter of Robert and Anne (Boote) Ralston, who was born February 16, 1825, and died November 15, 1867. Children by first marriage: Emily, Anna, William, mentioned below; George Washington, Louisa Whelan, died young; Louise Whelan; by second marriage: Mary Love, Robert Ralston, Emily de Berdt and Henry Seymour, of whom all but four died unmarried.

William Reed, eldest son of William B. and Louisa (Whelan) Reed, was born June 7, 1838, in Philadelphia. He graduated from the University of Pennsylvania in 1856, and was admitted to the bar of Philadelphia, May 5, 1860. When his father, Hon. William B. Reed, was appointed United States minister to China, young Mr. Reed accompanied him to the Orient and acted as secretary of the legation. In 1868, he removed to Baltimore, where he passed the rest of his life, becoming prominent in business and social circles. For many years he was a member of the well-known railroad supply firm of Morton, Reed & Company. Mr. Reed was a member of the Maryland Club, joining in 1869, and for a number of years was one of its governors. He married, April 25, 1871, Miss Emilie McKim, a descendant of an old and distinguished family of Maryland.

RICHARD ISAAC DUVALL

FIVE generations of American ancestors preceded Richard Isaac Duvall in Maryland. The original ancestor, Mareen Duvall, came from France to Anne Arundel county, about the middle of the seventeenth century. He was a man of strong religious principles as the sequel shows, and of a family of note, bearing arms:

Arms—Gules, a chevron argent between two mullets pierced, and a battle axe of the last.

Crest—A lion sejant, per pale argent and gules sustaining a shield as in the Arms.

Motto—*Pro Patria.*

Richard Isaac Duvall, of the sixth generation of the family in America, was of a strong and sturdy type of character, honorable and upright, and unflinching in his advocacy of any cause he deemed a righteous one. That trait of his Huguenot ancestor was transmitted to him unweakened by the lapse of time.

Mareen Duvall, the first of the family who settled in Maryland, is said to have come from the neighborhood of Nantes, Brittany, and some support is lent to this statement by the fact that he gave to the first piece of land patented to him the name of "Lavall," and there is a town called "Val" and a chateau "Laval" some sixty or seventy miles from Nantes. The name "Mareen" is clearly a corruption of the French "Marin" and he was undoubtedly a French Huguenot. Although the Edict of Nantes was not repealed until 1685, those of "the religion," as the Huguenots called themselves, were nevertheless severely oppressed by the government, and many of them emigrated to other lands. It was doubtless for this reason that Mareen Duvall settled in Maryland, to round out his days in peace, safe from the persecution that prevailed in his native land. The date of his arrival in Maryland is not recorded, but it was certainly before 1659 and probably not far from 1650. At any rate he made his demand for land, July 25, 1659, and this being duly laid out for him he had a patent, January 22, 1659-60, for a tract called "Lavall" on the west side of South river, in Anne Arundel county (Land Office, Lib. 4, fol. 431). Other tracts patented to him were "Middle Plantation," 600 acres, on the south side of South river, patented 1664 (Land Office, Lib. 7, fol. 450); "Duvall's Addition," 165 acres, on the west side of South river, patented August 8, 1670; and "Duvall's Range," 200 acres on east side of north branch of Patuxent river, in Anne Arundel county, patented September 10, 1672 (ibid. Lib. 14, fol. 22; Lib. 17, fol. 290).

Another tract called "Rich Neck," and containing 200 acres, was surveyed for Mareen Duvall and William Young, on the south side of South river, May 25, 1664 (Rent Roll, Lib. 1, fol. 33). In 1678 the Maryland Assembly passed an act appropriating a large amount of tobacco, then serving as currency, in payment of the service of those who had taken part in the recent expedition against the Nanticoke Indians (Md. Arch. vii, 87), and Mareen Duvall was paid eighty pounds of tobacco for his participation in the expedition (ibid 96). September 13, 1681, Thomas Francis and Nicholas Gassaway, writing to the Council about Indian outrages, state that in Anne Arundel county the Indians have killed a negro and wounded two white men—one mortally. The people are in great distress, since the Indians keep them constantly terrorized, and attack their dwelling houses, especially those of Mr. Duvall, and Richard Snowden (Md. Arch. xvii, 24). In 1683 an act was passed by the Assembly, and approved by Governor and Council, for the encouragement of trade by establishing with great liberality towns and ports of entry

in all the seaboard counties, and under the terms of this act
Mr. "Marien Duvall" is appointed one of the Commissioners
for establishing towns and ports in Anne Arundel county
(Md. Arch. vii, 611).

In one instance a glimpse is afforded of the immigrant's
political views. Colonel Nicholas Greenberry, in a communication to the Governor dated July 25, 1692, asserts that the
principal rendezvous of the leaders of the Jacobite party
were at "Darnall's, Chew's, Dorsey's and one Mareen Duvall's" (Md. Arch. viii, 343). During his long residence
in Maryland, Mareen Duvall acquired a large landed estate
by purchase, in addition to the tracts taken up by him, and
was thus able to provide handsomely for his large family of
twelve children. He styles himself "merchant" in his will,
and he doubtless engaged in the export of tobacco, a very
profitable occupation in those days, and one that stood in high
repute both in Virginia and in Maryland.

Mareen Duvall was three times married. The name of
his first wife has not been preserved. His second wife,
Susanna, is named in his will as the mother of his son, Mareen,
the younger, or Mareen II., as he is usually designated. His
third wife, Mary (Stanton) Duvall, sister of Daniel Stanton,
of Philadelphia, was married to him about 1693, the year
before he died, and bore him no children. According to
Judge Duvall, who left a thoroughly reliable genealogy of
the Duvall family (and of whom later) his grandfather, Benjamin Duvall, was born in 1692, and was the son of the immigrant by his second wife, Susanna. In all probability,
therefore, Mrs. Susanna Duvall died at the birth of her
youngest son, Benjamin, in 1692, and Mareen was married to
his third wife, Mary Stanton, in 1693. Mareen Duvall died
in August, 1694, and the following year his widow, Mrs.
Mary Duvall, married Colonel Henry Ridgely, in proof of

which we have the following: 9 October, 1695, "came Major Henry Ridgely, of Anne Arundel county, who intermarried with Mary, relict and executrix of Mareen Duvall, late of said county, deceased, and exhibited the inventory of said deceased's estate, etc. (Test, Proceedings). Major Henry Ridgely was soon promoted to Lieutenant-Colonel, and in 1695 his landed property, formerly in Anne Arundel county, was included in the newly formed county of Prince Georges'. He died in 1710, and by his will, dated April 30, 1705, and proved July 13, 1710, appointed his wife, Mary, his sole executrix. She soon married her third husband, Rev. Jacob Henderson, rector of Queen Anne Parish, Prince Georges' county, and afterward Commissary for the Province under the Bishop of London. Rev. Jacob Henderson died August 21, 1751. Mrs. Henderson survived until 1762. As she was married to Mareen Duvall in 1693, she must have been very old at the time of her death."

The order of the birth of Mareen Duvall's children followed below is that given by Judge Gabriel Duvall, and is shown by deposition filed in Provincial Court records. It is believed, on the same authority, that Mareen Duvall's first wife was the mother of the first five children, while Susanna was the mother of the remaining seven. It is to be noted that the immigrant had two sons named Mareen, both named in his will, and that Susanna was the mother of the younger. Mareen Duvall, who died in 1694, had issue by his first wife: 1. Mareen, "the elder," born in 1662, married, 1685-86, Frances, daughter of Captain Thomas and Mary (Wells) Stockett, of Anne Arundel county. 2. John, buried April 20, 1711; married, before August, 1685, Mary, daughter of William Jones, of Anne Arundel county. 3. Eleanor, married, before 1694, John Roberts, of Virginia. 4. Samuel, born 1667; married, June 18, 1697, Elizabeth Clark. 5. Susanna, married, before 1694, Robert Tyler, of Prince Georges' county.

Mareen Duvall and his second wife, Susanna, had issue: 6. Lewis, married, March 6, 1699, Martha, daughter of Robert Ridgely, principal secretary of the province; removed to South Carolina. 7. Mareen, through whom descent is traced. 8. Catherine, married, October 22, 1700, William Orrick. 9. Mary, married, July 5, 1701, Rev. Henry Hall, rector of St. James' Parish, Anne Arundel county. 10. Elizabeth, apparently unmarried in 1694. 11. Johanna, married, August 12, 1703, Richard Poole. 12. Benjamin, born 1692; died 1774; married, 1713, Sophia Griffith. The latter were the grandparents of Justice Gabriel Duvall, of the Supreme Court of the United States.

Justice Gabriel Duvall was born December 6, 1752. He married (first) a Miss Bryce, daughter of Captain Robert Bryce, of Annapolis, July 24, 1787. He married (second), May 5, 1795, Jane Gibbon, daughter of Captain James Gibbon, of Philadelphia. Beginning when very young he spent sixty-one years of his life in public service. In early life he was clerk to the Conventions in Maryland, clerk to the Council of Safety, and clerk to the first House of Representatives under the new Government. Later he was member of Congress. Then after serving as Judge of the General Court of Maryland and Comptroller of the Treasury of the United States, he was appointed Associate Judge of the United States Supreme Court, and held this honorable position from October, 1811, until his resignation in 1835 or 1836. He died March 6, 1844.

Mareen Duvall, "the younger," eldest child of Mareen Duvall, the Huguenot, and his second wife, Susanna, was born in Anne Arundel county, Maryland, in 1680. He is styled of "Great Marsh," but he removed to and died at his plantation, "Pleasant Grove," Queen Anne's Parish, Prince

Georges' county, Maryland, in June, 1741. He married, October 21, 1701, Elizabeth Jacob, who died in Prince Georges' county in February, 1752, daughter of Captain John Jacob. Children: Mareen, born March 14, 1703, married, November 25, 1725, Ruth Howard; Susannah, born September 12, 1704, married (first) Mr. Fowler, (second) Mark Brown; Elizabeth, born July 20, 1706, married Dr. William Denune; Samuel, through whom descent is traced; Anne, born May 10, 1709; Benjamin, born April 4, 1711, married Mary Wells; Jacob, born April 19, 1715, married Miss Bourne, of Calvert county, Maryland; Mary, born March 22, 1717; Lewis, born December 3, 1721, married Miss Hardesty; Gabriel, born September 13, 1724, died unmarried.

Samuel Duvall, son of Mareen and Elizabeth (Jacob) Duvall, was born at the parental estate, "Pleasant Grove," Prince Georges' county, Maryland, November 27, 1707, and died in November, 1775. He was a substantial planter and a man of influence, spending his entire life in Prince Georges' county. He married, May 16, 1732, Elizabeth Mulliken, born September 25, 1711, died after November 20, 1775, daughter of James and Charity (Belt) Mulliken, and granddaughter of James Mulliken, the Virginia settler. Children: James, born March 31, 1733, married his cousin, Sarah Duvall, daughter of Mareen and Ruth (Howard) Duvall; Charity, born May 6, 1734, married Mr. McDougal; Elisha, died January 8, 1837, married and left a son Benjamin; Elizabeth, born May 15, 1738, married Mr. Gover; Samuel, of further mention; Margaret, born January 30, 1742, married Mr. Denune; Jacob L., born May 13, 1744; Jeremiah, born August 24, 1745; Jesse, born April 4, 1748; Gabriel, born October 20, 1751.

Samuel (2) Duvall, son of Samuel (1) and Elizabeth (Mulliken) Duvall, was born July 7, 1740, and was a successful and influential planter of Prince Georges' county, Maryland. He was a soldier of the Revolutionary War, serving in the Maryland Line, went safely through his military experiences, and finally passed away in September, 1804, near the place of his birth. He married Mary Higgins, born in 1741, died prior to July 26, 1800, daughter of ——— and Sarah Higgins. Children: Richard, died in 1832, unmarried; Tobias, married, February 5, 1795, Sarah Willett, and died in 1835; Walter; Colmore, married, February 5, 1791, Elizabeth Peach; Samuel, died in 1838, married Miss Hall; Barton, of further mention; Beale, a merchant of Baltimore City, married (first) April 28, 1800, Margery Belt, (second) April 11, 1806, Elizabeth Williams; Levi; Sarah, married Samuel Peach; Elender, married William Williams; Rachael, married a Mr. Hill; Ann; Elisha, married and had issue.

Barton Duvall, son of Samuel (2) and Mary (Higgins Duvall, was born in Prince Georges' county, Maryland, in 1776, died October 15, 1831, a planter. He married, November 26, 1811, Hannah Isaac, born in 1788, died March 10, 1826, daughter of Richard Isaac, Jr., Esq., of Prince Georges' county, and Anne (Williams) Isaac, his wife, her mother a daughter of Stockett and Mary (Waters) Williams, of Anne Arundel county, Maryland. Children: Mareen, born in 1812, died August, 1831, unmarried; Richard Isaac, of further mention; Dr. Philip Barton, born July 17, 1816, died in 1851, married Mary E. Hopkins; Samuel Higgins, born May 30, 1818, died in 1890, married Christine Crowley; Dr. Joseph Isaac, born May 16, 1821, died in 1883, married Mary A. Mitchell, daughter of John Mitchell, of Prince Georges' county, Maryland; Mary Ann, born October 28, 1822; Henrietta, born in 1823, died October 17, 1826.

Richard Isaac Duvall, second son of Barton and Hannah (Isaac) Duvall, was born September 4, 1814, and died January 23, 1870. He was educated under private instructors in Prince Georges' county, where he lived until about 1845, when he removed to Anne Arundel county. He was a man of great determination and force of character, honorable and generous in all his business transactions. Though he never had the advantages of a college education, he was possessed of wide and varied information, and was an entertaining conversationalist, taking an active part in public affairs. For many years he was engaged in farming near Millerville, Anne Arundel county, and was one of the three originators, a founder, an original stockholder and trustee of Anne Arundel Academy, a famed school situated near Millerville. He served as a justice of the peace for Prince Georges' and Anne Arundel counties; was for several years a school commissioner; a commissioner of the Levy Court for two terms, and register of wills from 1861-62 until 1867. He was an extensive slaveholder, and at the outbreak of the Civil War his sympathies were with the Southern States. As a result of his candid and unconcealed expressions of opinion in favor of the cause of the Confederacy, he suffered arrest and imprisonment a number of times.

Richard Isaac Duvall married (first), October 2, 1833, Sarah Ann Duvall, born August 1, 1817, died January 2, 1854, daughter of Tobias Duvall. He married (second) Rachel Maria Waring, born March 21, 1828, died May 2, 1865. He married (third) June 12, 1867, Mary Amanda Mitchell, born in 1837, died February 22, 1903, daughter of Henry and Lavinia (Duvall) Mitchell. Children by first marriage: 1. James Monroe, born June 25, 1834, died February 9, 1901; married (first) January 6, 1858, Martha A. Basford, daughter of John and Sarah (Isaac) Basford; married (second) November 24, 1881, Rosa Neal, born October 3, 1844, died May 16, 1900, daughter of Robert Ellett and Susan Garland (Gilman) Neal. 2. Philip Barton, born November 19, 1836, died April, 1863; he graduated from Anne Arundel Academy, read medicine with his uncle, Dr. Joseph I. Duvall, also later with Dr. Samuel Chew, of Baltimore, and was graduated M.D. from the University of Maryland; went south at the beginning of the war, joined the Confederate Army in 1861, and on the day of his promotion to be assistant surgeon of Captain Dement's company, he was killed on the battlefield at Chancellorsville, Virginia; he was unmarried. 3. Samuel Fulton, born October 20, 1838, educated at Anne Arundel Academy, joined the Confederate Army in 1861, served until the close of the war, then again went south; he was wounded at the battles of Seven Pines and Gettysburg. 4. Joseph Comstock, born October 21, 1840, died November 5, 1840. 5. Richard Joseph, born December 19, 1841, died September, 1851. 6. Richard Marcellus, born March 20, 1844, died January 27, 1857. 7. Daniel Clayton, born May 15, 1845, died in Virginia, in April, 1901; was educated at Anne Arundel Academy; married, February 13, 1866, Mary Elizabeth Rosa Gantt, daughter of Thomas and Mary Gantt, of Anne Arundel county, Maryland. 8. Mary Emma, born January 18, 1848, died young. 9. Henry Willett, born July 3, 1850, died September 12, 1851. 10. Mary Virginia, born May 9, 1851, died July 29, 1853. 11. Sallie. Children by second marriage: 12. Richard Mareen, born November 1, 1856, near Millerville, Anne Arundel county, Maryland; married, October 30, 1895, Julianna Webster Goldsborough, daughter of Dr. John Schley and Julianna W. (Strider) Goldsborough; he was educated by private instructors and at Anne Arundel County Academy, and the State Normal School at Baltimore, and from 1877 to 1883 taught in private and public schools; he began the study of law in January, 1880, with Judge William H. Tuck, of Annapolis, was admitted to the

Maryland bar in January, 1883, removed to Baltimore the following September, and began the practice of law in that city; he is a member of the Maryland Historical Society, the Maryland Original Research Society, the American Bar Association, the Bar Association of Baltimore, the Maryland State Bar Association, is a trustee and member of the executive committee of Anne Arundel Academy, member of the Society of Colonial Wars, Sons of the Revolution, University Club and St. Andrew Society. 13. Marius Turner (twin with Richard M.) was born in Anne Arundel county, Maryland, November 1, 1856, died in Hanover county, Virginia, September 20, 1901; he was educated by private instruction and at Anne Arundel Academy, and was a substantial planter; he married Mary Elizabeth Sled, daughter of John Sled, Esq., of Hanover county, Virginia. 14. Everett, born August 3, 1858, in Anne Arundel county, Maryland; educated at the public schools and Anne Arundel Academy; he married, November 27, 1895, Libbie Mersereau, of Virginia. 15. Herbert, born April 17, 1861, in Anne Arundel county, died in Virginia, unmarried, March 30, 1901. 16. Barton Lee, born in 1863, in Anne Arundel county, died in Hanover county, Virginia, June 8, 1903. 17. Rachel Frances, born January 1, 1865, died in infancy. Child by third wife: 18. Hannah Lavinia, born in 1870; married James Hutchison, of Washington, D. C.; they have one child, Fulton.

JAMES WILLIAM THOMAS

THE ancestor of the Thomas family of St. Mary county, Maryland, was Thomas Thomas, who came from England about 1652, and was among the early settlers on the Pautuxet river. In the Revolution, sons of the family displayed their patriotism in council and field of battle, and during the conflict between the States, sons of the seventh generation won fame by their loyalty, devotion and valor in the Confederate army. Three brothers, sons of Senator Richard Thomas, of Mattapany, and grandsons of Major William Thomas, an officer of the Maryland Line during the Revolution, are of special mention for valiant service; Colonel Richard Thomas, who served under the name of Zarvona by act of the Virginia Legislature; Captain George Thomas, of Company A, Second Maryland Regiment, Confederate Army, and Sergeant James William Thomas, also of Company A, to whom this review is dedicated. After the war the survivors of Company A formed the Murray Confederate Association, and after the death of their comrade the association adopted resolutions to the memory of James William Thomas, as follows in part:

Be It Resolved: That in the death of Sergeant James William Thomas, the Murray Confederate Association deplores the loss of one of its most honored members. A gallant soldier and a true gentleman.

Profoundly devoted to the cause of the South, he shouldered his musket at the beginning of the war, and, as one of Murray's men of the Maryland Infantry, C. S. A., followed the Stars and Bars during the memorable four years of heroic struggle. Of the many beardless youths who left their homes and their firesides in "Dear Old Maryland," when the War between the States began, none carried into the conflict a more unfaltering devotion and loyalty than Sergeant Thomas. He was an ideal soldier, alert and intelligent in the performance of every duty, always at his post, and in the storm and stress of battle displaying the fortitude and coolness character

J. Wm Thomas

istic of the name he bore and worthy of the Maryland Line that charged at Cowpens and Camden.

Our comrade has crossed "over the river," to take his honorable place in the fast filling ranks of those, who, living and dying, loved the Cause, leaving behind him an untarnished name, and a record that must ever be the pride and boast of his descendants.

James William Thomas was of the seventh generation of the family founded in Maryland by Thomas Thomas, who secured a warrant for one thousand acres situated on the north side of the Pautuxct river, near Buzzard's island, March 31, 1656, and became prominent in the affairs of the colony, serving as one of the high commissioners of the Provincial Court held at Pautuxet.

He was succeeded by his son, James Thomas, of Ware, Charles county, Maryland, who was born in England prior to 1651. His will, dated June 7, 1701, was probated November 29, 1701. By his first wife, Teratia, he had children: John, of further mention, and Thomas, died prior to February, 1723.

John Thomas, son of James and Teratia Thomas, was born in 1682, and his will, dated April 30, 1756, was probated July 7, 1757. He married and had issue: John, of Ware, Charles county, Maryland, married Mary Wilson; Leonard, of Bowling Green, moved to the State of Georgia; James, died in 1782; Jane, who died prior to 1756, married Edward Swan; Elizabeth, died prior to 1756, married Benjamin Wood; William, of further mention.

Major William Thomas, son of John Thomas, was born in 1714, died at his residence, at Deep Falls, St. Mary's county, Maryland, March 25, 1795. He was commissioned captain of the county militia, in 1752, and major in 1754. He was elected a member of the committee of correspondence for St. Mary county, June 5, 1774, was a delegate to the Revolutionary Convention, 1775, member of the Maryland House of

Delegates, 1761, 1768 to 1776, and member of the General
Assembly of Maryland from 1777 until 1781. For forty
years he was a vestryman of King and Queen Parish. He
married Elizabeth Reeves, born in 1714, died in 1808, daughter of Thomas and Mary Reeves. They were the parents
of five children: 1. Colonel John Thomas, of Charles county,
Maryland, died in 1797; was an officer of the Continental
Army, member of the Maryland Legislature many years, president of the State Senate, 1795 to 1797. 2. William, of further
mention. 3. George, born in 1764, member of the Maryland
House of Delegates, 1787-88. 4. James, died in 1781; was a
soldier of the Continental Army, wounded at Yorktown. 5.
Elizabeth, died September 26, 1792; was wife of Major William Courts, an officer of the Maryland Line, Continental
Army.

Major William Thomas, Jr., of De La Brooke Manor,
St. Mary's county, Maryland, was born at Deep Falls, Maryland, in 1758, and died August 1, 1813. He was a lieutenant
in the Continental army, and later major in the famous Maryland Line; he was a prominent Free Mason and first master
of Hiram Lodge at Leonardstown, Maryland, elected grand
master of Maryland, 1809, and re-elected the following year;
was judge of the Orphans Court of St. Mary's county from
1797 to 1800, resigned to become chief judge of the County
Court, in which capacity he served from 1800 to 1802; president of the board of trustees for Charlotte Hall Academy;
member of the General Assembly from St. Mary's county,
Maryland, 1791 to 1796; and from 1802 to 1813 served in
both houses; president of the Maryland Senate from 1806 until
his death, August 1, 1813. He married, in 1782, Catherine
Brooke Boarman, born 1760, died in 1812, heiress of "De La
Brooke Manor," daughter of Richard Basil and Anne (Gard-
iner) Boarman. Children: James, of Deep Falls, St. Mary's

county, Maryland, three times Governor of Maryland, was born March 11, 1785, and died December 25, 1845; he married, June 25, 1808, Elizabeth Courts. 2. George, born in 1791, died November 20, 1856; married Mary Tubman. 3. Dr. William, of "Cremona," St. Mary's county, Maryland, born March 8, 1793, died September 20, 1849; married (first) August 6, 1818, Elizabeth Tubman; married (second) April 8, 1828, Elizabeth Lansdale. 4. Richard, of further mention. 5. Anne, born in 1798, died July, 1862; married Hon. Thompson Mason, of Loudoun county, Virginia. 6. Matilda, married Colonel George Brent. 7. Catherine, married United States Senator William Duhurst Merrick.

Richard Thomas, of Mattapany, St. Mary county, Maryland, son of Major William Thomas, Jr., was born in 1797, and died October 30, 1849. He was for many years a member of the Maryland Assembly from St. Mary's county; speaker of the House of Delegates, 1830, after which he was elected to the Senate, was president of that body from 1836 to 1843, and was president of the Maryland Colonization Society; he married Jane Wallace Armstrong; they had three sons: Richard, George and James William, of further mention. Richard Thomas was a commissioned colonel in the Confederate Army under the name of Richard Thomas Zarvona; his exploit in capturing the Federal steamer "St. Nicholas," is famous in the annals of the history of the Confederate service; after the Civil War he went to Europe and served with distinction under Garabaldi, and also in the Egyptian Army. Captain George Thomas, of Mattapany, born August 6, 1835, died May 14, 1903; was captain of Company A, Second Maryland Regiment, Confederate States Army; he married, October 23, 1866, Ellen Ogle Beall, born October 21, 1841, died October 30, 1909, daughter of Rev. Upton and Louisa (Ogle) Beall; they were the parents of eight children: Richard

Brooke, born January 27, 1868, died in 1875; John Henry, born August 3, 1869, of Mattapany, Maryland, Boston, Massachusetts, and New York City; Rev. Upton Beall, born March 31, 1871, married, Jnauary 22, 1907, Emily Hoffman; Tazewell Taylor, of the Baltimore bar, born September 9, 1872, married, September 23, 1903, Maria Antonia Vall-Spinoza; Edward Ogden, of New York; Louise Ogle, born December 20, 1875; Rev. William Matthews Merrick, of Rio Grande de Sul, Brazil, born May 3, 1878, married, October 25, 1904, Sara Elizabeth Cruishank; Kate, born September 10, 1879, married, September 15, 1910, Dr. Henry Nicholas Browse, of West Virginia.

James William Thomas, youngest son of Senator Richard Thomas, was born at Mattapany, St. Mary's county, Maryland, April 2, 1840, died at his estate in St. Mary's county, December 21, 1901. When war broke out between the States the three sons of Senator Thomas volunteered for service in the Confederate Army. Their mother remained at "Mattapany" until the same was occupied by Federal troops. James W. Thomas left his home on Wednesday, May 22, 1861, and arrived in Richmond, May 24. On the following day he was enrolled as a private in Company B, of the Maryland Guards. On June 17 he obtained a transfer to Company D, of which his brother, George, was first lieutenant, on June 19 was mustered in for the war, and on June 22 the company was ordered to join the First Maryland Regiment at Winchester, Virginia. He was first under fire on Sunday, July 21, at the battle of Manassas (First Bull Run), and he was continuously in the service until wounded at Gettysburg, July 3, 1863, and taken prisoner. Captain Murray was killed the same day, and George Thomas succeeded him in command of Company B. That company lost in the battles of July 2 and 3 their captain and eight privates killed, a lieutenant, two sergeants, and forty-seven privates wounded, and six captured. James W. Thomas was then first sergeant of the company. On July 19 he writes: "Several days since I was removed by Dr. Quinlan (a Federal surgeon) to the Presbyterian Church. Here I am comfortably fixed. Sisters of Charity attend here, everything is clean, and I get what I want. By Dr. Quinlan's directions they attend particularly to me. I could not be more fortunate unless I could go home. Mother has been with me some time." On July 23 he was sent east to David's Island, about twenty miles from New York, and was in the hospital until September 23, when he was sent South on parole. After partially regaining his health he took a clerkship in Major Anblers' office, Richmond, serving until February 9, 1864, when he rejoined the army, and on August 19 was taken prisoner in battle, and was confined at Point Lookout, a point of land lying between Chesapeake bay and the Potomac river. He was held a prisoner until February 17, 1865, when he was paroled, later exchanged and returned to Richmond. He again entered the army, and sixteen days later, on April 2, 1865, was again taken prisoner through a blunder of the captain commanding the brigade picket line. This ended his military service, as before he was released the war ended. He attained the rank of sergeant major. From the beginning of the war until May 26, 1865, Sergeant Thomas kept a diary, which long after the war he transcribed for his sons. He did not rewrite it, but added many valuable explanatory notes. This record, typed and paged, has been bound in morocco, and is a souvenir priceless to the family. After the war Mr. Thomas returned to St. Mary's county, Maryland, and there passed a quiet life in contentment and honor.

Mr. Thomas married, January 17, 1871, Fantelina Shaw, born October 9, 1842, daughter of Dr. Joseph Ford and Rebecca (Thomas) Shaw, of St. Mary's county, Maryland. They were the parents of Carroll, Armstrong, Richard Zarvona, Fantelina and Allison Ford. Carroll Thomas, born October 13, 1871, married, September 1, 1896, Margaret Ellen, daughter of Barclay and Eliza (Morton) Thomas, of Prince Georges' county, Maryland, and have one child, James W. Thomas, born February 8, 1903; Armstrong Thomas, born March 21, 1874, married, November 26, 1902, Rebecca Trueheart Ellerson, of Richmond, Virginia, daughter of Andrew Roy and Rebecca Lewis (Storrs) Ellerson; they are the parents of Ree Storrs, born April 18, 1905, died in infancy; Rebecca Lewis, born April 19, 1907; Armstrong, Jr., born April 8, 1909. Richard Zarvona Thomas, born November 8, 1876, died May 12, 1879. Fantelina Thomas, born October 30, 1879, died in July, 1888. Allison Ford, born March 27, 1881, married, April 1, 1916, Nell Aminta Kalbaugh; they have one child, Nell Allison, born May 19, 1917.

G. LANE TANEYHILL, M.D.

ALTHOUGH of Pennsylvania birth, Dr. Taneyhill's long and useful life was spent in Maryland, and from 1869 until his death in 1916, nearly half a century, in Baltimore. Aside from his eminence in his profession he was a prominent figure in the public life of the city, and in educational and religious affairs took an earnest, active part. The public schools of Baltimore owe much of their efficiency to his earnest efforts as commissioner to promote their advancement along modern lines.

Dr. G. Lane Taneyhill was born in Bellefonte, Pennsylvania, March 11, 1840, died at his home, No. 1103 Madison avenue, Baltimore, Maryland, March 2, 1916, son of Rev. Thomas Taneyhill, a minister of the Methodist Episcopal church. After completing his academic studies he began the study of medicine under Dr. John F. Petherbridge, of Calvert county, Maryland, his study of medicine having been in the intervals of teaching school in Calvert county. In 1863 he first came to the city of Baltimore, there entering the military hospital as a cadet. He completed his medical education at the University of Maryland, whence he was graduated from the medical department M.D., class of 1865. Soon afterward he was commissioned assistant surgeon of the Eleventh Regiment, Volunteer Infantry, by Governor A. W. Bradford, and ordered to duty at Fort Delaware.

After the war was over Dr. Taneyhill was appointed assistant physician to the Maryland Hospital for the Insane, remaining about three years. He then spent a year in Bellevue Hospital, New York City, returning to Baltimore in 1869. The next few years were employed in building up a private practice in Baltimore, and the subsequent years until death in meeting the demands of that practice. He became one of the best known and highly regarded general practitioners in the city, and ministered to a very large, influential clientele. He kept abreast of all modern medical discovery, and for many years was a prominent leader in the medical societies of Baltimore and Maryland. He took a deep interest in the proceedings and work of the Baltimore Medical Association, serving as its president, and in the Obstetrical and Gynecological Society of Baltimore, which he served as vice-president. He was for many years secretary of the board of trustees of the Medical and Chirurgical Faculty of Maryland; member of the American Medical Association; member of the United States Military Surgeons Association; treasurer of the Alumni Association of the University of Maryland; member of the Maryland Academy of Sciences; member of the Maryland Historical Society, and at the time of his death was a trustee of Dickinson College, and examining surgeon of the United States Pension Board. He was a whole-hearted, devoted physician, the soul of honor, and strictly observant of the ethics of his profession. No call upon his professional skill was ever disregarded, and many were the number of those he treated without hope of fee or material reward.

A Republican in politics, he took life-long interest in city affairs, but his chief interest was in the public schools. When elected school commissioner he labored most effectually to develop a modern school system to give to the youth of Baltimore greater opportunities for a practical education which would fit them for life's duties. He was a member of the Methodist Episcopal church from youth, and in Baltimore a long time member of the Madison avenue congregation, belonging to the official board. He was one of the vice-presidents of the City Missionary and Church Extension Society, president of the Laymen's Convention of Baltimore Conference of the Methodist Episcopal Church in 1915, and in church activity bore a leading part. He was a member and physician to the St. Andrew's Society, was a member of the Grand Army of the Republic, and ever took a deep interest in that organization. There were no idle periods in his life, every talent he possessed being consecrated to the service of his fellow-men.

Dr. Taneyhill married Caroline A. McAllister, of New York, who survives him, with two children: G. Lane (2) Taneyhill, M.D., Ruth Hollis Taneyhill, and one grandchild, Jean Cranston Taneyhill.

ROBERT CLINTON COLE

ROBERT CLINTON COLE, born November 16, 1857, in Baltimore, was a son of Robert Clinton and Ellen Louisa (Wise) Cole, of Baltimore, grandson of William and Cassandra (Smallwood) Cole, the former of Baltimore, and the latter of Charles county, Maryland, and great-grandson of James and Elizabeth (Clinton) Cole, the former of Cecil county, Maryland, and the latter of North Carolina. Mr. Cole was descended from an ancient English family, early planted in New England and Maryland. The name is derived from an ancient personal name of unknown antiquity.

Mr. Cole received his early education under private tutors. Subsequently he entered Dickinson College, at Carlisle, Pennsylvania, from which he was graduated in 1879 with the degree of Bachelor of Arts. He took a post-graduate course at Johns Hopkins Institute in political economy, and founded the Beta Theta Chi chapter there. Soon after he became principal of the old No. 12 grammar school of Baltimore, and while pursuing the duties of this position engaged in the study of law at the University of Maryland. In 1889 he completed the course and was admitted to the bar in that year. Two years previously his *alma mater* conferred on him the degree of Master of Arts. In the following year he became professor of history and political economy at Baltimore City College, continuing in that position until 1896, when he resigned to engage in the practice of law. While highly successful as a lawyer, Mr. Cole was best known as a factor in the educational life of the city and State. For nine years, 1904 to 1912 inclusive, he was a member of the State Board of Education, and his sober judgment was highly regarded during those years, when new problems were developing in the State educational system. In 1905 he retired from the practice

of law, and at the time of his death, December 16, 1914, he was president of the Calvert Mortgage Company, being associated with D. H. Doyle, J. Albert Hughes and Charles F. Hutchins in that organization. He was ever in touch with progressive educational work in the State, and contributed much to the establishment of the liberal educational quality maintained by the State. Mr. Cole was a familiar figure in the life of Baltimore, and was well known to most of the leading men of the city. Of tall and commanding figure, with gray hair and pleasant, kindly countenance, he was the object of considerate attention wherever he went. He was a member of the leading clubs of Baltimore, including the Maryland Club, Baltimore Club, Baltimore Country Club, Baltimore Athletic Club, of which he served as president, and Baltimore Chapter of the Dickinson College Alumni Association. He was a member of the Beta Theta Psi college fraternity, of the Sons of the Revolution, and the Society of the War of 1812. Popular in society, successful as a lawyer and business man, he died deeply regretted and widely mourned.

Mr. Cole married Elizabeth Rice, daughter of Frederick Rice, of Baltimore, who survives him.

WILLIAM WALLACE SPENCE

ON October 18, 1915, William Wallace Spence passed from the ranks of the nonogenarians to the honors of a centenarian, and in a quiet way celebrated the passing of the one hundredth milestone marking his journey through life. It was with great satisfaction that he reached that age, and feeling that Baltimore, where he had spent seventy of his one hundred years was the proper place to celebrate it, he returned from Hot Springs, Virginia, where he had been sojourning for several months. He spent the day in his bed resting, although not ill, smoked his customary cigar and greatly enjoyed the flowers and gifts which came from dear friends, particularly a small basket of heather, bracken and thistle, gathered in his native Scotland, and sent him by St. Andrew's Society. He only enjoyed the distinction of a centenarian a few weeks, his death occurring the following November 3, his life as full of honors as of years.

Mr. Spence sought the United States not as a refuge, but as a believer in America's opportunities and her institutions. He prepared himself to embrace these opportunities by obtaining a good education, then despite the strong arguments of his honored father and his many friends broke away from the home traditions of his race. But he was a loyal Scot and everything pertaining to the "auld Highland," as he was fond of calling his native land, appealed to him and warmed his heart. In Druid Hill Park, Baltimore, stands a heroic statue of the Scotch patriot, William Wallace, whose name he bore, presented by his namesake, and he made many visits to the land of his birth.

In Baltimore he won business reputation and fortune, first as a shipping merchant, then as a financier, was closely associated with Johns Hopkins in many important business ventures, and was a tower of strength to the Mercantile Trust and Deposit Company, of which he was vice-president until his death. Until 1875 he was intimately connected with the business world, not only as a member of Spence & Reid, shipping merchants, but with other leading mercantile concerns. But from 1875 until his death he was practically free from business cares. He retained his vigor surprisingly, and even when in his ninety-fifth year it was no uncommon sight to see him, formally dressed and with as much care as the youngest man in his party, occupying his box at the opera. For seventy-three years he worshipped with the congregation of the First Presbyterian Church, and it was a very rare event for him to be absent from the Sunday morning service. While he kept well abreast of the times, there were certain old-fashioned customs to which he remained loyal. One of these was his carriage and pair, he with a very few Baltimoreans refusing to adopt the automobile even after it became the "vogue." He was extremely fond of a game of whist and even the best masters found him a strong opponent. He made many journeys abroad after surrendering business cares, and during these tours added to the art treasures in which his home abounded and in which his soul delighted. There stands in the rotunda of Johns Hopkins Hospital a heroic statue of the "Divine Healer" that few know was the gift of Mr. Spence. While attending Divine service in Copenhagen with his friend, Dr. Daniel Coit Gilman, then president of Johns Hopkins University, now with his friend in the spirit land, the beauty of a staute of the Christ proved wonderfully fascinating to Dr. Gilman. "If you like it so much," said Mr. Spence, "I will have a similar one made for the rotunda of the hospital." This promise he kept, gave an order for an exact reproduction to the sculptor, Theodore Stein, and there it stands, a symbol of mercy, greeting every visitor to the institution, whose mission is one of mercy.

Mr. Spence was a believer in and a warm friend of young men. On his ninety-second birthday he urged upon them ambition and high purpose. "Be ambitious, prepare yourself for greater things so that you may be ready when opportunity comes. Aim high and put all the energy you possess into the accomplishment of your object. Be honest, work hard, and you will succeed." Could the secret or mainspring of his own success in life be reduced to words, it could be epitomized in his own words: "Always be prepared to take advantage of an opportunity." His was not a sordid nature, but he knew the value of money and the blessings it could bestow, and the great wealth he gained was wisely used. He was identified with many charities and philanthropies, but beneath his qualities, which made him a commanding figure in Baltimore's business world, beneath his kindness, capacity for friendship and his generosity, lay a deeply religious nature and principle, firm as the granite rock. His piety, wise counsel and material aid were woven into seventy years of the history of the First Presbyterian Church, and at a thousand other points touched the history of other churches.

He was a man of few words, direct in his utterances and expecting equal directness from those who would have business dealings with him. He was deliberate in his judgments, but when he had decided was as adamant. He held firmly the control of all affairs with which he was connected, and would never forsake a proved and sound business principle for an untried one. In like manner he possessed the gentleness of a woman, and in all the years of his active business life no instance is recalled of bad temper. This wonderful self control extended even to argument, and he would end a discussion with the same placid ease that he began it. His determined spirit was proverbial, and it was that spirit which carried him past his one hundredth birthday. During the last decade every purpose of his life was vigorously maintained, and during his last two years he became so feeble that many of his friends believed that only his will power enabled him to reach his ambition to attain the century mark. He was not only determined to see his one hundredth birthday, but to spend it in his Baltimore home, and he did. While he passed the day quietly in his bedroom, he was remembered by his friends of St. Andrew's Society, whose annual meetings he rarely missed; by the Maryland Historical Society, of which he was a life member; by the session of the First Presbyterian Church, and by his many personal friends. Perhaps the feature of his birthday which pleased him most came from the church, who held birthday services the day before that they might on the same day celebrate the one hundredth anniversary of the founding of its Sunday school. The following resolution was passed and sent to Mr. Spence:

The session of the First Presbyterian Church gladly avails itself of this occasion of the near approach of the one hundredth anniversary of the birthday of its honored and beloved senior member, William Wallace Spence, to offer him its hearty congratulations upon the unusually long term of years which he has been permitted to spend so happily and usefully in the Master's service in this congregation, seventy-three years as a member, and sixty-seven as ruling elder. It wishes also to place on record this expression of the deep appreciation felt by all its members of the loyal devotion to the interests of this church so fully displayed by him during the whole period of membership; of the affectionate regard and esteem they one and all entertain for him personally, and their gratitude to our Heavenly Father for the many spiritual and temporal blessings wherewith He has crowned his days.

William Wallace Spence was born in Edinburgh, Scotland, October 18, 1815, and died at his home, No. 1205 St. Paul street, Baltimore, November 3, 1915, his father a practicing physician of Edinburgh. He had all the advantages of education, but he had formed his plans for coming to the United States, the wishes of his father holding him until his eighteenth birthday. He then carried his plans into effect and seventy days later landed in New York City, but did not long remain there, going six months later to Norfolk, Virginia, where he remained seven years engaged in the shipping trade. In 1840 he decided Baltimore offered a wider field for his energies, and in that year he began business with his brother, John F. Spence, their place of business, No. 5 Rowlew's Wharf, the firm name, W. W. Spence & Company. Later John F. Spence withdrew and went west, his place being taken by Andrew Reid, the firm trading as Spence & Reid, shipping merchants and large importers of coffee. In 1847 the firm made a great deal of money in corn, they having purchased heavily at a figure which more than doubled. This was the cornerstone of the great fortune Mr. Spence accumulated, although Spence & Reid continued a large and prosperous business for more than twenty-five years. In 1875 he retired from commercial life and devoted himself to his private affairs, to charity, philanthropy, travel and the development of the finer side of his nature. He was one of the organizers of the Mercantile Trust and Deposit Company, was suggested as its first president, but he gave way to his son-in-law, General John Gill, who held the office until 1911, Mr. Spence serving as director and trustee. He rarely missed a meeting of the board and his judgment was both sought and deferred to until the end. He was also an official of the Eutaw Savings Bank, and so regular was he in his visits that if his carriage did not draw up before the bank at 10 o'clock each morning, the officers knew he was either indisposed or out of the city. He was regarded as one of the able financiers of the city and made so few mistakes that his reputation ever endured. In his business affairs he made use of all the aids of steam, electricity and modern invention, but could never be persuaded to adopt the automobile.

He took little part in civic affairs as an official, but his interest extended to every department of city life. He served three years as finance commissioner in association with Enoch Pratt, both voluntarily resigning. This office, to which he was appointed during Mayor Latrobe's second term, was his only public position. His charity was far-reaching and his interest extended to many philanthropies. He was president of the Presbyterian Eye, Ear and Throat Hospital; president of the Home for Aged Men; president of the Home for Aged Women; director of the House of Refuge; director of Egerton Orphan Asylum; senior elder of the First Presbyterian Church and its oldest member; life member of the Maryland Historical Society; member of St. Andrew's Society. He was an enthusiastic patron of art, and with Theodore Marburgh and others organized the Municipal Art Society, of which he was long a director. His gift to the city included the statue of his ancestor, William Wallace, which stands on the Lake Front in Druid Hill Park, his other notable gift, "Christ the Divine Healer," in the rotunda of Johns Hopkins Hospital.

So a wonderful life was passed, wonderful in its achievement, wonderful in its duration. None envied him his success for it was fairly earned and generously used. He began life with a definite purpose, but when the goal was reached he withdrew and long lived to enjoy the fruits of his enterprise, good judgment and ability. He held his honor sacred, and his record bears no trace of unworthy sacrifice for worldly gain, and freely as he received freely he gave; his life is an inspiration and his memory a rich inheritance.

Mr. Spence married (first) Mary A. Winkley, of Virginia, who died November 1, 1859. He married (second) Charlotte Morris, daughter of Charles Morris, of the firm James & Charles Morris, contemporary with Spence & Reid in the early forties. Mr. Spence left three children, all by his first marriage: Louise Wallace, married General John Gill; William Wallace (2) ; and Mary S., widow of O. N. Butler, all residents of Baltimore. Thirteen grandchildren also survive him.

ROBERT VANDERBURGH McKIM, M.D.

DR. McKIM was a native son of New York and a resident of the city of New York during more than the last quarter of a century of his long and useful life. He was a veteran surgeon of the Union Army, holding the rank of major. He was a man of considerable means and for many years preceding his death lived a retired life in the city of New York, devoting himself to the pursuits congenial to a man of culture and refined tastes. His progenitors were men of wealth and prominence in the business affairs of Philadelphia and Baltimore, descendants of Sir John McKim, born in Londonderry, Ireland, in 1655, knighted by his King for valiant service during the historic siege of Londonderry, raised July 30, 1689. Sir John McKim had by his second wife sons, Alexander and Thomas, the latter the founder of his line in America from whom descend the Philadelphia and Baltimore McKims.

Judge Thomas McKim was born in Londonderry, Ireland, October 10, 1710, died at Brandywine, Delaware, in September, 1784. He came to this country, October 3, 1734, landing in Philadelphia, Pennsylvania, where he resided until about 1739, when he moved to Brandywine, Delaware, where he resided until his death. He was a man of influence in his community, a justice of the Court of General Sessions and judge of the Court of Common Pleas for many years. He left children: John, of further mention; Robert, Eliza, Alexander, and Jane, all born in Brandywine, Delaware.

John McKim, of the second American generation, son of Judge Thomas McKim, was born in Brandywine, Delaware, in 1742, died in Baltimore, Maryland, in 1819. In 1785 he located in Baltimore, there rising to eminence in commercial life. He was the founder and first president of the

Union Manufacturing Company of Baltimore, organized in 1808, a company which operated one of the first cotton mills built in the United States and is still one of the successful manufacturing corporations of the city. He was also president of the Baltimore Water Company and one of the open-handed, public-spirited men of his day. His greatest philanthropy was the founding and endowment of a free school for the education of children of both sexes without regard to religious creed, an institution known as "The Mc-Kim School," a worthy monument to a worthy man. He married Margaret Duncan, daughter of Isaac and Margaret Duncan, of Philadelphia. She bore him two sons, Isaac and William Duncan. The eldest son, Isaac McKim, was born in Philadelphia in 1775, and came to Baltimore with his father in 1785. He entered his father's counting room at an early age and developed those qualities which made him the industrious, energetic, intelligent and successful merchant which he afterward became. He was a great shipping merchant in the East India trade. He took great pride in his vessels and had some of great celebrity as fast sailers. In 1836 he built one of the first of the clipper ships, the widely known "Ann McKim," which was named after his wife. During the War of 1812, he was in active service as an aide-de-camp to General Samuel Smith, commander in chief of the forces defending Baltimore, and advanced $50,000 to the city to aid in its defense.

He was one of the promoters of the Baltimore & Ohio Railroad, and one of its first board of directors. He took a warm interest in politics and was a prominent and influential member of the Democratic party. He served as State Senator and was twice elected to Congress, of which he was a member at the time of his death. He was eminently social in his nature and his generous and elegant hospitality was freely extended to a large circle of friends, as well as to all strangers who were in any way entitled to it. He died in 1838, at the age of sixty-three.

William Duncan McKim, youngest son of John and Margaret (Duncan) McKim, was born in Philadelphia, Pennsylvania, in 1779, died in Baltimore, Maryland, in November, 1834. After completing his education he joined his father in his various business enterprises and became one of the leaders of the commercial world. He was one of the founders of the Baltimore Gas Company, which he ably served as a director, also serving in that capacity in various banks, insurance companies and several public institutions of the city. Like his father, he was a man of noble, generous impulse and identified with many philanthropic movements. He married, in 1806, Susan Hazlett, of Caroline county, Maryland, whose ancestors, like his own, came from Londonderry, Ireland. They were the parents of six children: John, Hollins, Isaac, Hazlett, Margaret, married Alexander Gordon, and Robert.

Robert McKim, youngest child of William Duncan and Susan (Hazlett) McKim, was born in Baltimore, Maryland, May 25, 1816, died in New York City, April 23, 1893. He was a man of wealth and education, his connection with the business world that of an investor only. He married, November 7, 1838, Charlotte Vanderburgh, daughter of Dr. Federal Vanderburgh, and granddaughter of Colonel James Vanderburgh, an officer of the Continental Army during the Revolution. They were the parents of Susan Hazlett, born August 11, 1839, married, in November, 1859, William Mackay; Robert Vanderburgh, of further mention; Mary Helen, born September 14, 1843, died June 12, 1884, married, October, 1867, Richard Church; Clarence, born July, 1853, married, December, 1887, Caroline Lawrence;

deceased; Laura Vanderburgh, born July 22, 1860, married, November 26, 1884, S. Morris Pryor.

Robert Vanderburgh McKim, eldest son of Robert and Charlotte (Vanderburgh) McKim, was born at Rhinebeck, Dutchess county, New York, August 19, 1841, died in New York City, October 20, 1915. He was educated in Baltimore and New York City schools, chose medicine as his profession, receiving his M.D. from New York Medical College. At the outbreak of War between the States, he offered his services to the Federal government and was commissioned assistant surgeon of the Fifty-seventh Regiment, New York Volunteer Infantry, in October, 1861. In February, 1862, he was commissioned surgeon with the rank of major and saw hard service with the Army of the Potomac during the Seven Days fighting of the Peninsular campaign at Second Bull Run and Antietam. He was acting brigade surgeon during this period and later was in charge of a division hospital at Harper's Ferry, Virginia. He ever retained his interest in the militia and from March 5, 1883, until his resignation, honorable discharge, January, 1898, was brigade surgeon on the staff of General Louis Fitzgerald, commanding the First Brigade, New York National Guard. He was a member of the Military Order of the Loyal Legion of the United States, the Colonial Order, the Union Club, the Metropolitan Club, and secretary of the Kennel Club of New York. He was a man of highest character and agreeable personality, highly esteemed by his professional brethren and dear to an extensive circle of friends.

Dr. McKim married, at Baltimore, December 28, 1858, Mary Schroeder Albert, who died at sea, May 17, 1907, daughter of Jacob and Eliza Margaret (Shroeder) Albert, of Baltimore. Dr. and Mrs. McKim were the parents of seven children: Robert Albert, born September 15, 1863, married,

February 28, 1889, Caroline Ransom; Mary Albert, born May 30, 1865, married, April 28, 1888, George C. Wilde, of Baltimore; Albert Vanderburgh, born February 14, 1867; Susan Isabel, born March 10, 1869, died in 1872; William Julian Albert, born September 3, 1870, married, November 9, 1893, Maud S. Lee; Charlotte Albert, born August 7, 1872, died in 1881; Augustus Albert, born 1875, died 1879.

CHARLES WESLEY GALLAGHER, D.D.

A NATIVE son of Massachusetts, Dr. Charles Wesley Gallagher, an eminent Divine of the Methodist Episcopal church and the honored president of the Maryland College for Women, won his reputation as minister, scholar and educator beyond the confines of the State of his birth. He entered the ministry after the completion of his college course, continuing until 1889, having attained the dignity of a presiding elder ere he laid aside his priestly duties for those of an educator.

His first call was from Lawrence University, Appleton, Wisconsin, and for four years he was president of that institution. From that time until his death, in 1916, he continued in educational work as college executive, his connection with the Maryland College for Women beginning on June 1, 1908, after wide experience in the executive management of co-educational institutions and women's college, which peculiarly fitted him for the position he was to fill at Lutherville. He was a man of deep learning, and for two years after coming to the Women's College, he continued to instruct classes in psychology, logic and ethics, he having made a comprehensive study of those subjects before, and for a number of years taught them to classes in different institutions. He also gave special attention to the Bible in the Hebrew and Greek languages and ranked with the eminent scholars of his day. But his usefulness to the cause of the church and education was not alone his learning, his piety nor intellectual ability, but also in his executive quality, his business sense and his sound judgment, which won him the support of the friends of religion and education, and his appeals never were disregarded by those to whom they were addressed.

Charles W. Gallagher

Seventy years was the span of his life, and it contained no blank periods, every page of his record being filled with honorable, useful endeavor to raise higher the standards of religion and education. He was a powerful advocate of the causes he championed, was an eloquent platform speaker and in frequent demand at church conventions, conferences and educational gatherings, while his powers of literary expression and theological argument are wonderfully expressed in his "Theism or God Revealed," published in 1899, when he was in the full prime of his splendid powers. During most of the years spent as president of the Women's College, his duties were solely executive, the importance of that work demanding his release from class teaching.

Dr. Gallagher, along maternal lines, traced his ancestry to the Foster family of Colonial fame, who dated in Massachusetts from the year 1628. His paternal grandfather, John Chartres Gallagher, of the Gallagher family of 1765, was proprietor and principal of the first academy in Sackville, New Brunswick, Canada, where a very important educational institution has been developed. Dr. Gallagher's father, Samuel Chartres Gallagher, married Rooxby Moody Foster, and resided in the vicinity of Boston, Massachusetts, where his son, Charles Wesley Gallagher, was born. The parents were devoted members of the Methodist Episcopal church, and when a name was to be chosen, "Charles Wesley," brother of John Wesley, the founder of Methodism, was selected as an honored name they would have their son bear. The name was worthily borne, and who can say that there was not an inspiration in it which impelled the young man in his course toward high ministerial dignities.

Charles Wesley Gallagher was born in Chelsea, Massachusetts, February 3, 1846, and died in Lutherville, Maryland, at his home on the Campus of the Maryland Women's

College, December, 1916. He completed public school courses, finishing with high school, and with this preparation he went West and taught school in Austin, Nevada, being for one year of that period principal of an academy. On his return East he entered Wesleyan University, Middletown, Connecticut, graduating A. B., class of 1870. He pursued divinity studies at Wesleyan, was regularly admitted to the ministry of the Methodist Episcopal church, later was formally ordained, and entered upon pastoral duty at New Haven, Connecticut. In 1873 he was awarded his A. M. degree. From New Haven he was assigned to Hartford, Connecticut, under the Methodist rule of the itineracy, going thence to Providence, Rhode Island, his pastorate there being followed by charges in Brooklyn, New York, and in New York City. Wesleyan University conferred the honorary degree, Doctor of Divinity. He grew in intellectual strength and power along with ministerial usefulness, his brethren elevating him to the important office of presiding elder of the New Bedford district. During his years in the ministry he had become well known as a strong friend of the cause of education, this reputation, coupled with his learning, piety and eloquence, rendering him an ideal head of an educational institution of high degree. In 1889 there came a first call from the educational field, Lawrence University, Appleton, Wisconsin, offering him the presidency of that institution. The call seemed one that should be heeded, and after fully considering the matter he resigned from the active ministry and accepted the presidency of the University. He remained at Appleton for four years, then transferred his services to Maine Wesleyan Seminary and College, there remaining until 1897, when he became associate principal of LaSalle Seminary, Auburndale, Massachusetts. Four years later, in 1891, he accepted the presidency of the National Training School for Missionaries and Deaconesses, in Washington, D. C., remaining executive head of that institution until June, 1908, when he was elected president of the Maryland College for Women at Lutherville, Maryland.

For two years after becoming president of the Women's College, Dr. Gallagher taught psychology, logic and ethics, but from that time until surrendering his trust he was occupied entirely in executive duty. He succeeded in raising the standard of the Maryland College for Women during his incumbency, and brought the college through some difficult periods. After the fire of 1911, he threw himself whole-heartedly into the work of replacing the ruined buildings and met with success. He ended his days in honor and usefulness, his memory forever enshrined in the hearts of the thousands of young men and young women who went out from under his teachings to carry the light to others. He continued in the active discharge of his duties until about three weeks prior to his death, when a severe breakdown followed a severe bronchial attack. Funeral services were held from the college under the direction of Dr. George Preston Mains, author and minister of Harrisburg, Pennsylvania, a life-long friend and classmate. His remains were interred in Druid Ridge Cemetery, Maryland.

Dr. Gallagher served during the Civil War with a regiment of Massachusetts Volunteer Infantry, and was a member of the Grand Army of the Republic. He belonged to many societies and organizations, educational, religious and literary, was well known and greatly beloved by a very wide circle of friends.

Dr. Gallagher married (first) Emily Anne Hubbard, who died May 13, 1890. He married (second) Evangeline Corscaden, who died November 24, 1914. His only surviving child is E. Louisa Gallagher, who married Professor Beekman Oliver Rouse, the able successor to the presidency of the Maryland College for Women. Their only son is Oliver Wesley Rouse.

CHARLES E. HILL

IN 1871, when Charles E. Hill first came from New Hampshire to Maryland, there were some of his new neighbors who looked askance at one of the "Yankees." It was only seven years after his father's death on the Chattanooga Battlefield when he left a northern college to become Assistant Professor at the United States Naval Academy at Annapolis, and much of the bitterness of the Civil War still lingered, but, in 1909, when ill health forced him to live again in the New Hampshire hills, he had seen all that bitterness pass, and among his closest friends and business associates were men whose fathers had given their lives for the Confederacy as his had for the Union. When he died, April 6, 1917, at his house in Temple, Hillsborough county, New Hampshire, he had been for forty-two years a member of the Baltimore Bar and he had borne his part in the development of the city he had learned to love.

Pedigrees are interesting only as they explain individual character. The Massachusetts Archives and the Records of the Society of the Cincinnati show that Samuel Hill, Hope Brown and Ebenezer Bancroft bore their share of military service throughout the War of Independence. Samuel Hill's son, Ebenezer Hill, married November 18, 1795, Ebenezer Bancroft's daughter, Rebecca, and one of the twin sons of this marriage, Joseph Bancroft Hill, married, August 26, 1845, Hope Brown's great-granddaughter Harriet. Charles Ebenezer Hill, the first child of this last marriage, was therefore, of purely "American" and typically New England antecedents.

Samuel Hill was a great-grandson of Ralph Hill, who came to Plymouth from Devon before 1638, and grandson of Captain Ralph Hill who fought in the Indian Wars and was a Representative in the Massachusetts General Court from 1689 to 1694. Both Hills were among the petitioners to Governor Bellingham for the incorporation of the Massachusetts town of Billerica. They were born in England and came of a family whose most distinguished member, probably, was Sir John Hulle (or Hylle) of Kyton, Devon, one of the judges of the King's Bench, 1389-1407. The Browns and the Bancrofts are the same sort of people as the Hills. All were members and many were ministers, elders or deacons of "The Church," for the Congregational Puritan Church was in those days supported by general taxation and civil rights depended upon church membership.

Hope Brown was fourth in descent from William Brown(e), who settled in Sudbury about 1638, and was of the lineage of the Brownes of "Hawkedon," Bury St. Edmunds, Suffolk. The first church in Sudbury was founded by the brothers, William and Edmund Brown, in 1640, Edmund becoming the first minister, and William being elected the first deacon. William Brown afterwards was a representative in the Massachusetts General Court. One of his sons, Hopestill, transmitted his typically Puritan name in a shortened form to his descendant, Hope Brown, who April 19, 1775, then a corporal, marched with his company to Concord. Hope Brown's grandfather, Colonel Josiah Brown, had been signer of the church covenant in 1724, had commanded his regiment in the French and Indian Wars in 1755, and was one of the original grantees of the town of Mason, Hillsborough county, New Hampshire, with which his Hill descendants later became prominently identified.

Colonel Ebenezer Bancroft did not, like Hope Brown, march to Concord on April 19, 1775, for at that time he held the King's commission as captain, but the battle of Lexington absolved him from his oath, and, although wounded at Bunker

Hill, he commanded Massachusetts troops in Rhode Island, was in the battle of Bennington, commanded the guard which conducted the Hessian troops to Cambridge and continued in the service until the close of the war. He was a descendant of Lieutenant Timothy Bancroft, who joined the Reading settlement in 1652, and among his co-descendants were such men as the Rev. Aaron Bancroft, D.D., Chief Justice Fuller and George Bancroft, the historian. The early Massachusetts families were much inter-married, and Henry Adams of Braintree, forefather of two Presidents, John Whitney and Elder Edward Howe of Watertown, Andrew Stevenson of Cambridge, the Warrens, Proctors, Pattersons, Cutlers, Fletchers, Farwells, Paines, Pages, and Parkers, all contributed a little of their Puritan steadfastness to descendants who have done their part in the development of the land their progenitors helped settle. The career of Charles E. Hill was thoroughly consistent with his heritage from these and others like them. In their lives, as in his, *service* of some sort was the primary object of life, whether that service were to Church, State, family or neighbors.

Mr. Hill was born in Colebrook, in the extreme northern part of New Hampshire, where his father was then minister, but he spent part of his childhood at his grandfather's house in Mason, Hillsborough county. This town lies on the boundary line between New Hampshire and Massachusetts, farther in the hills than Groton and not quite so far as Temple and Dublin, its near neighbors. Colonel Brown had been an original grantee of Mason, and Ebenezer Hill became its minister soon after he graduated from Harvard College (A.B., 1786; A.M., 1789). In accordance with the custom that then prevailed, he remained as minister of "The Church" for sixty-four years, and also represented Mason in the New Hampshire Legislature. His first wife died, and he married

Rebecca Bancroft, widow of Samuel Howard, who bore him, November 26th, 1796, twin sons, Joseph Bancroft and John Boynton Hill. These two graduated at Harvard College (A. B.) 1821 in the same class, both were in the first seven of the Phi Beta Kappa; both were members of the "Institute of 1770" and the "Hasty Pudding Club," and, on graduation, both studied law and were admitted to the bar. John Boynton Hill continued practice, became a partner of John Appleton, afterwards Chief Justice of Maine, was speaker *pro tem* of the Maine Legislature in 1855 and finally returned to the Mason homestead, where he died in 1886. Joseph Bancroft Hill was admitted to the Tennessee bar in 1828, but later returned to Mason and became colleague with his father in the ministry of the church. When the war came, although over sixty, he joined the Army of the Cumberland in the service of the United States Christian Commission and was killed in a hospital train accident at Chattanooga, June 16th, 1864.

Mr. Hill was then sixteen and upon him fell much of the responsibility for his mother and two younger brothers, who were then living in Temple. He prepared for college from 1863 to 1867 at the Appleton Academy in New Ipswich, of whose trustees his grandfather Hill had been president. He had expected to enter Harvard, of which his father and grandfather were graduates, but changed his plans and entered the freshman class of Dartmouth College in 1867. Of his life at the academy and at college, Honorable Melvin O. Adams, his classmate and roommate wrote:

The literary programs of those days show his trend. He never rode a Greek or Latin Oration where if both horse and rider were thrown—the audience still sat in awed unwisdom. He took a full-sized theme requiring something to be said and he stood up and said it. Graduating at the Academy his oration was on "True Glory." At another time he made his appeal for "Energy." Still in his boyhood at the Academy, at a mock murder trial he was counsel for the defense and got away with it. The functional events

of college days were what we call Sophomore Prize Speaking; and The
Junior Exhibition.   He competed as a Sophomore, rendering that old
sonorous declaration: "Virginius to the Roman Army;" while at The Junior
Exhibition his oration was "The Heroic Age of American History."   These
illustrate.   He was scholarly and his scholarship was flexible.   If he excelled
in Greek and Latin he was no less good in mathematics and physics.

At college he was a member of the Alpha Delta Phi.
On March 8th, 1871, Captain Carter, the commanding officer
at the Naval Academy, reported to Secretary Robeson that
he had examined Mr. Hill and found him duly qualified to
fill the position of "Assistant Professor of Ethics and English
Studies" at the Naval Academy, and recommended that his
appointment be forwarded to him as such.   He left college
before graduating to accept this postion, but years later his
college conferred upon him the A.B. degree.   In 1871 the
old Naval Academy, founded by his father's cousin, Secretary of the Navy Bancroft, was a quaint, delightful place
with ancient, tree-shaded houses and green lawns.   The mild
climate of Annapolis was a great contrast to the rigorous
New England winters, and for four years Mr. Hill taught
history to future officers and studied law for himself.   It was
his original intention to practice in Boston, but dread of its
cold winters, and his engagement to a Maryland girl led
him to select Baltimore as a permanent home.   He resigned
from the navy, to take effect on September 15th, 1874, was
admitted to the Baltimore Bar, February 13th, 1875, and
November 23rd married Kate (Keturah) Watts, daughter
of Philip Coleman Clayton, sixth in descent from John Clayton, Attorney-General of Virginia, 1714-37, whose son,
Samuel, married Philip Pendleton's daughter, Elizabeth.
Mrs. Hill was born April 25th, 1849, in Annapolis, and such
Marylanders as Colonel Henry Ridgely, Richard Wells, Captain Thomas Stockett, John Brewer and Major John Welsh
were among her progenitors.

For the thirty-four succeeding years he lived in Balti-more and spent the summer vacations in New Hampshire, first at Mason, and after the death of his uncle, John Boynton Hill, at Temple. Those thirty-four years were devoted to his pro-fession, church and family life, with a participation in the duties of citizenship. At first alone, then with Mr. Fred-erick P. Ross, and finally as head of the firm of Hill, Ross & Hill, he lived the usual lawyer's life. His work was mostly what is known as "business law," but he appeared in many important litigated cases in the local courts and the Court of Appeals. Perhaps the best known of these was "The Berry Will Case," which occupied various courts for long periods and resulted in important decisions on testamentary law by the Court of Appeals. In this case with ex-Governor Wil-liam Pinckney White and Mr. Edgar H. Gans, he repre-sented the Safe Deposit and Trust Company, executor. On the business side of law he helped organize various corpora-tions, in some of which he took an active interest. At his death he was still president of the Maryland Color Printing Company, and a director of the C. J. Youse Company, the one a large manufacturer of all sorts of colored labels and the other of all manner of paper boxes. When he was forced by ill health to give up active business, he was engaged in the development of the suburb known as Howard Park, and he founded the water service which later grew to be The Artesian Water Company, and which supplies the greater part of the suburbs adjoining the city to the northwest.

He worked hard during the week at his office, first, 16 East Lexington street, then in the Central Savings Bank Building, and finally in the Keyser Building, but he worked as hard, if not harder, on Sunday with his church duties. After graduating from Harvard, in 1879, his brother, Wil-liam Bancroft Hill, came to Baltimore, was admitted to the bar and practiced with him for a time. He shortly, however, followed their father's example and left the law for the church. Mr. Hill often jestingly asserted that his brother's change from law to theology was due to the influence of his law office.

Outside of New England, the Congregationalist usually becomes a Presbyterian, and when Mr. Hill first came to Maryland he attended the latter church. Bishop Ames was then, however, a powerful preacher and to hear his sermons Mr. Hill attended the Methodist Episcopal church, with which he later became closely identified. About 1885, the time of the building of the present First Methodist Episcopal Church, he became one of the trustees and continued this relation until his death. January 3rd, 1886, he was elected superintendent of its Sunday school. "A born teacher and a devout student of the Bible from boyhood, he not only," in the words of the Rev. Dr. Hugh Johnston, "built up a great school, but became thoroughly identified with the mighty movements of the church and the benevolent work of the city." He was trustee of the Women's College, now Goucher College, from 1891 to 1914; for many years trustee and special treasurer of the Home for the Aged of the Methodist Episcopal Church, as well as a trustee of the Baltimore Annual Conference, the Ashbury Sunday School Society and other church and benevolent agencies. For a number of years he lectured on "Medical Jurisprudence" at the Maryland Homœopathic Hospital.

His inherited Republicanism was very much tempered by the strong Southern Democratic views of his wife, and he took no part in what is known as active politics. He was, however, an early member of the Reform League and of the Civil Service Reform Association, and was actively engaged in the political revolution in Maryland in 1895, which overthrew the old city and State rings. Soon after coming to Baltimore, he took up his residence in what was then No. 80 Charles street in Baltimore county, one door from Brown street and three blocks above the "Boundary." Here he resided until forced to spend most of his time in New Hampshire. Later, No. 80 became No. 308 and finally No. 2120 North Charles street. Brown street became Third, and then Twenty-second street, and the boundary became North avenue when that part of Baltimore became a portion of the "Annex," and of the old Twenty-second Ward. The "Good Government Movement," in 1895, for a time was thought to have great promise of political regeneration for the country. It started in New York, and in Baltimore, under the leadership of Honorable Charles J. Bonaparte, it was taken up by the governing body of the Reform League, and Good Government Clubs were organized in various parts of the city, perhaps as many as ten or twelve altogether. In each case the nucleus was furnished by the members of the Reform League and Mr. Hill organized and became president of the Good Government Club of the Twenty-second Ward. He was also a member of the executive committee of the general movement.

Although he belonged at various times to the Maryland, University, Country, Merchants and other clubs, he used them rarely, and took his recreation with his family. Brought up in the country, he rode well, was an excellent whip and devoted to horses. When bicycles came into use he gave up his daily drive and rode with his sons, but when bicycling fell into disuse, he again took up driving and riding, and rode daily before breakfast. Part of the summer vacation was always spent in a two or three weeks' driving trip in the White Mountains or other portions of New England. After his forced retirement to New Hampshire, he did considerable writing, and translated and annotated the larger part of a History of the French Revolution, which he intended to publish. At the same time he transformed an old golf course on his place into a scientifically planted fruit orchard of several hundred acres and became a local authority on fruit culture, keeping up a constant correspondence with the State Agricultural authorities.

The death of his wife, April 6th, 1907, was a blow from which Mr. Hill never fully recovered. He spent the summer of 1908 in England and France and returned in September, in apparent improved health, but soon contracted a cold he was unable to throw off. He made short trips to Savannah and Asheville and resisted the idea that there was anything the matter with him. Finally, however, he became convinced that his health was seriously impaired and spent the spring of 1909 in the Blue Ridge. He remained there until July and then feeling much improved, went to his house in New Hampshire. During the remaining eight years of his life, despite his invalid condition, he lived an active life, made a number of trips to Baltimore and took a keen interest in his affairs there and in New Hampshire. His death, April 6th, 1917, occurred just ten years to a day after that of his wife, and he was buried beside her in Greenmount Cemetery.

He had three sons to whose education and interests he gave unremitting care, and whose companionship he constantly sought,—John Philip Hill (Major and Judge Advocate, N. G. Md.), formerly United States Attorney for Maryland; Dr. Eben Clayton Hill (Captain U. S. A.), of the Medical Staff of Vassar Hospital at Poughkeepsie; and Bancroft Hill, consulting engineer, treasurer of The Artesian Water Company of Baltimore. He was survived by his brothers, Rev. William Bancroft Hill, D.D., professor of Biblical Literature at Vassar College, and Joseph A. Hill, Ph.D., Chief Statistician, Census Bureau, Washington, D. C.

George Morrow

GEORGE MORROW

Passed out to softer summers than we know,
Passed out to sweeter countries than we've seen;
Passed out to golden cities with their glow
Of Jasper and of beryl and onyx sheen.
Passed out with all your gentle sweetness, friend,
A brave and smiling comrade to the end,
A faithful soldier in this life that signs
Above the toil and all the care it brings.
Passed out from such a circle as drew around
Your heart in love so earnest and profound,
Respecting you because of worth that drew
All men who loved true worth in work to you.
Passed out, but not forever from our hearts;
Already there a flower of memory starts
That holds as sweet and dear as memory can
Your golden record as a friend and man.
Passed out from faithful service through the years,
Passed out to leave us unashamed of tears
That flow from one so worthy of a grief
In which our hearts cry out on Death, the thief.
Passed out to sunny slopes where childhood smiles,
To Daisied fields and slopes where song beguiles
The Noble hearted and the leal and true—
Good night: Bon voyage: from all your comrade crew.

THUS wrote Folger McKinsey, the "Bentztown Bard," on the death of his friend, George Morrow, dean of the local editorial staff on the Baltimore "Sun," and one of the best known newspaper men in Baltimore.

George Morrow was born in Washington county, Pennsylvania, July 23, 1853, and died in the city of Baltimore, Maryland, August 3, 1915. He began his newspaper career as a boy on the "Echo Pilot" of Greencastle, Pennsylvania, learning the printer's trade in that office. He came to Baltimore in 1870, and for a short time was employed on the old

Baltimore "Gazette." He left the "Gazette" to go to St. Louis, Missouri, but after two years in that city returned to Maryland, becoming owner and editor of the Baltimore "County Democrat," published at Towson. Later that paper passed under the control of William Ruby, and in 1882 Mr. Morrow became a reporter for the Baltimore "Sun" and was connected with that paper until his death, a period of thirty-three years. He served in every capacity from reporter to editor, his newspaper experience in Baltimore gaining for him a wide circle of friends in every station in life. For many years he was court reporter, covering some of the most stirring and important proceedings that has ever occurred in the Baltimore courts. His intelligent and accurate accounts of the happenings in the courts won him the friendship of every prominent member of the bar practicing at that time and of every judge on the bench. Among his close friends won during that period, which were ever retained, was Judge Stewart, Judge Phelps, Bernard Carter, William Pinckney White, Edgar H. Gans, former mayor of Hayes, and the older members of the bar, all of whom knew him well and esteemed him.

At the time Mr. Morrow joined the "Sun" the founder and owner, A. S. Abell, made it a point to know personally every man connected with the news and editorial departments of the "Sun." The "Sun's" reputation was built on accuracy, attention to detail, conciseness and impartiality, and these he would discuss with the men frequently, pointing out to a writer just where he thought an article had fallen short of what he conceived such an article should be, and he had no patience with mistakes in names. It was that kind of training Mr. Morrow received practically at the beginning of his career, and to the last day he remained at the office of the "Sun" he remained faithful to it. As a reporter, as telegraph editor, night editor, and assistant city editor, with the duty of editing local "copy" and preparing it for the printers, his constant striving was for accuracy and conciseness. His long training seemed to have given him a sixth sense for the detection of errors in copy that passed through his hands. When an error in name or fact was suspected he invariably looked it up, and then with his kindly, friendly manner that left no sting of reproof would call the attention of the writer to his error in order that he might not repeat it. Scores of men that he trained in this way passed out of the "Sun" office to positions in all parts of the United States, and then practiced the habits of accuracy and fidelity he had impressed upon them.

He was not an unsympathetic task-master, no man being quicker to recognize merit in a story than he. The reporters whose work it was his business to edit felt the warmest friendship for him, and among the younger men in the office he was known as "Uncle George." In later years his hair turned a silvery white, although he was not an old man, and his standing form was as erect as it had ever been. He was the friend of every man who was in earnest, and no one was so well pleased with the success of advancement of the younger men or so willing to call general attention to a particularly good piece of work. Dissipation on the part of one of his boys always grieved him, and in a manner devoid of offense he took advantage of the first opportunity to point out to the young man where such a course would invariably lead. His influence was strong for good in the "Sun" office, and the idea did not prevail there that dissipation was a part of the curriculum, but on the contrary that such a course would utterly ruin a newspaper career.

Mr. Morrow was a serious, thoughtful, moral and upright man, genial in manner and with a keen sense of humor. He had no vices, coarse jokes offended him, and he never could tolerate humiliation or hardship placed upon any human being for the sport of others. The hardships of children particularly grieved his tender heart, and in all things he was a gentleman of the highest type, kindly, courteous and unassuming, an honor to his profession. There were many older residents of Baltimore who had known him from youth and followed his rise with gratification. His knowledge of Baltimore and its history during more than a quarter of a century of residence was wonderfully interesting and authentic, while his memory for names was remarkable. For many years he was a member of St. Peter's Protestant Episcopal Church. He had the personal friendship and respect of every man who had been in control of the "Sun" from founder down to the present owners, and until stricken with his last illness was rarely away from the office.

Mr. Morrow married, January 4, 1882, Amanda C., daughter of Lewis A. and Mary Ann (Burdick) Howser, of Washington, D. C., her mother, a daughter of Henry and Lydia (Hoadley) Burdick, who were married about 1843, Henry Burdick, a soldier of the War of 1812. Henry and Lydia Burdick had eight children: Caroline, married Matthias Jeffers; Cornelia, married John Murphy McCreary, of Cincinnati; Elizabeth, married (first) Mr. Newton, (second) William Gordon, of Virginia; Mary Ann, married Lewis A. Howser; Lydia Amanda, married George R. Cinnamond; Virginia, married Abner L. Ross, of Lebanon, Ohio; William Henry, unmarried; Maria Louise, married William Eickelburger. Lewis A. and Mary Ann (Burdick) Howser had children: Lydia; Virginia, married Louis R. McClure, of Baltimore; Lewis A., married Julia V. Keller; Emily Louisa, died unmarried; Mary Cunningham, married John M. McCreary, and had two children; Lewis Howser and Emma Ross McCreary, married Albert Romosher, and has one child, Gertrude Ross; Amanda C., married George Morrow, and has children: Mary Burdick, married H. Evans Smith, of Baltimore; Gertrude Howser, married Peter Corbin Chambliss, and has a son, Peter W.; Kathry Allen, who, with her widowed mother, resides at the family home, No. 2434 Madison avenue, Baltimore.

The following article, which appeared in the editorial columns of the Baltimore "Sun," is a testimonial of the esteem with which Mr. Morrow was held by the paper of whose editorial staff he was so long a member:

A FAITHFUL SERVANT

The highest commendation given in the New Testament is the commendation bestowed on the good and faithful servant. Conscientious fidelity to duty, loyalty to the trust committed and the task assigned is still, with all our uplift, too rare a virtue to go unmarked and unpraised.

An unchanging and unostentatious example of this noble virtue of fidelity was contained in the quiet, steadfast, straightforward life of George Morrow, a member of the "Sun's" staff for more than a generation, who completed life's assignment yesterday. He was one of the few members of the "Sun's" present staff whose connection with the paper extended back to the life of its founder, Mr. A. S. Abell, and his passing breaks one of the few links with that period. Trained in that early school, he retained its virtues while keeping pace with the progressive ideas and methods of the present. He regarded the "Sun" as an institution, and was as loyal to its service as the soldier to the flag of his country. An honorable and upright gentleman, duty and fidelity were the golden words in the lexicon of his life.

When we can "leave our brother sleeping" the sleep of the just with the supreme praise of the Supreme Teacher of the centuries as his epitaph and eulogy, our regret at his passing is mingled with just pride in his fine and manly record. May we all deserve one which means as much.

CHARLES CHRISTOPHER HOMER

FAR from the scene of his own birth and successful life, but near the birthplace of his parents in Germany, Mr. Homer drew his latest breath and closed a long career of honor and usefulness that firmly fixed his name among the great financiers of Baltimore, his native city.

The business world knew him as a wise and upright banker, his fellowmen as a public-spirited citizen foremost in advancing any enterprise which promised a bigger, better Baltimore, but to his friends he was the frank, genial gentleman, holding sacred the ties of home and friendship, delighting to serve those near and dear to him. He was the man of culture in business, the student of the problems of his business, widely informed and grounded in its laws and equally so on all economic questions bearing any relation to national finance or the public welfare. He was not a dreamer or an idealist, but from his study and his experience chose those things which were sound, practical and proven. Thus ever keeping his feet on the solid rock, he became a recognized force in the financial world, his opinions, views and ideas being sound, carried weight when presented to those with whom he discussed public problems, before congressional committees or before monetary conventions.

He bore the crucial test of success nobly, and ever preserved the charm of his winning personality and bore all his varied responsibilities with modest dignity, fidelity and honor, winning public esteem to an unusual degree. He was taken away in the full prime of his splendid manhood and intellectual strength, his death hastened by the mobilization preparations going on in Germany at the outbreak of the present European War. He had sailed for Europe on July 8, 1914, to benefit his wife's health, and the events and unusual strain of the next two months brought on a nervous break-down, from which he did not recover. He was a son of Christopher and Dora (Malo) Homer, both of German birth, who, in early youth, came to the United States. Christopher Homer became a successful business man of Baltimore and to posterity left an honored name.

Charles Christopher Homer was born in Baltimore, Maryland, November 1, 1847, died in Bremen, Germany, September 13, 1914. He was educated in Baltimore private schools and the University of Georgetown, whence he was graduated A.B., class of 1867, later receiving from his *alma mater* the Master's degree. He began his business career as a glass and paint salesman, changing at the end of one year to a line of hardware. He soon abandoned that line also and established the provision house of Foss & Homer. That house continued in business until 1880, when it dissolved, Mr. Homer from that time devoting himself entirely to finance. He had been elected a director of the Second National Bank in 1878, and during the two years he continued in business after his election he made a deep study of national finance and banking, thus when later he was called to official relation with the bank it was not a tyro called, but a man of practical knowledge well grounded in the principles and practice of the business he was to administer. In 1886 he was elected vice-president of the Second National Bank. He remained the executive head of that institution for twenty-five years, a period of great growth and expansion for both institution and executive.

He was a commanding figure in his native city's financial affairs, and his wisdom as an executive was sought by other institutions. He was vice-president of the Savings Bank of Baltimore at the time of his death; an ex-vice-president of the Safe Deposit and Trust Company, and from 1897 until

1911 was president of the Baltimore Clearing House, re-elected annually, only his positive declination to again serve the Clearing House as president caused his retirement. He was chosen chairman of the Baltimore committee that drafted a plan for the "Creation of a Safe and Elastic Currency," known as the Baltimore plan, a plan which was unanimously endorsed by the association. With this endorsement he appeared on December 12, 1894, before the Congressional Committee on Banking and Currency and made the final argument in favor of its adoption by Congress. He was an active member of the Baltimore Board of Trade and a delegate representing the board at the monetary convention held at Indianapolis, January 25, 1898.

During the "free silver" agitation of 1896, Mr. Homer, as president of the Second National Bank, voiced the sentiment of that institution and so sound and weighty were his opinions and so highly was he regarded as an authority on national financial policy that the substance of the sentiment was incorporated in the first act of the newly-formed Maryland Bankers Association as follows: "Resolved, That we are unalterably opposed to the free coinage of silver and to every debasement of our currency in whatsoever form it may be presented; that we firmly and honestly believe that the true interest of our country will be best served by its rigid adherence to the gold standard of value, the continuance of which will not only preserve its financial integrity and the future welfare of its citizens, from the wage earner to the capitalist, but will insure through the prompt restoration of confidence, that rapid development of its resources which will eventually place it among the first nations of the earth."

With the modesty of a truly great man, he bore himself when at the height of success with the same frank, genial kindliness of manner as when striving for his first business success as a merchant. His course was marked by quiet dignity, fidelity to his trusts, and honorable performance of every duty. He did not strive for the world's applause, but won it from those who opposed his views as well as from his friends. His business responsibilities were heavy, but he never wavered in his public-spirited loyalty to the interests of his native city and in a larger way to his State and Nation. He served as a trustee of the Sheppard and Enoch Pratt Hospital, and was a member of the Maryland Historical Society. He abjured partisanship in politics, but supported the men who stood for the measures and principles of government he believed in, and were themselves best fitted to fill the office sought. His hand was ever extended to relieve the needy, but in his benevolence, as in his every deed, he was so unostentatious and gave so quietly that publicity was avoided and many of his good deeds remain unknown. He loved his home, and with his wife, a woman of attractive personality, dispensed an abundant and charming hospitality. He looked on life from a broad point of view, recognized and appreciated the good in others and viewed with sympathy the frailties of human nature. His friends were legion, and it is not a forced sentiment that "none knew him but to love him."

Mr. Homer married, March 4, 1869, Frances M. Holthaus, born in Baltimore, September 7, 1847, daughter of Francis Theodore and Maria E. Holthaus, both born near Osnabruck, Hanover, Prussia, but married in Baltimore, both coming to that city in youth. In 1914, Mrs. Homer being in poor health, the devoted couple journeyed abroad and at Bad-Beynhausen, Germany, spent the weeks intervening between their arrival and the outbreak of hostilities between the European nations. The conditions were trying to an American and the warlike preparations seriously affected Mr.

Homer. He made his way to Bremen, intending to take passage home, and there was completely prostrated and never rallied. Five children were born to Charles C. and Frances M. Homer, four sons, and a daughter who died in infancy. The sons, eminent in finance, law, medicine and commerce, are factors in the life of their native city and worthy successors in the third generation of a name never to be forgotten in Baltimore annals. The sons are: Charles Christopher (2), who was his father's close business associate, vice-president of the Second National Bank and his successor; Francis Theodore, member of the law firm of Willis & Homer; Henry Louis, resident physician at Union Protestant Infirmary; Robert Baldwin, president of the R. B. Homer Lumber Company.

Douglas H. Thomas Jr

DOUGLAS H. THOMAS, JR.

SINCE the invention of order in Architecture by the Greeks, to whom the world owes all that is great, judicious and distinct in the architectural orders, the ability to follow the laws of those orders and the style of the different periods has been the foundation upon which to base the claim to be designated an "architect." But in addition to that ability, there frequently have arisen men of creative genius who have made the profession an art and who, given limit of cost, location, purpose, material and surroundings, would design buildings which, correct in architectural detail, so fitted the location in which it was placed, so harmonized with its surroundings, was so well adapted to the purpose intended and so agreed in its style with the material of which it was built, as to stamp its creator not only as an architect, but as an artist as well. To this class belonged Douglas H. Thomas, Jr., of Baltimore. While as a member of the firm, Parker, Thomas & Rice, his personal ability was merged with that of his associates, the touch of his personal genius is seen in many of the fine public and business buildings designed by the firm in Baltimore and elsewhere. He possessed that creative genius in a high degree and will ever rank among the foremost architects of his day.

Perhaps the personal quality of his work is best seen in the buildings at Johns Hopkins University, his firm being the winners of the first open competition for the general development of Homewood. Himself an alumnus of the University, he devoted himself personally to the designing of the new buildings and unsparingly gave of his talent and of his genius to a scheme of buildings which would be in keeping with the great fame of the University. To this labor of love as well as of professional obligation, he brought all his art, all his skill, his trained taste, and from every viewpoint labored to produce an artistic, practical and harmonious whole. The complete Academic or Gilman Building in its dignity and effectiveness stands as a monument to his taste and appreciation of what a University building should be.

Douglas H. Thomas, Jr., son of Douglas H. Thomas, Sr., president of the Merchants-Mechanics Bank of Baltimore, and his wife, Alice Lee (Whitridge) Thomas, was born in Baltimore, in March, 1872, died there, the victim of an automobile accident, June 11, 1915. He attended private schools until sixteen years of age, then went abroad and for one year was a student at the University of Lausanne, Switzerland.

After his return from Lausanne, he entered Johns Hopkins University whence he was graduated with the customary degree, class of 1893. He continued his studies at the Massachusetts School of Technology, Boston, specializing in the study of architecture, now a profession in which a follower must also possess the knowledge of a constructive engineer. After graduation from the Institute of Technology he again went to Europe, studied at the Ecole Des Beaux Arts, and afterwards to Greece, the fountain-head and inspiration of architectural art, completing his studies. He then returned to Baltimore and in partnership with J. Harleston Parker began a brilliant career as an architect which only terminated with his death. Parker & Thomas maintained offices in Baltimore and Boston, and as the years progressed took a leading position among the foremost architects of the United States. Later Arthur Wallace Rice was admitted to a partnership, the firm then becoming Parker, Thomas & Rice.

Monuments to the skill, ability and high standing of the firm may be seen in different States and cities, but in Baltimore and vicinity they exist on every hand. Among the more notable are the "Belvedere Hotel" (Baltimore's largest and most beautiful hostelry), Baltimore & Ohio building, Gilman County School, the Bank building of Alexander & Sons, Savings Bank of Baltimore, Baltimore Trust Company building, Metropolitan Savings Bank, and The New State Normal School at Towson, Maryland. They also designed several buildings for Harvard University, Cambridge, Massachusetts, and for Johns Hopkins University, at Homewood. They designed and erected government buildings and Virginia State building at Jamestown Celebration, and all buildings at Jamestown, except the buildings of the separate States.

Mr. Thomas personally took a deep interest in the development of Homewood, designing and erecting the Academic and the Administration buildings. His last work, left unfinished, was the new building to be erected by the Consolidated Gas and Electric Light and Power Company, on Lexington street, Baltimore.

In speaking of his work at Homewood, an official of the university said: "The death of Douglas H. Thomas is a very great loss to Johns Hopkins University. Himself an *alumnus* of the institution, he has, since 1906, given ungrudgingly of his talents and energy to the scheme of Homewood's general development, having made it a labor of love rather than a mere professional obligation. The Academic building, in its great dignity and effectiveness, is a monument to his taste and appreciation of what a University building should be. When the power house plan was completed and bids for its construction were in, he saw a way to improve its appearance and reduce its cost, not heeding the fact that it would also reduce his commission. He served the University with an unselfish devotion and gave to his *alma mater* the best of himself and of his talents. His death is not only an official loss but a personal one to all of us."

Mr. Thomas was president of the Maryland Institute of

Architects, and a member of other professional and scientific societies. He possessed an ease and grace of manner, was quiet, courteous and friendly, was very popular in Baltimore, where he had a host of friends. His clubs were the Maryland, Baltimore, Merchants and Eldridge Kennels.

He married, at the Church of the Advent (Episcopal), Boston, in 1901, Elizabeth Lyman Chadwick, who died very suddenly in Biarritz, France, in 1912, daughter of Dr. J. R. Chadwick, of Boston, Massachusetts, leaving four daughters: Catherine, Rosamond, Alie and Elizabeth.

JOHN PRENTISS POE

THE Poe family has long been identified with Maryland, and has contributed many distinguished citizens to that commonwealth. Burke's "Landed Gentry" gives an extended account of the ancestry of this family, and shows that Dr. Poe, physician to Queen Elizabeth, who came from Donegal, was a member thereof. David Poe, of Dring, Ireland, died in 1742. He was a son of John Poe, for whom he named a son. This son, John Poe, grandson of John Poe, married, in September, 1741, Jane McBride, of Ballymoney, County Antrim, sister of that McBride who was Admiral of the Blue and a member of Parliament for Plymouth in 1785.

In 1743 John Poe and his wife set out for America, and arrived at New Castle, Delaware, accompanied by two sons, David and George. They located first in Lancaster county, Pennsylvania, and afterwards removed to Cecil county, Maryland, later to Baltimore, where John Poe died in 1756. The first city directory of Baltimore, published in 1796, contains the name of Jane Poe, widow, German street, between Harvard and Hanover. This property was owned by the family. She died July 17, 1802, aged ninety-six, and is buried in Westminster Churchyard, lot 129. Their eldest son, David Poe, married Elizabeth Cairnes, and they were the parents of David Poe, who married Elizabeth Arnold. Edgar Allan Poe, the poet, was born of this marriage, in Boston, Massachusetts, January 19, 1809.

George Poe, second son of John and Jane (McBride) Poe, was born in Ireland, and was brought by his parents to America when only two months old. The family afterward removed to Cecil county, Maryland, where, about 1773, George Poe married Catherine Dawson. Soon after their marriage they moved to Baltimore and lived first on Thomas street,

MD.—13

Fells Point, west of Broadway, as it is now, and afterward on their own property, No. 183 Market street. This lot is now on the south side of Baltimore street, about three doors east of Hanover street. He was a private in Captain Case's company, on duty, 1775-76. David Poe, his brother, was a sergeant, later in Captain McClellan's company. David Poe was lieutenant; George Poe, sergeant, and William Poe, private. On June 11, 1776, George Poe was commissioned captain in the Thirty-fourth Battalion, militia of Frederick county. George Poe died at the home of his son, Jacob Poe, at Elmwood, Frederick county, August 20, 1823, aged about eighty-two years, and was buried in the burying ground of the Brick Meeting House, near Walkersville, same county. The loss of the family Bible by fire makes it impossible to give the exact date of his birth. Catherine (Dawson) Poe, his wife, was born in Cecil county, Maryland, May 13, 1742, and died at the home of her son Jacob, which was then at Havre de Grace, Maryland, August, 1806, and was buried in lot No. 129, Westminster Churchyard, Baltimore. Children: Jacob, mentioned below; George, born November 14, 1778, died July 21, 1864; Harriet, March 28, 1785, died January 6 1816; Stephen, died in infancy.

Jacob Poe, eldest child of George and Catherine (Dawson) Poe, was born October 11, 1775, on Thomas street, Baltimore. As a young man he was employed by a merchant, and made several voyages as supercargo; afterward he became a farmer, first near Havre de Grace, and in 1817 at Elmwood, Frederick county. He married, in Baltimore, January 4, 1803, Bridget Amelia Fitzgerald Kennedy, daughter of John and Amelia (Fitzgerald) Kennedy, born June 10, 1775, in County Tipperary, Ireland. Her father sailed from Dublin in the ship "Neptune," April 30, 1784, and landed at Baltimore, May 30, following. Her mother was Amelia, daughter of George Fitzgerald, counselor at law. She died at Salisbury, Eastern Shore, Maryland, 1790. John Kennedy died at St. Croix, West Indies, while on a visit to his brother James. Jacob Poe died at the home of his son, Neilson Poe, Lexington street, Baltimore, July 25, 1860, aged eighty-five years. He was buried at the Brick Meeting House, near Walkersville. Bridget A. F. (Kennedy) Poe died December 25, 1844, at her home, Elmwood, Frederick county, and was buried in the Brick Meeting House Churchyard. Children, first six born in Baltimore: George, November 10, 1803, died February 6, 1804; John, March 4, 1805, died September 12, 1807; George, March 20, 1807, died January 10, 1879; Amelia and Neilson (twins), August 11, 1809, former married Dr. Charles Goldsborough, and died November 2, 1883; James Mosher, January 3, 1812, died October, 1885; Harriet Clemm, August 6, 1817, in Frederick county, Maryland, died December 1, 1878.

.Neilson Poe, son of Jacob and Bridget A. F. (Kennedy) Poe, was born August 11, 1809, in Baltimore, and in early life was a student at law in the office of William Gwynn, a noted counselor and editor of the "Federal Gazette." Afterward he was assistant editor, then editor and owner of the Frederick "Examiner," and on his return to Baltimore, in 1835, became editor and proprietor of the Baltimore "Chronicle." He was admitted to the bar before attaining his majority, and practiced in Baltimore until 1878, when, at the request of Governor Carroll, he accepted the chief judgeship of the Orphan's Court, which place he filled until shortly before his death, January, 1884. He was a constant contributor to many journals, and was distinguished by the beauty of his style and elegance of his diction. He married at Elmwood, November 30, 1831, Josephine Emily Clemm, daughter of William, Jr., and Harriet (Poe) Clemm, born August 13,

1808, at Mount Prospect, Baltimore county, the home of her grandfather, Colonel William Clemm. She died January 13, 1889. Children: Amelia, born October 1, 1832, in Frederick county; Neilson, September 6, 1834, in Frederick county, married, November 7, 1867, Alice Henrietta Morris; John Prentiss, mentioned below; Josephine Clemm, March 10, 1838, in Baltimore, married, April 10, 1860, George Gibson Casey; Harriet Clara, July 4, 1840, in Frederick county, died May 1, 1846; William Clemm, December 4, 1843, in Frederick county, married, October 13, 1868, Eleanora Hennen Robertson, died January 20, 1906; Kennedy, May 3, 1845, died February 26, 1846; Robert M., January 31, 1847, in Baltimore, married, November 27, 1872, Sarah Graham Wingate, died April 10, 1884; Charles, August 4, 1851, in Baltimore, married, October 10, 1877, Ellen E. Conway.

The character and career of John Prentiss Poe are most beautifully and aptly described in a memorial address delivered by Honorable Henry D. Harlan, November 11, 1909, at the University of Maryland, as follows:

John Prentiss Poe was born August 22, 1836, in Baltimore. He grew up under happy influences, having before his eyes a rare example of domestic felicity, refinement, culture and the many graces of Christian character. His first teacher was his accomplished mother. For a short while he was a pupil in the public schools of Baltimore, and at an early age entered the French and English Academy of Professor Boursaud. Later he attended St. Mary's College, and subsequently matriculated at Princeton College, from which he graduated with the class of 1854, being then in his eighteenth year. On the fiftieth anniversary of his graduation his *Alma Mater* conferred upon him the degree of Doctor of Laws.

On his return from college, the young graduate secured a clerkship in a bank, and during this time read law under the supervision of his father. He was appointed librarian of the Law Library, where he had an excellent opportunity to pursue his studies and familarize himself with the literature of the law. He was admitted to the bar of Baltimore in the superior court on the twenty-first anniversary of his birth—August 22, 1857—and in December of that year was admitted to the court of appeals of Maryland, and to the supreme court of the United States in the succeeding January. In every department of the law he was equipped to serve his clients, and no one served them with greater fidelity. In their behalf no task was too great to undertake; no amount of research too arduous; no attention to details too exacting. He brought to the trial of their causes a mind richly stored with the learning of the profession; a thorough acquaintance with the rules of practice and the technicalities of pleading; a capacity for clear and exact statement that was unexcelled; a memory that was little short of marvellous, combined with reasoning powers of a high order, and a diction that was singularly pure and copious. He could speak in the convincing language of logic, or when the occasion required, employ the persuasive voice of eloquence. He could denounce fraud and wrong with telling effect, and uphold justice and right with overpowering force. His manners were gracious and winning. While maintaining the interests of his clients, he was fair to his opponents, courteous to his adversaries, deferential and respectful to the court. He was an adept in the art of cross-examining. Small wonder that he had many cases to try in the State and Federal courts. * * *

Mr. Poe was a great master of our profession, but he was more than an eminent lawyer, he was the codifier of our whole body of statute law —public general and public local, as well as of the ordinances of the City Council of Baltimore. He was the draftsman of many forms in legislation, and a legal author of note. His books have been of inestimable value to the profession. There is in our State no practitioner, even of the smallest pretentions, and no judge who does not keep his works on pleading and practice at hand, and refer to them constantly. For many years he was one of the school commissioners of Baltimore City, a city counsellor, a member of various tax commissions, served in the State Senate, and was attorney-general of Maryland from 1891 to 1895. No record of his life, however brief, would be complete without reference to his well-known party fealty. He was a life-long Democrat, advocating the election of candidates of that party, and supporting its measures when many did not; he believed in party government, and while he recognized the existence of public evils and the necessity for reform, he thought this could best be secured within the party lines, not from any personal motives—for he gave his party more than he ever received from it—but because he thought the supremacy of the party was for the interest of the State. In political contests he was a frequent and an effective public speaker, and as is not unusually the case, was at times the target of severe and much unjust denunciation. This he accepted with equanimity, and never did a public man bear so little resentment. His connection with Maryland University is especially interesting. It was here that for forty years he did his great work as a teacher. The story of the Law School before he became associated with it is soon told. A Law Faculty was first constituted and annexed to this university in 1813. * * * No school of instruction in which lectures were given to students was opened until 1823. This ceased in 1836, and in 1869 the surviving members of the Law Faculty, Messrs. George W. Dobbin and John H. B. Latrobe, determined that the time had come to revive the School of Law. They selected Messrs. George William Brown, Bernard Carter, H. Clay Dallam and John Prentiss Poe to fill the existing vacancies in their faculty. The first course of instruction began on the first Monday in February, 1870, with twenty students in attendance, and continued till the summer vacation. From the time of his election to the Law Faculty, Mr. Poe was the leading spirit in the reorganized Law School, carrying to the close of his life the great burden of the work. In the fall of 1870 he offered to give a course of lectures on Pleading and Practice at Law, and his offer was gladly accepted. His entire course of lectures upon the two branches assigned to him was delivered at night for a whole scholastic year, to a class sometimes as small as three, and never larger than seven, and without compensation. Mr. Poe had, however, entered upon the task convinced that the interest of his profession required the establishment and maintenance of a law school of high order in this State, and his enthusiasm was undaunted. After many years of faithful work, always preserving the same courage and taking the same interest as at the beginning, he beheld the school grow, largely as the result of his own attractive personality, and his capacity as a lecturer and teacher, until it became recognized as one of the important institutions of learning in the commonwealth, both by the reason of the number of its graduates, and the influence it has exerted in raising the standard of legal education. Its graduates up to the present time number over thirteen hundred. All of these came under his teaching, and it may be justly said that no man in his generation has so deeply touched and moulded the life of the bar. He was the friend of the students, and ever ready to share with them his knowledge and experience, and in the concern with which he watched them enter upon their professional careers and the delight with which he welcomed their successes was exhibited that paternal solicitude which endeared him so strongly to the student body and to the alumni as a whole.

Mr. Poe was not content to be a good lecturer. He desired to impart knowledge to his students in a permanent form. This led him first to print a syllabus of his lectures on Pleading and Practice. This was followed by the preparation of his comprehensive work on "Pleading and Practice in the Courts of Common Law." The first volume "Pleading" appeared in 1880, the second volume on "Practice" was published in 1882, and the fourth and last edition of this invaluable treatise appeared in 1896. Mr. Poe was made dean of the Law Faculty on the death of the venerable George W. Dobbin, in 1884. But his activities were not confined to the Law School. As a member of the Board of Regents, every department of the university engaged his attention. There was no movement for its development that did not have his sympathy and co-operation. At the meetings of the board, of which he was long the secretary, his attendance could always be counted on. If there was work to be done he never avoided it. In all the years I have known him, I have never heard him urge the excuse that he was too busy to undertake a task that fell to his lot. He would sleep a few hours less and work a few hours more—that was all. Fortunately, he had a strong constitution and his capacity for work was almost incredible. He was so ready and capable that it was natural to turn to him, and he would not only do what he was asked to do, but do it uncomplainingly and well. If legislation was required to add a new department, or to expand the chartered powers of the university, he was at hand to draw the necessary bill. If an orator was desired for a commencement occasion, who could so well conduct the necessary correspondence? His associations with his colleagues were of the most delightful kind. Envy was absolutely foreign to his generous nature. He rejoiced in every honor which they won, and the meetings of a social character in which they participated in common were made memorable by his vivacity and general wit.

Turning for a moment from his public to his private life, we find a devoted son, husband, father and brother, and a staunch friend. To work unsparingly of himself for those he loved was to him a pleasure. If I were asked to sum up the principal characteristics of his life I should say activity, industry, integrity, devotion to his family, devotion to his profession, devotion to the Law School of this University, devotion to his party, cheerfulness of spirit and conscientious performance of duty in every station of life to which it pleased God to call him, were dominant. His was a long life. More than three score years and ten, and a full life lived nobly and in the fear of God. The end was not unfitting. He labored to the last. His step may not have been quite so quick, his heart action not quite so strong, but his eye was as bright, his smile as sweet, his presence as cheery, his hand-clasp as warm as ever when we last saw him, and he retained all his alertness, mental vigor and happy disposition.

All the sons were graduates of Princeton, all distinguished as football players, and all of the survivors now occupying prominent and successful positions in life. The third son, John Prentiss Poe, being possessed of a spirit of adventure, lost his life, September 25, 1915, while fighting under the British colors at the battle of Loos. He was a gentleman, first and last, but could not settle down to the easy life of the metropolis. The force which enabled him to win many football games for Princeton led him wherever there was adventure to be had. He found this in the rough mining camps of the western frontier, in the snowy wilderness in Alaska, in the swamps of Cuba, and in the Philippine jungles; in torrid Nicaragua, and at last under the crimson banner of England, floating over the shrapnel-torn trenches "somewhere in France." Soon after graduating from college he went to Nevada, where he soon joined the mounted police of the State. On one occasion he led the mounted police into a stronghold of desperate cattle thieves and captured the gang at the point of a pistol. Men soon learned to know that he could be relied upon. While prospecting in the western gold fields he made a trip to the famous Death Valley, in New Mexico. Subsequently he became a member of the governmental expedition which surveyed the boundaries between Alaska and British Columbia. When war was declared between Spain and the United States, he returned to Baltimore, and enlisted in the Fifth Maryland Regiment. He then joined the Sixteenth Infantry Regiment, with which he went to the Philippines. In 1903 he enlisted in the Kentucky State militia, and was ordered to service in the mountains. He enlisted in Marine Corps at headquarters, Washington, D. C., December 24th, 1903. Was promoted same date to sergeant. Transferred to Marine Barracks, League Island, same date. Served in Panama until discharged at Washington, D. C., "upon settlement of accounts," February 27th, 1904, as a sergeant with character "excellent." In the war between Honduras and Nicaragua in 1907, he was commissioned a captain of infantry in the Honduras army, and gained special distinction at the siege of Amapal. In the following year he participated in the fiilibustering expedition against Castro, the dictator of Venezuela. In September, 1914, he sailed for England, and soon enlisted as a private in the heavy artillery. In June, 1915, he secured a transfer to the Black Watch, the famous Scottish Highlanders Regiment, which has been distinguished in battlefields throughout the world. In speaking of his death, Samuel McCoy, of the Philadelphia "Public Ledger" of November 14, 1915, said: "In the report received from the British War Office, no details of his death were given—only the date, September 25, 1915. It is believed, however, from the terms of a letter written by a captain in the Black Watch, that his death came as the Black Watch charged the German lines with the fury of demons, and with the thrilling music of the bagpipes leading them on to glory. But all the Princeton men who knew Johnny know that he must have died as he lived—a man to whom gentleness was a creed and yet one to whom the call to heroic deeds sounded as compelling as it did to the knight-errants of old. So he must have died, fearless as he was on the football field, merry as he was in his last words: 'I trust I shall be on hand at the next round-up to tell you how the play came up. I looks toward you all and also bows. I also hopes I catches your eye?' "

JOHN S. ENSOR

THE late John S. Ensor, lawyer and philanthropist, was was a man whose universal good will and benevolence toward all mankind were evinced during his entire lifetime. By that very element in his character was he brought to meet his death, October 27, 1915. While on his way from Arlington, Maryland, to Govans, to attend a political mass meeting at which he was to be the principal speaker, an accident occurred in which a man was injured, and while hurrying to secure aid for him, Mr. Ensor was struck and killed by a trolley car, and thus was ended a career of activity and usefulness.

John S. Ensor was born May 28, 1868, at Towson, and received his early education in the public school of his native place, where his early life was passed. He was enthusiastic and active in all out-door sport and recreation. He graduated from Lafayette College, Easton, Pennsylvania, as honor man and orator of his class, in 1888, and was graduated at the Maryland University Law School in 1890. At the age of twenty-two he engaged in the practice of law in Baltimore, and applied himself with such diligence and ability that he was appointed assistant United States district attorney at Baltimore at the age of twenty-three. He entered upon the duties of this position with enthusiasm, and conducted important trials in both the lower and appellate federal courts. He was ever a student and continually strived to keep in touch with everything that pertained to his profession, and in an active practice of twenty-five years built up a very thriving business and was popular with members of the bar and the courts. His cases were always tried with ability and courtesy, and he enjoyed the sincere esteem of all who were privileged to know him. At a very early period he began to manifest an interest in the public welfare and especially in the promotion of the interest of future citizens in the person of the boys about him. He was very much interested in the Boy Scouts, for some time had been a scoutmaster and was one of the most energetic and enthusiastic in this movement. It was very natural that he should be called to the public service, for he was ever the friend of the people, and the unrelenting foe of corruption in public life. In 1895 he was nominated by the Baltimore County Republicans for State's attorney, in a convention which was torn by factional troubles. He surmounted all difficulties and received a handsome majority, being the first Republican to be elected as State's attorney since the Civil War. It is said his service as prosecuting officer was vigorous, and his work and methods won him many friends. After retiring from the office of State's attorney, Mr. Ensor continued to manifest an interest in public affairs and to labor for the promotion of good government. He had been particularly earnest in the advocacy of good roads, and was an earnest worker in behalf of neighborhood improvement associations. He was one of the leaders in the fight against the Mount Washington sewerage deal, which has been a scandal in the political history of his home city. As a trustee of Mount Washington Presbyterian Church he was active in promoting the moral works of that body. His broad mind and generous spirit were demonstrated in his affiliation with numerous prilanthropic and benevolent orders, including the Independent Order of Odd Fellows, the Junior Order of United Mechanics, the Masonic Fraternity, and the Benevolent and Protective Order of Elks, of which organizations he was an active worker. He was for many years a member of the Baltimore Country Club and the Mount Washington Club. In all these organizations he took a leading position and filled various important official stations. His breadth and fairness are indicated by his advocacy of non-partisan judicial election, and with other broad-minded Republicans he urged the support of Judges Burke and Duncan, who were Democratic nominees. While he was earnest and faithful in support of his principles, he believed in good men and good government before partisan advantage. In the fall of 1915 he was the nominee of his district for State Senator, and his fellow candidates adopted the following resolutions of respect and condolence:

Whereas, an Allwise but to a mysterious Providence has permitted death to invade our county and to remove from our midst John S. Ensor, one of its most highly respected citizens,

Resolved, Therefore, by his surviving colleagues of the Republican county ticket that they mourn the loss of him whose noble qualities of mind and heart have endeared him to his fellow men.

Resolved, That in his death the State has sustained the loss of one of its most loyal and devoted sons; and that his fidelity to principle and ideal standard of citizenship should be an inspiration to those who live after him.

A newspaper said of him:

Mr. Ensor's fight for the taxpayers against the Mount Washington sewerage deal, and his splendid campaign for the judgeship in the fall of 1914, in which he carried this formerly strongly Democratic county and was only defeated by a few votes excess majority for his opponent in Hartford county, are all well-known and recent matters. He was a foremost advocate of good roads and had much to do with the movement which has put this county so far to the front in this line. He was a patriot to the core, loving the country, its flag and all its traditions. He was a devoted friend to boys and was earnest in all efforts to make them better and more useful citizens, being prominent in the Boy Scouts' activities.

The character of Mr. Ensor is aptly and beautifully expressed in the following account from "The Sun" of Baltimore:

A high tribute was paid yesterday to the memory of the late John S. Ensor by the judges of the Circuit Court for Baltimore county and the members of the bar at a memorial meeting in the courtroom at Towson. Resolutions of respect as prepared by a committee composed of States's Attorney George Hartman, William M. Lawrence and T. Scott Offutt were read by Mr. Hartman and ordered spread on the minutes of the court and a copy sent to the family. Judges N. Charles Burke, Frank I. Duncan and Allan McClane were on the bench. After the addresses of the members of the bar, Judge Burke, speaking for the court, said in part: "The court fully concurs in what has been so well and justly said of Mr. Ensor in the resolutions read and in the remarks of gentlemen of the bar. His death was so pathetic, so inexpressibly sad as to touch the hearts of the whole people of the county. It is fitting that his professional brethren, who stood in close relationship and association with him, should meet in this room which witnessed his most arduous labors, the scene of his triumphs and disappointments, to pay a just and affectionate tribute to his memory. Mr. Ensor was not a great or profound lawyer, but he was more than a mere lawyer. He had a combination of qualities which attracted and attached to him a vast number of his fellow citizens. His genial nature, his kindliness and warm-heartedness endeared him to the people generally and secured for him a great personal popularity. In his private life he was clean, upright and above reproach and stood for the best things of life; his professional career was honorable, and characterized by fidelity to all the interests committed to his charge. His impulses were generous, and in the discharge of his public and private responsibilties he was actuated by high motives." The United States Court at Baltimore also adjourned in respect to the memory of Mr. Ensor, who was formerly assistant district attorney.

Following are newspaper editorial tributes to Mr. Ensor:

The tragic and untimely death of Mr. Ensor, Republican candidate for the State Senate, in the very prime of vigorous manhood has shocked and saddened the people of this county. For years Mr. Ensor had been a part of its public life, widely known to the people for his interest in their civic and social welfare. Notwithstanding the call of his profession and the many demands of a full and active life, he always found time for earnest and useful endeavor in matters relating to the welfare and social betterment of his fellows.

Devotedly attached to children, he took a prominent place in the Boy

Scout movement. He believed it had an effective influence for training boys to be truthful, manly, self-reliant and obedient, and his death will be mourned by none more deeply than by his little friends—the boys.

His energy and simple manliness, his buoyant and cheery good nature and his ready and sincere sympathy endeared him to thousands of friends who will long remember and long miss the bright, ringing and infectious laughter which was one of the many characteristics of "Johnny" Ensor.

The following beautiful tribute is extrated from an article entitled "Here Was a Man":

As he lived, so he died. Throughout his life he had striven for the welfare of mankind, with a big heart overflowing with kindness and hands and feet active to carry out the promptings of his helpful nature. At the moment when he was stricken he was in the act of seeking to administer aid to a fellow being, regardless of the fact that his own important affairs were waiting. All who knew him deplore what seems to us his untimely removal from among us, but although the future held bright promise of high honor and even increased usefulness for him, his career could not have been more consistently closed had he lived for a century. We will realize this more fully after the fresh poignancy of our shock and grief has passed.

Mr. Ensor married Irma Risley, of Philadelphia, and left besides his widow, two young sons, John S., Jr., and Risley.

ROBERT HENRY SMITH

FOR forty-seven years an honored member of the Baltimore bar, and recognized as the most eminent exponent of Admiralty law connected with that bar, it is not as the learned lawyer, nor the financier, that he was best known to thousands of Baltimorans, but as the superintendent of the Sunday school of the Second Presbyterian Church for forty-seven years, and as an elder of that church for nearly half a century. At a memorial meeting of the bench and bar, held in his honor, United States District Attorney Samuel K. Dennis, in presenting the memorial resolution, characterized Mr. Smith as a soldier, a teacher and lawyer, whose life was blameless, who had "less original sin than any of us and more charity than most of us." "His most lasting success," said Mr. Dennis, "was outside the law and lay in the good he did." Former Judge Alfred S. Niles, once a law student in Mr. Smith's office, said that on one occasion Mr. Smith said to him: "If I had to choose between my practice and my work in church and Sunday school, I should not hesitate an instant to give up my practice." Said Daniel H. Hayne in part: "Mr. Smith's precept and example were constant incentives toward the best efforts of those with whom he came in contact and still survives him, an active force for good."

Mr. Smith's ancestry on both sides was Scotch-Irish Presbyterians from the north of Ireland, who settled in York county, Pennsylvania, some of them coming in time to engage in the second war with Great Britain, 1812-14. He was a son of Robert and Sarah (Ross) Smith of Chanceford, York county, Pennsylvania. His father was a farmer and merchant, deeply interested in public affairs, and a loyal Presbyterian. Of his early life at home Mr. Smith once said: "Though raised on the Shorter Catechism my early life was not made irksome, but most happy."

Robert Henry Smith was born at the homestead in Lower Chanceford township, York county, Pennsylvania, December 1, 1845, and seventy-two years later, on October 9, 1917, died in the house in which he was born. His brother, Samuel resides in the old homestead, and Robert H. was there convalescing after a severe illness at his Baltimore home, No. 1230 North Calvert street. He grew to manhood at the home farm, attended good schools, and remained at home under the influence of a good mother, his whole after-life being a tribute to that strong beneficial influence. He attended public schools until the age of fourteen, then attended York Academy until his enlistment in July, 1864, in the 194th Regiment, Pennsylvania Volunteer Infantry, serving one hundred days. After receiving an honorable discharge he returned home, entered Lafayette College, Easton, Pennsylvania, there continuing until graduated A.B., class of 1867, A.M., 1870. In the winter of 1862 he taught a term in the public schools and after graduation he taught one year in York Academy, although his intention all through his college years had been to prepare for the medical profession. But he met with little encouragement from his friends, and some opposition, and during the year at York Academy, he decided to study law. In 1868 he began to study law in Baltimore, Maryland. Two years later he was admitted to the bar, September, 1870, and at once began practice in that city. He was very ambitious, and in selecting a branch of the profession, in which to specialize, chose Admiralty law, a branch of the profession in which he became famous. He acquired a wide and accurate knowledge of Admiralty law, served a very large clientele of marine merchants and shipowners, and was a recognized authority. His genial, affable manner, uprightness and integrity, were equally important factors in his success; men liking and respecting him for his virtues as well as for his professional skill and ability. Said his friend, Mayor Randolph Bailton, at the memorial meeting previously referred to: "I do not hesitate to say that there is hardly a man in the whole country who stood in the front rank with a greater right on the question of character, and on the point of setting an example of how a man could go through all the vicissitudes of business—money-making if you please to call it so—and yet come out stainless." At the same meeting Judge Rose responding for the bench said: "For many years he was the undisputed leader of the admiralty bar of this court. He probably seldom thought evil of any one until the evidence of such a person's conduct was absolutely conclusive. He certainly never gave expression to any such thought if he entertained it. Very many men and women have been better men and women because they came in early life under the influence of Robert H. Smith. I wonder after all, if any other work we can do really lasts so long and counts for so much." Such was his career at the bar and such the estimation in which he was held by his brethren of the bar. In addition to the demands of a larger practice he was a professor of Admiralty Federal Procedure and Legal Ethics at Baltimore Law School, 1900-1910; was appointed a member of the Court House Commission in 1893, that Commission having in charge the erection of a City Court House; in 1893 he became a member of the Board of Trustees of the McDonough School, and in 1907 was chosen president of the Board. He knew nearly every boy in the school and some of them he aided in establishing themselves as prosperous business men and financiers. In 1896 he was elected president of the Board of Supervisors of Election for the city of Baltimore, and in 1904 he was chosen a member of Tome Institute, at Port Deposit, Maryland. Other philanthropies which received the benefit of his interest and legal knowledge were the Presbyterian Eye, Ear and Throat Hospital, which he served as a member of the Board of Governors, and the Presbyterian Association, which he served as legal counsel. In the business world he was a director of the National Bank of Baltimore; the Title Guarantee and Trust Company; the American Bonding Company. His fraternity was Zeta Psi; his club the University. He was a member of the local, state and national bar associations and for many years president of the local association. He was a Republican in politics, taking an active interest in city politics and in 1904 was the successful candidate of his party for Congress. But politics was little to his liking and his connection more a matter of civic duty than personal preference.

There is little question that the deepest interest of his life outside his home was the Second Presbyterian Church and Sunday School. He joined that church soon after coming to Baltimore in 1868, and was a faithful consistent member and strong pillar of support, until his death forty-nine years later. Nearly that entire time he was superintendent of the Sunday School and an elder of the church. In addition he was interested in other affairs of the Presbytery and well known in all religious denominations, although strict in his devotion to the tenets of his own church. The fruit of his zeal and devotion is in evidence in the large Sunday School of the Second Church, built up and held together through his personal efforts and the teachers whom he inspired.

Mr. Smith married, April 23, 1873, Helen A. Alford, who survives him, a resident of Baltimore. Mr. and Mrs. Smith are the parents of two children, one deceased, and a daughter, Helen, now wife of Dr. Henry J. Walton of Baltimore.

When Mr. Smith's death was announced in the United States Court, adjournment was at once ordered and a committee appointed by Judge Rose to draft a suitable memorial. All of the committee were present at the later memorial meeting except former United States Attorney General, who sent a letter regretting his inability to be present, but endorsing the resolution submitted by the Committee as they "expressed clearly and with entire accuracy the high regard entertained for Mr. Smith by his brethren of the bar and their regret at his death." A layman's memorial service was held at the Second Presbyterian Church, Sunday evening, October 14, 1917. The funeral services were held at 3 P. M., October 11, and all that was mortal laid at rest.

A fitting close to this tribute of respect to a good man is his word of advice to young men: "There can be no success unless they are faithful and honest. I believe that character has more to do with a man's success than his genius."

EDWIN WARFIELD

THE history of the Warfield family of Maryland, of which Edwin Warfield, former Governor of Maryland, and president of the Fidelity Trust Company of Baltimore, is representative, is ancient and honorable to the highest degree, and needs no reinforcing from the records of the past. It is a fact, however, that it is one of the oldest families of Great Britain, the surname being derived from the Manor of War-welt (modern name Warfield), in the Hundred of Ripples-mere, Barrochescire (Berkshire), England. At the time of the Domesday Survey in 1085, this manor was vested in the Crown (William the Conqueror) as tenant-in-chief, the Saxon holder having been Queen Eddid (Edith or Eadgyth), Queen of Edward the Confessor, the eldest daughter of God-wine, Earl of Wessex, and his wife Gytha, the sister of Harold. Warfield Manor afterwards came into the possession of the Nevilles, who were of Norman descent. Windsor Forest, Berkshire, is one of the five forests mentioned by name in the Domesday Survey. The forest was at that time divided into sixteen walks, among them "Warfeilde" or "Walfelde Walke."

In "The Annals of Windsor" there are many interesting references to this name showing its prominence at an early period in the history of England. On the 25th of September, 1216, "King John sent orders from Scotter, in Lincolnshire, to Engelard de Cigony, to deliver Hugh de Polested forthwith, in prison at Windsor, to John de Warfield, brother of Elye de Warfield, unless he should be ransomed in the meantime." (Patent Rolls 18 Johann. M. 2). In 1271, "the Prior of Merton held Upton in free gift of the grant of Pagan de Warfield." (Hundred Rolls 39 Henry III).

The Norman conquerors introduced the "de" into England, but it must not be supposed that the prefix meant that they were always of Norman origin, for very many families of British, Saxon and Danish descent also used the prefix until it was almost completely dropped or discarded in the fourteenth and fifteenth centuries for brevity and with the disappearance of Norman French.

Warfield is a village and parish, in the Hundred of Wargrave, and about eight miles to the southwest of Windsor. It contains Warfield Park, Warfield Hall and Warfield Grove.

(I) The American history of the family begins with Richard Warfield, who came from Berkshire, England, in 1662, and was doubtless a member of the family which originated in that county. He settled upon the banks of the Severn in Anne Arundel county, Maryland. The Howards and other old Maryland families settled in the same region, many of the first families of Maryland and other states tracing to these families through intermarriages.

Richard Warfield acquired a large estate, all of which came to him by purchase or exchange. The lands were in the finest agricultural section of the state, his several estates being known as "Warfield's Plains," "Warfield's Range," "Warfield's Increase," and "Warfield's Addition." A century later his descendants led in the struggle for independence. Richard Warfield was more zealous in the service of the church than in the state. He was a member of the first vestry of old St. Anne's, built under the act of assembly, of 1692, which divided the counties into parishes, and ordered the chapels built. He was a generous contributor to all religious causes, and from his large means gave bountifully to all public activities. His will, probated 1703-04, shows him to have been possessed of all the luxuries of the day, including valuable slaves and indentured white servants, and his fealty to English tradition is shown in the willing of "My Gold Seal Ring to my son John," the head of the house.

He married Ellen Browne, daughter of Captain John Browne, of London, who came from England, in 1673, a descendant of Sir John Browne, who brought over emigrants in 1659, receiving from Governor Philipp Calvert a grant of five hundred acres. Descendants of the marriage are connected with all the distinguished Maryland families and with many in Virginia, Kentucky, and other states.

(II) The line of descent to Governor Warfield is through John Warfield, son of Richard and Ellen (Browne) Warfield. He was of "Warfield's Plains," in 1696, later of "Warfield's Forest," and in 1704, of "Warfield's Range." He married Ruth, daughter of John and Ruth (Morley) Gaither, her father a Colonial official of Virginia, who moved to Anne Arundel county, Maryland, there receiving patents for large tracts of land prior to 1662.

(III) Benjamin Warfield, son of John and Ruth (Gaither) Warfield, of "Warfield's Range," Howard county, Maryland, was a member of the vestry of Queen Caroline Church. His wife, Rebecca, was a daughter of Judge Nicholas and Sarah (Worthington) Ridgely. Her father was Chancellor of Delaware, grandson of Colonel Henry and Katherine (Greenbury) Ridgely and great-grandson of Colonel Henry Ridgely, who died in 1710, a justice in 1667, member of the Dover House in 1698, and captain of the "Foote." Colonel Henry Ridgely married (first) Elizabeth Howard, of England, and (second) the widow of Mareen du Val.

(IV) Captain Benjamin (2) Warfield, son of Benjamin (1) and Rebecca (Ridgely) Warfield, was of Cherry Grove, his death occurring in 1806. He bought and added to the estate known as "Fredericksburg," the original patent which is owned by Governor Edwin Warfield. The old hipped roof house which he built in 1765 is still standing, and is owned and occupied by John Warfield, brother of Governor Warfield. He held a captain's commission in the Revolutionary Army, dated March 2, 1778. He commanded the Eldridge Battalion, Severn Militia. The men of the Warfield family during this period were leaders in developing the patriotic spirit of the state to oppose the English oppression. They bitterly opposed the Stamp Act, "Liberty and Independence or Death in Pursuit of It" their motto. In the Severn Militia alone during the Revolution were Captain Benjamin Warfield, Lieutenant Robert Warfield, Ensign Charles Warfield, Launcelot and Thomas Warfield, Lieutenants, Ensign Joseph Warfield. Dr. Walter Warfield was a surgeon in the Revolutionary Army, and an original member of the Society of the Cincinnati; Elijah and David, sons of Colonel Charles Warfield, were captains in the Fifth Maryland Regiment Militia and were on guard in Baltimore in 1812. Dr. Charles Alexander Warfield paraded the battalion, of which he was the major in the upper part of Anne Arundel county, wearing in their hats labels bearing the motto, "Liberty and Independence or Death in the Pursuit of It." This was the spirit of the Warfields during the Revolution, and in every war they have promptly rallied to the support of their country's cause.

Captain Benjamin Warfield married Catherine Dorsey, born November 30, 1745, daughter of Philemon and Catherine (Ridgely) Dorsey. Her father, who died in 1772, was a captain of "The Hundred," and resided near Dayton, his estate consisting of over ten thousand acres, extending from Clarkeville to Florence in Anne Arundel county. Catherine (Dorsey) Warfield was a granddaughter of Joshua and Ann (Ridgely) Dorsey, of "Barnes Folly," and a great-granddaughter of Major Edward and Sarah (Wyeth) Dorsey. Major Edward Dorsey was a judge of the Maryland High Court of Chancery, member of the Maryland House of

Burgesses from Baltimore county in 1705. He was a descendant of Sir John d'Arcy, whose three sons came over in 1661. Captain Benjamin Warfield had three sons: Joshua, Philemon Dorsey and Beale, the last two named served in the War of 1812.

(V) Joshua Warfield, son of Captain Benjamin (2) and Catherine (Dorsey) Warfield, was born September 11, 1781, died March 19, 1846, being known as Joshua Warfield of Cherry Grove. He married, March 12, 1816, Lydia Welsh, born October 23, 1790, a descendant of Nicholas Wyatt, who came over in 1600, also of John McCubbin, a Scotch baronet, and of John Howard, who took up Timber Neck, now a part of Baltimore. Lydia Welsh was a daughter of John and Lucretia (Dorsey) Welsh, of Upper Howard county, Maryland, granddaughter of John and Hannah (Hammond) Welsh, of South River, Maryland, great-granddaughter of John and Rachel (Hammond) Welsh. Captain John Welsh was a merchant of South River, and a partner of his cousin, Richard Snowden. Rachel (Hammond) Welsh was a granddaughter of Major General Hammond, Justice of the Provincial Court in 1667; member of the Council in 1668; member of the Court of Admiralty in 1700. Captain John Welsh was a son of Major John and Mary (Welsh) Welsh, the former of the "Quorum," 1671-81, and high sheriff of Anne Arundel county, 1676-78.

(VI) Albert Gallatin Warfield, son of Joshua and Lydia (Welsh) Warfield, was born in the old homestead of the Warfields, at Cherry Grove, February 24, 1817, and died at his residence, "Oakdale," Howard county, Maryland, November 3, 1891, inheriting as a part of his patrimony a large number of slaves, and was one of the largest slave owners in his section, yet he was opposed to the doctrine of slavery, and let each one free as he reached the age of forty years. He inherited also a part of the home plantation upon which he built "Oakdale," and there he lived his long and honorable life. He was especially kind to his slaves and gave himself entirely to the management of his large estate, real and personal. He never accepted but one public office, that of president of the country school board in 1869. "Oakdale," a beautiful estate, was noted for the open-handed hospitality there dispensed, the courteous, refined, cultivated host and the gentle, womanly hostess vieing in their efforts to make "Oakdale" a place of fond recollection.

Mr. Warfield married, August 25, 1842, Margaret Gassaway Watkins, a descendant of John Watkins, son of the founder, who came over in 1667. He married Ann, daughter of Major Nicholas Gassaway, who came to Maryland in 1649, member of the Upper House of Lord Baltimore's council, and deputy governor. The line of descent is through Nicholas Watkins, son of John and Ann (Gassaway) Watkins, born March, 1691, and his wife Margaret; their son, Nicholas (2) Watkins, born August 20, 1722, died in 1766, and his wife, Ariana Worthington; their son, Colonel Gassaway Watkins, and his wife, Eleanor Bowie Claggett; their daughter, Margaret Gassaway Watkins, wife of Albert Gallatin Warfield, and mother of Governor Edwin Warfield.

The Worthington ancestry of Mrs. Margaret G. Warfield is interesting. Ariana Worthington, born December 25, 1729, married, in 1743, Nicholas (2) Watkins. She was a daughter of Thomas and Elizabeth (Ridgely) Worthington, her father, who died in March, 1753, was a member of the House of Burgesses and major of Anne Arundel county militia. She was a granddaughter of John and Sarah (Howard) Worthington, the former a member of the "Quorum" also of the House of Burgesses, and captain of the Severn Militia. Sarah Howard was a daughter of Matthew and Sarah (Dorsey) Howard, who came in 1650, and granddaughter of Robert

Howard, duke of Norfolk, and a descendant of Thomas
Plantagenet, of Brotherton, a son of King Edward I. Ariana
Worthington was a great-granddaughter of Rev. John Worth-
ington, master of Jesus College, Cambridge, England, and a
great-great-grandaughter of Roger Worthington, son of
Thomas Worthington, of Worthington and "The Bryn."

Colonel Gassaway Watkins, father of Margaret Gassaway (Watkins) Warfield, veteran of both the first and second
war with Great Britain, served in the Revolutionary Army in
Colonel Smallwood's regiment, from January, 1776, and was
actively engaged in the battles of Long Island, White Plains,
Germantown, Monmouth, Guilford Court House, and
others. He was an original member of the Society of the
Cincinnati, and for a number of years president of the Maryland Society. He died at Walnut Grove in 1840. He married, April 26, 1803, Eleanor Bowie Claggett, daughter of
Wiseman and Priscilla Bowie (Lyles) Claggett, granddaughter of Edward and Eleanor Bowie (Brooke) Claggett, great-
granddaughter of John and Mary (Millikin) Bowie, the
former the son of the founder who came from Scotland in
1705-06, and a great-great-granddaughter of James Millikin,
the American founder of the family of the "Levels," Prince
George county, Maryland.

"Oakdale," the home of Mr. and Mrs. Albert Gallatin
Warfield, was not only where a place of hospitality and order
reigned, but was a home made so attractive that the children
loved to dwell in it, even when business and their own families
made it necessary to live elsewhere. Mrs. Warfield was widely
known for her gentleness, kindness and charity. She was the
friend of everyone in sorrow or need, and ever ready to minister to their wants. She was a friend of the ministers to
whom she gladly extended the hospitality of "Oakdale," and
a friend of the church to which she generously contributed.

She died at the home of her youngest daughter in Westchester, Pennsylvania, while on a visit, surviving her husband five years. At the funeral of Mr. Warfield at "Oakdale" every class and condition gathered to honor his memory, and all were mourners.

Mr. and Mrs. Albert Gallatin Warfield were the parents of eleven children, three died in infancy, and eight survived, four of whom are: 1. Albert Gallatin, a major in the C. S. A. 2. Joshua Nicholas. 3. Gassaway Watkins, died at Camp Chase, Ohio, a soldier of the Confederacy in 1864. 4. Edwin, of whom further.

(VII) Edwin Warfield, son of Albert G. and Margaret G. (Watkins) Warfield, was born May 7, 1848, at "Oakdale." He was educated in the public schools and St. Timothy Hall, Catonville, Maryland. He was admitted to the Maryland bar, 1881; was Register of Wills, Howard county, Maryland, 1874 to 1881; State Senator, 1882-1886; president of Senate, 1886; Surveyor of the Port of Baltimore, 1886-1890, appointed by President Cleveland. He was the founder of the Patapsco National Bank of Ellicott City, Maryland; founder of the Fidelity and Deposit Company of Maryland, its president, the largest surety company in the world; Governor of Maryland, 1904-1908, declining renomination. He is a member of the South River Club of Anne Arundel county, Maryland (one of the oldest in the world), a member of the Society of the Cincinnati, also of the Sons of the American Revolution, the Society of War of 1812, the Maryland Historical Society, of which he is president, American Bar Association, also Maryland and Baltimore City Bar Association, and has many other business and social connections.

Mr. Warfield married, November 24, 1886, in Baltimore, Emma Nicodemus, daughter of J. Courtney Nicodemus, a grandson of Lieutenant Frederick Nicodemus, of Washington county, Maryland, an officer of the Revolution, and his wife, Mary J. Montandon, a descendant of Albert Montandon, a Huguenot, who settled in Philadelphia, Pennsylvania, in 1720. Children of Governor Warfield are: Carrie; Emma; Louise; Captain Edwin Warfield, of the 110th Field Artillery, now in France; Alice, married M. Gillett Gill; John; Clarence; Margaret Gassaway, married Herman Hoopes, of Philadelphia; Marshall T., married Lucy W. Holland. The family home is "Oakdale," Howard county, Maryland, Governor Warfield's birthplace and the family homestead for generations far into the past.

JAMES ELLICOTT TYSON

ALTHOUGH one-half the life of James Ellicott Tyson, an eminent native son of Baltimore, was spent retired from active business life, there was never a time when he was not deeply concerned for the welfare of the city. In a day when commercialism was believed to be the prevailing American characteristic, he laid aside business cares, content with the fortune he had amassed, and although he lived to the great age of eighty-nine, he never tired of the delights his country estates gave him. He was a man of fine presence, most courtly manner, lovable in character and gentle in disposition—a true gentleman of the old school, greatly esteemed by all. His career in the business world was one of honorable success, but his heart lay away from the marts of trade, and he there remained only until he could retire with sufficient competence to gratify his love of the pleasures and recreations of the great out-of-doors furnished by his own broad acres, travel and kindred pursuits. He was of distinguished ancestry, tracing to the days of William Penn in Pennsylvania, to early Maryland days, and to a long line of English ancestors.

(I) Reynear Tyson, the first of the family by this name in America, was a member of the Society of Friends, having been converted by the preaching of William Penn, at whose request he emigrated to Pennsylvania, arriving on the ship "Concord," October 6, 1683. Reynear Tyson's own statement regarding the date of his arrival in Pennsylvania is given in "Watson's Annals of Philadelphia," as follows:

We whose names are to these presents subscribed do hereby certify unto all whom it may concern, that soon after our arrival in this province of Pennsylvania, in October, 1683, to our certain knowledge, Herman ap den Graff, Dirk ap den Graff and Abraham ap den Graff, as well as we ourselves, in the cave of Francis Daniel Pastorious, did cast lots for the respective lots which they and we then began to settle in Germantown; and the said Graffs (three brothers) have sold their several lots each by himself; no less than a division in writing had been made by them. Witness our hands this 29th day of November, A. D., 1709. Leanart Arets, Thomas Hunder, Abraham Tunis, Jan Lensen, William Streygert, Jan Lucksen, Reynear Tyson.

William Penn, proprietor of Pennsylvania, named Reynear Tyson as one of the incorporators in his patent for Germantown, October 12, 1689, by which Francis Daniel Pastorious, Reynear Tyson and others were authorized to form a court and sit once a month; they were constituted a body corporate by the name of Bailiff Burgesses and Commonality of Germantown in the county of Philadelphia. Under this charter he was a burgess 1692-93-94-96. The government of Germantown began October 6, 1691, and ended February 12, 1707, when the borough and court records of Germantown were ordered to the recorder's office, Philadelphia, by Act of Assembly. He was one of the signers of the certificate issued by the quarterly meeting at Philadelphia, addressed to the London yearly meeting, which Samuel Jennings bore with him to London in 1693, concerning the Keith controversy. Some years before his death, Reynear Tyson removed from Germantown to Abingdon, Philadelphia county, where he became a large landowner and active business man, and was associated with the Friends' meeting of that place. He lived beloved and honored to a ripe old age, dying July 27, 1745, aged about eighty-six years. He married Margaret Kunders, a lady of good family and high social position. Children: Mathias, mentioned below; Isaac, born September 7, 1688; Elizabeth, August 7, 1690; John, October 9, 1692; Abraham, August 10, 1694; Derrick, September 6, 1696; Sarah, December 19, 1698; Peter, March 6, 1700; Henry, March 4, 1702.

(II) Mathias Tyson, eldest son of Reynear and Margaret

(Kunders) Tyson, was born June 3, 1686, at Germantown, Pennsylvania, and preceded his father to the grave by many years. He received a good estate from his father, and moved to Abingdon, Philadelphia county, where he lived the quiet life of a country gentleman. He married in Abingdon, Mary Potts, daughter of John Potts, of Llanidoss, Wales, by whom he had the following children: Margaret, born July 7, 1708; Mary, March 25, 1710; Reynear, June 24, 1711; John, December 20, 1712; Sarah, October 10, 1714; Elizabeth, September 14, 1716; Isaac, mentioned below; Matthew, July, 1720; Martha, March 12, 1722; Elizabeth, October 25, 1723.

(III) Isaac Tyson, third son of Mathias and Mary (Potts) Tyson, was born August 21, 1718, in Philadelphia county, died in Baltimore county, Maryland, in 1784. He settled in Upper Dublin township, Philadelphia county, Pennsylvania, where he was living at the time of his removal to Maryland. In the year 1774 Isaac Tyson purchased a tract of land in Baltimore county, on which was a saw mill, situated on the falls of the Little Gunpowder River. He did not remove to Maryland until the year 1783, the year after purchasing an additional tract of two hundred and fifty acres from his son, Elisha Tyson, who had settled in Baltimore county about the time of his father's first purchase, which was in the year 1773, according to the Baltimore records. He brought with him to Maryland a certificate from the Horsham Friends Meeting, Philadelphia county, to Friends of Gunpowder Meeting, Baltimore county, dated July 2, 1783, with certificates for his sons, George and Jesse Tyson. Although a newcomer in Maryland, he became one of the influential and prominent men of his community. He died honored and respected by his neighbors in Baltimore county. He married, March 28, 1748-49, Esther, daughter of Isaac Shoemaker, of Shoemakertown, Pennsylvania. Children: Elisha, men-

tioned below; Tacy, born May 20, 1752; Aneas, May 20,
1754; Jacob, October 1, 1755; Nathan, January 10, 1757;
Sarah, September 16, 1758; Jesse, July 20, 1761; Elizabeth,
September 21, 1768; Dorothy, February 18, 1770; Mary,
1772; George, 1775; William.

(IV) Elisha Tyson, son of Isaac and Esther (Shoemaker)
Tyson, was born December 18, 1750, in Philadelphia county.
He lived at Jericho on the Little Falls of Gunpowder River,
in Baltimore county, and later moved to Baltimore, Maryland.
He built a mill at Jones Falls near what is now Druid Hill
Park. Always a member of the Society of Friends, he was
full of wisdom and courage in every-day life, and was the first
of the family to come to Maryland, having preceded his father
here by ten years. The approximate date of his arrival is determined by the certificate which he presented from Abingdon
Friends Meeting to the Gunpowder Monthly Meeting of
Friends in Baltimore county, March 3, 1773, in which he
was recommended as a member of the Society, by which meeting he was received. He prospered greatly in this world's
goods and became one of the wealthiest men in Baltimore, his
estate at his death being valued at nearly three hundred thousand dollars. Philanthropist and humble Christian, Elisha
Tyson's constant endeavor was to redress the wrongs of suffering humanity, and he devoted much of his life to efforts in
behalf of the persecuted son of Africa, suffering persecutions
himself on their account. A complete biography has been
written of this devoted friend of emancipation, who, though
far ahead of his time in his horror of slavery, yet remained
unshaken by the adverse criticism of his contemporaries. He
left a farewell address to the colored population of Baltimore,
and at his death was mourned by ten thousand of those whose
cause he had so valiantly espoused. He married (first) November 5, 1776, Mary Amos, who died April 17, 1813, daugh-

ter of William and Hannah (McComas) Amos, and grand-daughter of William Amos, Sr., founder of the Amos family in Maryland. He married (second) October 22, 1814, Margaret Cowman, who died January 29, 1853. Children: 1. Isaac, born October 10, 1777; married, November 8, 1797, Elizabeth Thomas, who died May 12, 1812, daughter of Evan and Rachel (Hopkins) Thomas; he died June 30, 1864. 2. Esther, born February 23, 1779, died in childhood. 3. Lucretia, born January 9, 1780; married John Wilson. 4. William, born October 2, 1782, married Elizabeth Ellicott, daughter of Jonathan and Sarah Ellicott. 5. Mary, born September 4, 1785; married Enoch Clapp. 6. Nathan, mentioned below. 7. James, born March 4, 1790, died young. 8. Sarah, born August 19, 1791, died young. 9. Elisha, born January 28, 1796; married Sarah S. Morris. 10. Deborah, born March 12, 1798, died May 12, 1801.

(V) Nathan Tyson, son of Elisha and Mary (Amos) Tyson, was born November 14, 1787, and died January 6, 1867. He was reared and educated in Baltimore, and became one of its most prominent citizens. He was the first president of the Baltimore Corn and Flour Exchange, now known as the Chamber of Commerce. He also held a prominent place in the social life of the city. The following resolution was passed at a meeting of the Baltimore Corn and Flour Exchange, January 8, 1867, on the death of Nathan Tyson:

RESOLVED, That the members of the Corn and Flour Exchange have learned with deepest sorrow of the death of Nathan Tyson, our first venerated President, to whose zealous and active co-operation we were indebted for the successful organization of our Association.

RESOLVED, That in the character of the deceased we recognize the true type of all that is upright and honorable in the merchant, true and noble in the Christian gentleman, and one who has in addition to his beautiful illustration of the relations of life, entirely filled the measure of his whole duty in his connection with us as a merchant and a citizen, and we are gratified that it was permitted him to attain a fullness and maturity of years but seldom reached.

RESOLVED, That the deceased presented to us in his daily conduct his known integrity, his uniform courtesy and goodness of heart, an example by which we should be benefitted and which, if followed, would enable us to pass away as he has done from the scene of active life universally lamented and respected, an example which we urge upon all to emulate.

RESOLVED, That this Association tender to his bereaved family our deepest and most sincere sympathy and condolence in their loss and that a copy of these resolutions signed by the Chairman and the Secretary be conveyed to them and the same published in our daily newspapers.

JAMES HOOPER, JR., *Chairman.*

HENRY M. WARFIELD, *Secretary.*

Mr. Tyson married Martha Ellicott, September 27, 1815, born September 13, 1795, died March 15, 1873, daughter of George and Elizabeth (Brooke) Ellicott. She was a descendant of Robert Brooke, of De La Brooke Manor, Maryland (see Brooke line). Martha Ellicott is described as having worn at her wedding a white corded silk dress shading into opal tints, a white fichu crossed on her breast, and a white lace bonnet. Thus arrayed she is reputed to have presented a picture of lovely young womanhood. Children: 1. James Ellicott, mentioned below. 2. Elizabeth Brooke, born March 30, 1818; married, March 25, 1843, John Marsh Smith; died July 29, 1890. 3. Henry, born November 18, 1820; married, May 13, 1847, Mary Gillingham, who died December, 1891; he died September 1, 1877. 4. Isabelle, born March 17, 1823. 5. Anne, born February 26, 1825, died August 7, 1884; married, June 11, 1861, William Kirk, died July, 1879. 6. Mary, born August 11, 1826, died same year. 7. Frederick, born April 17, 1828. 8. Robert, born March 25, 1834; married (first) June 4, 1863, Jane Gambrill, died 1864; married (second) November 20, 1869, Sarah R. Smith. 9. Evan, born August 27, 1831, died May 6, 1832. 10. Lucy, born March 20, 1833; married Henry Maynadier Fitzhugh. 11. Nathan, born June 24, 1834, died March 27, 1835. 12. Nathan, born June 27, 1836, died March 9, 1837.

(VI) James Ellicott Tyson, son of Nathan and Martha (Ellicott) Tyson, was born August 21, 1816, in Baltimore, Maryland, and died at his country estate, "Warwick," in Howard county, Maryland, September 4, 1904, lacking but one year of attaining the honors of a nonagenarian. He was educated in private schools and prepared for college under Mr. Sams, but owing to certain obligations incurred by his father at this time he was obliged to forego his college course and enter into business. He did so with the determination of helping his father out of his financial difficulties. In this he was most successful, and through his energy and close application to work he not only succeeded in this but was able to build up the great firm that bore his name and carry it on through many prosperous years, until he was able to retire, an independent man. For many years Mr. Tyson was engaged in the flour and grain business in Baltimore, having large shipping connections with South America. He was also a ship owner, using his own vessels to transport cereals to the Latin American countries. He retired from active business life at the comparatively early age of forty-five, realizing a promise he had made to himself not to continue in business life once he had attained what he considered a fortune ample for the necessities and luxuries of his day. He was a man of commanding presence, and fine physique; had a keen sense of humor, was quick at repartee, an interesting reconteur and held broad views on the questions of the day. He was precise and fixed in his habits. His office was closed every day exactly at 3 in the afternoon, and all business ceased for the day. This was known to all his business associates, and none ever thought of calling upon him on business matters after that hour. He was an ardent sportsman and very fond of hunting. Almost any afternoon he could be seen gun on shoulder and dogs at heel, tramping about on one of his large estates in search of game. Farming was his hobby, his first venture in this line being a large plantation given to him by his great-grandmother, Elizabeth Brooke. In addition he owned a large amount of real estate in various localities, including the estate "Warwick," a farm at Ocean City, Maryland, large tracts in Pennsylvania, and valuable properties in Baltimore and elsewhere. He was very successful in most of his farming enterprises, and uniformly so in dealing in real estate properties, becoming widely known as having excellent judgment as to the value of real estate in general. "Warwick," where the last years of his life were spent, an estate of one thousand acres, granted to one of his Ellicott ancestors, was always kept in a high state of cultivation, and was his especial pride. He was excessively fond of books and a wide reader. He possessed an excellent library, the foundation being second hand books bought in the days when his means were limited, but his love of reading keen. In 1861 and 1862 Mr. Tyson traveled extensively abroad, visiting England, Ireland, France, Switzerland, Germany, Italy, Greece, the Holy Land and Egypt. Many most interesting letters written by him to his mother from these lands have been preserved by his daughter, Mrs. Lily (Tyson) Elliott. They show a broad grasp of the social and political events occurring in those countries, as well as of the great political and social upheaval in our own country at that time. He held true to the faith of his fathers, and was ever a faithful member of the Society of Friends. In political faith he was an ardent Democrat, and in the struggle between the states warmly espoused the cause of the South. He had no liking for political office, and never held such office of any kind. When his death was announced at the Chamber of Commerce, of which he was a member, by President Gorman at a general meeting, the following gentlemen were appointed to represent that body at the funeral: James J. Corner, James Lake, George Frame and W. G. Atkinson. He was buried from the Friends Meeting House in Baltimore, on Park avenue, Tuesday, September 6, 1904.

James Ellicott Tyson married (first) September 23, 1847, Frances Helm Jolliffe, daughter of John and Frances (Helm) Jolliffe, of Frederick county, Virginia. Children: Frances Jolliffe, born June 17, 1848, died, unmarried, July 27, 1878; Lily, mentioned below; Martha, died July 15, 1866. After the death of his first wife, Mr. Tyson married (second) Frances E. Williams, who also pre-deceased him.

(VII) Lily Tyson, daughter of James Ellicott and Frances Helm (Jolliffe) Tyson, was born in Baltimore, married (first) October 2, 1879, Gaston Manley, of distinguished family, and (second) Dr. Marshall Elliott, of Johns Hopkins University, whom she survives. Children (all by first marriage); Elizabeth Brooke, Martha, married Myron Melvin Parker, Jr., of Washington, D. C.

(The Brooke Line).

(I) Richard Brooke, of Whitechurch, Hampshire, England, is the first of the family by this name of whom there is definite record. His will was proved May 6, 1594. He married Elizabeth Twyne, whose will was proved June 2, 1599, a sister and heir of John Twyne. A cross erected in the church at Whitechurch by their youngest son, Robert, records that Richard Brooke died January 16, 1634, after forty-one years of wedded life, and his widow Elizabeth died May 20, 1599. Children: Thomas, mentioned below; Richard, Robert, of London; Elizabeth, Barbara, Dorothy.

(II) Thomas Brooke, son of Richard and Elizabeth (Twyne) Brooke, was born 1561. He matriculated, Novem-

ber 24, 1581, at New College, Oxford, and received degree of
B.A., May 4, 1584; was a barrister and of the Inner Temple,
1595; bencher, 1607, and Autumn reader, 1611. He was a
member of Parliament for Whitechurch, 1604-1611. His
will is dated September 11, 1612, and proved the November
following. He was buried at Whitechurch, September 17,
1612, and his wife the following day. A marble tomb upon
which their sculptured figures lie side by side is in the church
at Whitechurch. He married Susan Foster, daughter of Sir
Thomas Foster, Knt., of Hunsdon, Herts, judge of the common pleas, and Susan Foster, his wife, daughter of Thomas
Foster, Esq., of London, was therefore sister of Sir Robert
Foster, who was in 1663 chief justice of Kings Bench. Children: 1. Thomas, born 1599; matriculated at Oriel College,
Oxford, October 27, 1615; a barrister-at-law; buried January
25, 1665, at Whitechurch. 2. Richard. 3. Robert, mentioned
below. 4. John, born 1605. 5. William. 6. Humphrey. 7.
Charles.

(III) Robert Brooke, of "De La Brooke and Brooke
Place Manors," son of Thomas and Susan (Foster) Brooke,
was born June 3, 1602, in London, England, died July 20,
1655, at Brooke Place Manor, where he is buried. He matriculated at Wadhams College, Oxford, April 28, 1618, received the degree of B.A., July 6, 1620, and M.A., April 20,
1624. He arrived in Maryland, June 30, 1650, with his wife,
ten children and twenty-eight servants, all transported at his
own cost and charge. On July 22, 1650, with his sons, Baker
and Thomas, he took the oath of fidelity to the proprietary.
A commission had to be issued to him in London, September
20, 1649, as commander of a new county to be erected, also
a separate commission of the same date as member of the council of the province. On October 30, 1650, a new county named
Charles was erected, and Robert Brooke constituted its com-

mander. In 1652, when the province was reduced by the parliamentary commission, Robert Brooke was placed at the head of the provincial council instituted by him and served as acting governor of the province from March 29, 1652, until July 3rd following. He was a member of the council and commander of Charles county until July 3, 1654, when an order was passed revoking his commission and nullifying the act creating the county, in place of which a new county called Calvert was erected. He is said to have been the first to settle on the Patuxent River, twenty miles up at "De La Brooke." In 1652 he removed to "Brooke Place." During the period of the settlement of Marylan no one was treated with greater liberality or accorded higher honors by Lord Baltimore than Robert Brooke. In addition to the whole of Charles county, which was granted to him by Lord Baltimore, Robert Brooke received grants from the proprietary for manors in Maryland. On September 1, 1649, Brooke Place Manor, containing two thousand acres of land, with the privileges of holding Court Baron and Court Leet, was issued to Robert Brooke at London, and on the 18th of September, the same year, the grant of "De La Brooke" Manor containing two thousand, two hundred acres, with the same manorial privileges, was issued at London by the proprietary. Brooke Court Manor was another of the famous Brooke estates, known also in the records as "Aquasco," in that part of Southern Maryland which later became Prince George's county.

Mr. Brooke married (first) February 26, 1627, Mary Baker, born at Battle, County Sussex, England, and died 1634, daughter of Thomas Baker, Esq., and Mary Engham, his wife, daughter of Sir Thomas Engham, and (second) May 11, 1635, Mary Mainwarring, born at St. Giles in the Fields, London, and died November 29, 1663, at "Brooke Place

Manor," Maryland, daughter of Roger Mainwarring, Doctor of Divinity and Dean of Worcester, subsequently Bishop of St. Davids, who came in collision with parliament by reason of his zealous advocacy of the royal prerogative. Children by first marriage: 1. Baker, born November 16, 1628, married Anne Calvert, daughter of Leonard Calvert, Governor of Maryland. 2. Mary, born February 19, 1630, died in England. 3. Major Thomas, born June 23, 1632, married Eleanor Hatton. 4. Barbara, born 1634, died in England. Children by second marriage: 5. Charles, born April 3, 1636, died unmarried. 6. Roger, mentioned below. 7. Robert, born April 21, 1639, in London, England, died 1667, in Calvert county, married Elizabeth Thompson. 8. John, born September 20, 1640, married Rebecca Isaac, and died in 1677. 9. Mary, born April 14, 1642. 10. William, born December 1, 1643. 11. Ann, born July 22, 1645, married Christopher Beans. 12. Francis, born May 30, 1648, died unmarried, 1672. 13. Basil, born 1651, died in infancy. 14. Henry, born November 28, 1655, died unmarried, 1672. 15. Elizabeth (twin of Henry) married, before 1679, Richard Smith, Jr., of Calvert county, Maryland.

(IV) Roger Brooke, son of Robert and Mary (Mainwarring) Brooke, was born September 20, 1637, at Brecknock College, Wales, the Episcopal residence of his maternal grandfather, the Bishop of St. Davids, after whom he was named, and came to America with his parents when thirteen years old. He lived at Battle Creek, Calvert county, Maryland; was one of the justices of the county from 1674 to 1684; was commissioned to high sheriff, April 18, 1684, and served until May 30, 1685, when he was again commissioner of the quorum. He married (first) Dorothy Neale, daughter of Captain James and Ann (Gill) Neale; married (second) Mary Wolseley, daughter of Walter Wolseley,

Esq., and granddaughter of Sir Thomas Wolseley, of Staffordshire; she was also the niece of Anne Wolseley, first wife of Philip Calvert, from whose house she was married. Children by first marriage: 1. Roger, mentioned below. 2. James, died before 1709. 3. Dorothy, born 1678, died 1730; married (first) Michael Taney, died 1702; married (second) Richard Blondell, died 1705; married (third) Colonel John Smith. Children by second marriage: 4. John, born 1687, died 1735. 5. Basil, died 1711. 6. Ann, married (first) James Dawkins, (second) James Mackall. 7. Cassandra. 8. Mary.

(V) Roger (2) Brooke, of Prince George county, son of Roger (1) and Dorothy (Neale) Brooke, was born April 12, 1673. He married, February 23, 1702, Eliza Hutchins, second daughter of Francis and Elizabeth Hutchins. Her father, Francis Hutchins, was for many years a member of the House of Burgesses, representing Calvert county. Roger Brooke moved to Prince George county, and died there intestate in 1718. Eliza (Hutchins) Brooke married (second) Captain Richard Smith. Children of Roger (2) Brooke: 1. Roger, born December 8, 1703, died May 28, 1705. 2. James, mentioned below. 3. Elizabeth, born November 23, 1707, married Nathaniel Beall. 4. Dorothy, born July 5, 1709, married Archibald Edmondston. 5. Mary, born December 29, 1710. 6. Ann, born March 29, 1712, married William Carmichael, of Queen Anne county. 7. Roger, born June 10, 1714, died 1772. 8. Cassandra, born April 3, 1716. 9. Priscilla, born November 16, 1717, died 1783; married Charles Browne, of Queen Anne county, died 1766. 10. Basil (twin of Priscilla) died 1761.

(VI) James Brooke, son of Roger (2) and Eliza (Hutchins) Brooke, was born February 21, 1705, and was the first of the family seated at Brooke Grove, which estate was patented by Charles, fifth Lord of Baltimore, to him on April 11, 1745. James Brooke held many thousand acres of land in Prince George county, afterward Frederick and Montgomery counties. James Brooke never cared to hold public office, but lived the life of a country gentleman on his beautiful estate in Prince George county. He married Deborah Snowden, daughter of Richard and Elizabeth (Neale) Snowden, January, 1725. Children: 1. James, mentioned below. 2. Roger, born August 9, 1734, died September 7, 1790; married Mary Matthews, who died about April 25, 1808. 3. Richard, born July 8, 1736, died May 2, 1788; married, 1758, Jane Lynn, who died September 15, 1774. 4. Basil, born December 13, 1738, died August 22, 1794; married, May 1, 1764, Elizabeth Hopkins, who died August 17, 1794. 5. Elizabeth, born March 22, 1741, married, June 2, 1761, Thomas Pleasants, of Goochland county, Virginia. 6. Thomas, born March 8, 1744, died June 11, 1789.

(VII) James (2) Brooke, son of James (1) and Deborah (Snowden) Brooke, was born February 26, 1730, in Prince George county, and died in August, 1767. He was a devout Christian, and is said to have been the first gentleman in Maryland to free his slaves, liberating twenty-two, an action which it is stated greatly displeased his father, who was a large owner of slaves. Like his father he married a Quakeress, a daughter of Virginia. He married in Fairfax Meeting, Loudoun county, Virginia, October 30, 1759, Hannah Janney, daughter of Amos Janney, of Loudoun county, Virginia, granddaughter of Abel Janney, and great-granddaughter of Thomas Janney, a Colonial justice of Pennsylvania, who came from Chester county, England, in the ship "Endeavor," 7th month, 29th day, 1683. Thomas Janney was a celebrated minister of the Society of Friends, and companion of William Penn. James and Hannah (Janney) Brooke had three chil-

dren, one of whom, Elizabeth Brooke, married George Ellicott, and their daughter, Martha Ellicott, married Nathan
Tyson (see Tyson, V).

(The Ellicott Line).

(I) Andrew Ellicott, of Collumpton, Devonshire, England, came to Pennsylvania in 1730, accompaned by his son,
Andrew Ellicott, Jr. It was probably not his intention at
first to remain in the colonies, as he left his wife and children
in England, but owing to his son's desire to settle permanently
in the New World, he was finally persuaded to make his home
in Pennsylvania. He never returned to England, and his
wife, whose maiden name was Mary Fox, never joined him in
this country. He lived in Bucks county, Pennsylvania, and
died there in 1766.

(II) Andrew (2) Ellicott was born in England, and
came to this country with his father, Andrew (1) Ellicott.
He settled in Bucks county, Pennsylvania, where he met and
married Ann Bye, a Quaker maiden. The wedding took
place in the Friends Meeting House in Bucks county, June
17, 1731. Andrew Ellicott, Jr., died in 1741. His wife
married (second) George Wall, an Englishman, in June,
1744, by whom she had two children, George and Esther
Wall. She died in Bucks county, August 21, 1786. Children
of Andrew (2) and Ann (Bye) Ellicott: 1. Joseph, born
October 8, 1732, married, 1753, Judith Bleaker. 2. Andrew,
mentioned below. 3. Nathaniel, born February 17, 1736, married Letitia Harvey. 4. Thomas, born March 16, 1737, married (first) Anne Ely, (second) Mrs. Rebecca Wilkinson,
(third) Jane Kensey. 5. John, born December 28, 1739, married (first) Leah Brown, (second) Cassandra Hopkins.

(III) Andrew (3) Ellicott, son of Andrew (2) and Ann
(Bye) Ellicott, was born January 22, 1734, in Bucks county,
Pennsylvania, and died in 1809. In 1772, accompanied by his

brothers, Joseph and John, he removed from Pennsylvania to Baltimore county, Maryland, where they purchased large tracts of land, about ten miles west of Baltimore City. Andrew Ellicott did not remove his family from Bucks county until 1794, where he had a large and comfortable home, to which he is said to have traveled on horseback many times a year. The Ellicotts built large mills on the Patapsco river for grinding wheat and other grains. This was the site known as Ellicott's Mills, now Ellicott City, Howard county. At their own expense the Ellicotts opened a road for wagons from their mills to Baltimore, and on its completion laid out a road to Frederick City, which united at Ellicott's Mills with their road to Baltimore. They did a great deal to improve agricultural methods in Maryland, Andrew and his brothers being among the most progressive men of their time. Andrew Ellicott married (first) Elizabeth Brown, of Pennsylvania, (second) Esther Brown, her cousin. Children by first marriage: 1. Elias, born December 27, 1757, died young. 2. George, mentioned below. 3. Benjamin, born October 16, 1761, died 1838, unmarried. 4. Nathaniel, born January 10, 1763, married Elizabeth Ellicott. 5. Andrew, born December 9, 1764, died May 23, 1766. 6. Elizabeth, born January 18, 1766, died young. 7. Jonathan, born November 9, 1766, married Sarah Harvey. Children by second marriage: 8. Joseph, born June 22, 1768, died September 16, 1771. 9. Tacy, born May 3, 1770, married Isaac McPherson. 10. James, born August 24, 1772, married Henrietta Thomas. 11. Andrew, born October 2, 1776, married Hannah Thomas. 12. Thomas, born November 10, 1777, married Mary Miller. 13. John, born February 2, 1780, married Mary Mitchell.

(IV) George Ellicott, son of Andrew (3) and Elizabeth (Brown) Ellicott, was born March 28, 1760, in Bucks county, Pennsylvania. He came to Maryland with his parents and there lived his life, a gentleman of means, engaged in the management of his private property interests. The Patapsco Female Institute was founded by the Ellicotts for the site of which they gave seven acres of beautiful forest land near Ellicott Mills, and it was through George Ellicott that the State of Maryland empowered the principal to educate eight girls annually at the expense of the State. This beautiful mansion, long ago passed from public usefulness, is now the summer home of the great-great-granddaughter of George Ellicott, Mrs. Lily Tyson Elliott. George Ellicott married Elizabeth Brooke, daughter of James (2) Brooke, of Brooke Grove, Montgomery county, Maryland, and his wife, Hannah (Janney) Brooke (see Brooke, VII).

(The Jolliffe Line).

(I) John Jolliffe, son of Thomas Jolliffe, of Crofton Hall, England, came to Virginia, and about 1652 (January 22) received a tract of land of one hundred acres located on the Elizabeth river, by assignment from John Lawrence. He built the first grist mill in the Old Dominion. He married Mary Rigglesworth, daughter of Peter Rigglesworth, of Yorkshire, England, and of Norfolk county, Virginia, about the year 1664-65. They had seven children.

(II) Joseph Jolliffe, eldest son of John and Mary (Rigglesworth) Jolliffe, was born about 1664, in Norfolk county, Virginia. He is said to have been a well educated man and well versed in the law. He married Ruth ———.

(III) William Jolliffe, son of Joseph and Ruth Jolliffe, was born in Norfolk county, Virginia, on the family plantation, about 1695. In the year 1766 he was living in Frederick county, Virginia. On July 2, 1776, he patented 304 acres of land on the Drains of Babb's Creek. This was the Redhouse tract (taking its name from the color of the house) which has remained in the family for so many generations. He was one of the first lawyers enrolled in Frederick County Court, Virginia, November 11, 1743, when the court was first formed. Shortly after this he acquired five hundred acres of land north of the present site of Winchester. He married Phoebe (maiden name unknown). He and his wife were associated with Hopewell Meeting, Frederick county. They had several sons and perhaps daughters.

(IV) William (2) Jolliffe, son of William (1) and Phoebe Jolliffe, acquired large estates on Opequon, north of where Winchester was later laid out. He was one of the citizens appointed by the court held November 9, 1758, as overseers of the road from Cunningham's Mill to Robert Moseley's. He married Lydia (Hollingsworth) Ross, widow of John Ross, son of Alexander Ross, whose estate adjoined that of William (1) Jolliffe. Lydia Hollingsworth was a daughter of Stephen Hollingsworth, granddaughter of Henry Hollingsworth, and great-granddaughter of Valentine Hollingsworth, who came to Pennsylvania in the ship "Welcome" in 1682. William and Lydia (Hollingsworth-Ross) Jolliffe were married about 1750, by Friends ceremony in Hopewell Meeting, Frederick county. Children: 1. John, mentioned below. 2. Phoebe, born December 15, 1752, died young. 3. Gabriel, born May 19, 1755. 4. Phoebe, born February 12, 1758. 5. Lydia, died December 30, 1759.

(V) Captain John Jolliffe, son of William and Lydia (Hollingsworth-Ross) Jolliffe, was born December 18, 1751, in Frederick county, Virginia. He commanded a company in the Fourth Virginia Regiment; was stationed with his regiment at Suffolk, Virginia, and later was with General Washington's army before New York. He participated in the engagements and skirmishes of the American army during that eventful year. He fell a victim to the scourge of smallpox, which proved fatal to so many at Morristown, New Jersey, in the year 1776, in his twenty-sixth year. In recognition of his srevices his heirs received from the State of Virginia a tract of land situate in the Northwestern Territory of the United States, upon the waters of the Scioto river, containing 2,666 2/3 acres, which was located by virtue of a military warrant, August 2, 1787. Although born in the Quaker faith, he was married out of meeting by a Methodist minister to Mary Dragoo, the beautiful daughter of Peter Dragoo, a neighbor. Children: John, mentioned below; and William.

(VI) John (2) Jolliffe, son of Captain John (1) and Mary (Dragoo) Jolliffe, was born on the Red House Plantation, Frederick county, Virginia, February 26, 1775. He inherited all his father's estate, as well as the military warrant of nearly three thousand acres, and in addition a large amount of property from relatives who died without natural heirs, making him one of the richest men in Virginia in land, slaves and money. He was a justice in Frederick county in 1801, and served a short time as captain in the War of 1812. He married at Winchester, Virginia, Frances Helm, daughter of Colonel Meredith Helm, of Belville Farm, Frederick county, March 10, 1807. She was born June 24, 1787. Children: 1. Meredith Helm, married Margaret Hopkins. 2. Lavinia, married Samuel Hopkins. 3. William, married Catherine Newby, of Clark county, Virginia. 4. Selina, married William Overall, of Virginia. 5. Amos, married Mary Jones, of Virginia. 6. James, married Ann Overall, of Virginia. 7. Edward C., married Virginia Page, of Vrginia. 8. Frances Helm, married James E. Tyson (see Tyson VI).

JOHN HENRY THOMAS

THE fame of John Henry Thomas was won in general law practice, but it was as an admiralty lawyer that he gained national reputation. He very frequently appeared in notable cases in the federal courts, the Court of Appeals and in the Supreme Court of the United States, and in himself represented the best traditions of the Maryland bar. His long life of seventy-four years was devoted to the practice of law, his term of service at the Baltimore bar overlapping a full half century of years. The highest sense of personal and professional honor marked that and every period of his life, while a fine courtesy and dignity of manner were distinguishing characteristics. For thirty-five years he was a law partner of S. Teacle Wallis, with whom his name is inseparably associated in Baltimore's judicial annals. Mr. Thomas was one of those courageous, intensely public-spirited citizens, who never seeking the honors or distinctions of public life, yet never fail, especially in times of public trial and difficulty, to respond promptly and fearlessly to every call of duty. His reward came in the love and esteem of his fellow citizens, the consciousness of duty well performed and in unvarying respect in which his high legal attainment was held by his professional brethren of bench and bar. He was a son of Dr. William Thomas, whose estate "Cremona" is in St. Mary's county, Maryland.

John Henry Thomas was born at "Cremona," St. Mary's county, Maryland, July 4, 1824, died in Baltimore, July 14, 1898. After completing all courses at "Charlotte Hall," St. Mary's county, he came to Baltimore and pursued courses of study at St. Mary's Seminary on Paca street. He then went to Princeton College, once the College of New Jersey, now Princeton University. He was a member of the famous class of 1844, of which so many later rose to eminence. Among his intimates of the class were Dr. Charles Shields, Noah Hunt Schenk, Alfred H. Colquitt of Georgia, Carolus Woodruff and James Clark Welling. At Princeton Mr. Thomas, who was but twenty at graduation, displayed that clearness of mind, quick perception, strong reasoning power and oratorical ability, which later so distinguished his legal work. He ranked with the best debaters of the college and ended his course with high honors in scholarship.

After graduation, in 1844, Mr. Thomas returned to Baltimore and later in the year began the study of law under the preceptorship of S. Teacle Wallis. His natural talents were in accord with the profession he had chosen and he made rapid progress. Mr. Wallis conceived so high an opinion of the young man's ability that when he was appointed special envoy to Spain by the Government, he encouraged Mr. Thomas to take an examination, although it had been his intention to spend a year longer in preparatory study. He successfully passed the ordeal of examination, was admitted to the bar and taken into partnership with his former preceptor. During the early period of the partnership, Mr. Wallis was kept in Europe by his diplomatic duties, Mr. Thomas managing the law business of the firm. After Mr. Wallis returned from Europe the real partnership began, which continued for thirty-five years, terminating about the year 1881. From that time until his death in 1898 Mr. Thomas practiced alone, his activity continuing until his last illness. Wallis & Thomas became one of the best known and most successful law firms of Baltimore, and after the dissolution Mr. Thomas maintained the same high standards. He enjoyed a very large admiralty practice and in that branch of his profession ranked with the very ablest lawyers of the country. He appeared before the Supreme Court of the United States in a large number of cases, the records of that court showing that he was one of the ablest counselors who argued before it, and that he therein lost but one case. He defended Mrs. Wharton in the two trials in which she was the defendant charged with the murder of General Ketchum and the attempted murder of Eugene Van Ness. The first is one of the celebrated cases of Maryland jurisprudence, Mr. Thomas being associated with I. Nevett Steele and Judge A. B. Hagner for the defense. His speech to the jury was one of the crowning efforts of his career and is yet spoken of where olden time lawyers congregate. Mrs. Wharton was acquitted and retained the same counsel in her trial for the attempted murder of Mr. Van Ness, that trial also resulting in her acquittal. At a later period he represented the Maryland Steamboat Company in the investigation of the "Joppa-Gleam" accident in which Harrison Garrett of Baltimore lost his life. He was also counsel for the North German Lloyd Steamship Company, the Allan Line and for a number of other important corporations.

Mr. Thomas was a lifelong Democrat, but never took an active part in politics, except upon one or two occasions when his instincts were aroused against disorder and lawlessness or aid in some much needed reform. He was closely identified with the reform movement in 1859, when the first meeting of what was then the reform party was held at his house. He "stumped" the State at that time, and worked with other prominent men to overthrow the rule and break the power of the "Know Nothing" party. He was a candidate during that year for attorney-general on the reform party ticket against Milton Whitney. In 1882 he took a prominent part in the "new judge" movement, and his speech to an immense crowd at Concordia Hall was regarded as the ablest of that campaign.

Mr. Thomas married, in 1851, Miss Mary T. Leiper,

daughter of Judge George Gray Leiper of Delaware county, Pennsylvania, member of Congress, 1829-1831, and for many years lay associate judge for Delaware county, and there he died November 17, 1868.

Judge Leiper was a son of Thomas Leiper, born in Strathaven, Lanark, Scotland, December 15, 1745, came to Philadelphia, Pennsylvania, in 1763, became very wealthy, was a member of the First City Troop, and rendered efficient service as an officer of the Revolution. He was a prominent Democrat, presidential elector, director of the Pennsylvania and United States banks, United States commissioner for the defence of Philadelphia in 1812, president of Philadelphia Common Council, and in 1824 one of the first officers of the Franklin Institute. He died in Delaware county, Pennsylvania, July 6, 1825.

John Henry and Mary T. (Leiper) Thomas were the parents of a son, George Leiper Thomas, deceased, and a daughter, Eliza Snowden Thomas, now residing in Baltimore. George Leiper Thomas, the only son of John Henry Thomas, was born in Baltimore and there died sixty years later, September 10, 1912. After preparation in Baltimore institutions he finished his education abroad, receiving degrees from universities in Germany and Switzerland. On his return to the United States he pursued further courses at the University of Virginia, receiving from that institution the degree Bachelor of Arts at graduation. Deciding upon the legal profession he entered the law department of the University of Maryland, whence he was graduated with high honors LL.B. After completing so thorough a course of preparation he was admitted to the Baltimore bar and for many years he was associated with his honored father in practice. He was a man of cultured tastes, with a high sense of personal and professional honor and the center of a wide circle of intimate friends. He was a member of many societies, but quiet and reserved in nature and sought no political distinction. He never married, but with his sister, Miss Thomas, maintained a hospitable home in Baltimore.

Dr. William Thomas of "Cremona" was a brother of James Thomas, a Governor of Maryland, major of the Fourth Maryland Regiment Cavalry during the War of 1812 and brevet major-general, six times member of the Maryland Legislature, Governor, 1833-1835. Another brother, Richard Thomas, was a member of the House of Representatives, and speaker, State Senator and president of the Senate. The father of these sons, William Thomas, was the youngest son of John Thomas of Charles county, Maryland, a member of the House of Delegates, major of militia and a member of the Revolutionary Committee of Safety. William Thomas married Catherine Boarman, a granddaughter of Roger Brooke, a prominent descendant of Commodore Robert Brooke of the Patuxent, who in 1650 came over with forty servants as his bodyguard and built first "De La Brooke," but afterward moved to Brook Place."

Dr. William and Catherine (Boarman) Thomas were the grandparents of John Henry Thomas of Baltimore. Leonard Calvert's daughter, Ann, married, about 1664, Baker Brooke of "De La Brooke." Their daughter was the mother of Catherine Boarman.

W. H. Stanley.

CHARLES HARVEY STANLEY

THE gentleman of the old school is not a myth, although the originals are now becoming very rare. With the passing of Charles Harvey Stanley, of Laurel, Maryland, in the closing days of 1913, one of the true type of "old school" politicians and gentlemen disappeared from earthly view, but the memory of his life is green and will ever live in Maryland annals, and in the hearts of his fellowmen. Said Governor Crothers who appointed him State comptroller: "He was one of the best public officials I ever knew." Everybody in Southern Maryland knew him, and in Central Maryland almost everybody, but to "Southern Maryland" he "belonged," one of that rapidly disappearing "before the war" type, positive in his convictions, ready to fight for them to the end, rigid as a steel bar in carrying out the responsibilities of any trust imposed either by the people or his friends, yet so kindly hearted that no greater pleasure was his than helping a friend over a rough part of life's pathway.

Although of Connecticut birth, Mr. Stanley was a descendant of John Stanley, a younger son of the Earl of Derby, who came in 1653, and the following year became surveyor of the colony, Maryland. A descendant of John Stanley settled in North Carolina, and there John Wright Stanley fought for the cause of liberty, and is revered as one of North Carolina's Revolutionary patriots. John Wright Stanley's son was clerk of Craven county, North Carolina, court for fifty-four years, that son being the father of Rev. Harvey Stanley, a clergyman of the Protestant Episcopal church, father of Charles Harvey Stanley to whose memory this review of a noble life is dedicated. Mr. Stanley's cousin, Edward Stanley, was a member of Congress from North Carolina, and a great-uncle, John Stanley, was for many years president of the North Carolina

State Senate. Rev. Harvey Stanley, father of Charles Harvey Stanley, was born in North Carolina, married Mary Anne Kinne, a daughter of Charles R. Kinne, who in early life moved from New York to North Carolina, there engaging in the practice of law. Charles R. Kinne was a brother of William Kinne, editor of "Kinne's Blackstone." Rev. Harvey Stanley settled with his family in Prince Georges county, Maryland, when his son, Charles Harvey Stanley, was a boy, and there his after life was spent.

Charles Harvey Stanley was born in Saybrook, Connecticut, October 20, 1842, died at his home, at Laurel, Prince George's county, Maryland, December 20, 1913. His parents moved to that county, in 1851, and there he obtained a good education in local schools and under private tutors. When the questions which finally led to war between the North and the South were under discussion, he became greatly interested, and when the break came, cast his lot with the South, and until Lee's Surrender, rode, fought and suffered with Company B, of the First Regiment, Maryland Cavalry.

Returning to Prince Georges' county, in 1865, Mr. Stanley taught school and studied law, having as law preceptor, General Thomas Bowie. He filled the dual role of teacher and student until January 17, 1869, and then was admitted to the Maryland bar. Up to this period of his life, Mr. Stanley had been used to an out-of-door life, having grown up in the county, was familiar with all sorts of farm work, and fond of hunting and fishing, but inordinately fond of flowers. His three years as a cavalryman had hardened his body, but not his nature, and he bent himself to his ambition, a professional career, with a firm resolve to gain a profession and make a home for those depending upon him, which was one of the objects he ever kept in view, believing, as he once wrote: "A man without a home is little more than a brute." In boyhood, he had realized that success only came through application. His resolution to make a position for himself held him true from boyhood, and when he was admitted to the bar in 1869, he brought to the profession a learned, clear, clean mind, and a body trained to work and not to falter. Mr. Stanley's career at the bar was one of honorable success. As a lawyer, he was sound and able, having a large clientele in Prince George's county, Baltimore and Washington, and he won from his profession both fame and fortune. He was learned in the law, and loyal to the strictest ethical tenets of his profession, despising subterfuge, or any attempt to befog an issue. He held his professional honor as sacred as his private honor, and he was regarded as one of the fairest, but most to be dreaded, opponents. He made a client's cause his own, and to that cause gave himself without reserve.

With the passing years Mr. Stanley acquired other interests, business and political. He was the principal factor in the organization of the Citizens National Bank of Laurel, in the year 1890, and was president of that successful institution from the time of its organization until his death. He was a State director of the Baltimore & Ohio Railroad Company for several years, and had landed and business interests of importance. He was a trustee of the Maryland Agricultural College from 1882, and charter member of the Farmers' Club of Prince George's county. Educational affairs held a deep and sincere interest for him. He gave freely of his time and thought to the development of the county public school system, and to the Maryland Agricultural College, of which he had been a director for many years. He realized the possibilities of the college as few public men did, and he was ready to support any movement tending to any increase in the institution's usefulness. In his politics Mr. Stanley was as uncompromising as in his private life. He was a Democrat from principle, and loved his party with the devotion of a son for his father, and followed his party's flag wherever it led. Yet he was not a reactionary, he would follow, but he wanted his party to go the right way, and he believed firmly in the rule of the people. He made his first appearance in public official life in 1882, when he was elected a member of the Maryland House of Delegates, serving three years. From 1890 to 1894, he was mayor of the town of Laurel, president of the school board commissioners of Prince George's county from 1901 until 1911. His faith in the people was made very plain at the time he became a candidate for the Congressional nomination from the Fifth Maryland District in 1912. He had announced early in the year that he would be a candidate if the Legislature passed the Direct Primary law before then, being the first man in the State to make his candidacy contingent upon the passing of that law. He was unsuccessful in the primary and the honor went to another. Shortly afterward, Governor Crothers appointed him comptroller of the State to succeed William B. Clagett, also of Prince George's county, who had died in office. Mr. Stanley announced at the time of taking the office that he would not be a candidate to succeed himself, a voluntary promise which was kept. He was a perfect martinet in that office, spending a great deal of time at his office in the State house at Annapolis, and insisting upon being advised of the details of the work. He revolutionized methods used for making payments through his office, flatly refusing to allow payments unless the requisitions stated specifically the nature of the outlay, and were prepared with strict regard for the law, and for safe accounting.

In religion Mr. Stanley was of the faith of his fathers, and a vestryman of the Episcopal church of his town, the first chancellor of the diocese of Washington, which position he held until his death, and a member of the standing committee of the diocese from its organization. He was a member, and a pastmaster, of Laurel Wreath Lodge, Ancient Free and Accepted Masons; was a member of the Chapter of Royal Arch Masons; and a grand inspector of the Grand Lodge of Maryland.

Mr. Stanley married, November 26, 1871, Ella Lee Hodges, of Anne Arundel county, Maryland, who died in September, 1881. He married (second) in September, 1884, Margaret Snowden, daughter of John Snowden, of Prince George's county, who survived her husband with six children; Harvey; Charles Harvey (2); William; John; Margaret Snowden, and Elizabeth Hopkins, wife of James G. Boss, Jr. Thus in honor and usefulness Mr. Stanley's years, seventy-one, were passed, and at their close he went to his reward unafraid, but with a serene reliance upon the teachings of "the Book" which had long been one of his closest literary friends.

HENRY LONGITUDE SEAL OULD

HENRY LONGITUDE SEAL OULD, a son of Henry and Jane Ould, was born February 2, 1793, in Devonshire, England, and died in Georgetown, District of Columbia. His father was a mathematician and man of great inventive genius, and became celebrated as the originator of the "Graphor," an instrument for reckoning longitude, and for the publication of a book on the subject. Hadley is said to have used the Graphor in 1791. To his son he gave the name of "Longitude," to commemorate the invention of this instrument, and added the name "Seal" on account of the British seal attached to it, an honor conferred upon him for his useful invention.

Henry L. S. Ould was educated under the English schoolmaster, Joseph Lancaster, who originated a system of primary education known as the Lancastrian or Monitorial system, the principal feature of which was the instruction of younger pupils by the more advanced students, called monitors. This method of instruction found considerable favor in the United States in the early days of the nineteenth century, and a school was organized in Georgetown, District of Columbia. It was claimed in favor of this system that it allowed more time for recreation than under the old rigid rules then in vogue in the district schools, and besides was much cheaper, one teacher being able to supervise the instruction, it was said, of as many as three hundred pupils in the same class. This system, long since discarded, deserved the credit of causing the education of the masses to be looked upon as a thing attainable, and was without doubt the origin of our present free school system. In the year 1811 Mr. Lancaster was asked to send to this country an able teacher of the system. He chose two very capable young gentlemen, Mr. Robert Ould, and his brother, Mr. Henry L. S. Ould, both of whom came to Georgetown with the highest recommendations. They became naturalized Americans, lived long and useful lives, and died highly respected and beloved in the communities in which they resided. In response to a letter requesting him to send a schoolmaster to Georgetown, Joseph Lancaster writes:

On looking over all my schools I found but one young man answering the description, that was willing to go, and he was unwilling to leave England without his brother, a brother bound to him in affection from infancy, and to whom he has been a foster parent since the decease of his mother. Both young men have quitted respectable situations (Robert was librarian of the London Library and Henry was associated with the Bank of Wales), and connections to embark in your cause; they are in every respect worthy of your countenance and protection to which I commend them. The elder, Robert Ould, as well as his brother, Henry Ould, have been my pupils at an early age. I have been in frequent intercourse with them since they left school. They have lived amongst my friends, so that in every respect I can speak of their merits and characters on gratifying evidence of the most satisfactory kind. I trust it will be as great a pleasure to you to receive them as it is to me to recommend them to your protection.

During the War of 1812, both these gentlemen being British subjects and liable to be pressed into England's service, withdrew from Georgetown to Montgomery county, Maryland, where Robert Ould married Pauline Riggs Gaither, and became the father of Judge Robert Ould, of Richmond, Virginia. It is said that Henry Ould was at one time very much in love with Ann Riggs Gaither, at least he preserved some poems writen and signed by her that bear the date of 1815. Inscribed upon tiny sheets of paper and written in a delicate feminine hand, they are still treasured by his descendants. Subsequently he met the bewitching Elizabeth Cloud Peirce, and fell desperately in love with her, and lost no time in storming the citadel of her affections, as is attested by his eloping with her shortly afterward.

The Peirce family is one of the oldest Quaker families of the Middle States, and the coat-of-arms is as follows:

Arms—Argent, a fesse humettee gules, between three ravens rising sable.
Crest—A parrot, in its beak an amulet.
Motto—*Celer et audax.*

The Peirce family is descended from George Peirce (or Pearce, as he himself wrote it), who came from the parish of Winscomb, Somerset county, England. He married Ann Gainer of Thornbury, Gloucestershire, on the 1st day of the 12th month (February), 1679. With his wife and three small children he left Bristol, England, the seaport nearest his home, in 1684, and settled in Chester county, Pennsylvania, where a tract of 490 acres was surveyed for him in that year, in Thornbury township. This was undoutedly named from the English home of his wife to preserve early associations. They had arrived in Phildealphia as early as the 4th day of the 9th month (November), 1684, as on that date he presented two certificates to a meeting of Friends, held at the governor's house. One for himself was from the monthly meeting at Fifrenshay, in the county of Gloucester, and that of his wife was from Thornbury meeting. It is not probable that he settled on his new purchase in that year, as winter had now arrived. His name first appears at Chichester Friends Meeting in 1686, after which meetings were sometimes held at his house. He was very strict in attention to religious duties, and also gave some time and means to civil affairs and the improvement of the country. In the Provincial Assembly of 1706 he represented Chester county, and was one of a company which built "the Concord mill," the first mill erected in his neighborhood. About 1732 he removed to East Marlboro township, where he died in 1734. He obtained a patent of land in that township December 14, 1701, which included Peirce's Park, or "Evergreen Glade," as he named it. This was conveyed to his son in 1725, and thus passed down through several generations of his descendants. Part of the original dwelling, which was constructed of brick in 1730, is still standing. To his daughter Betty, and her husband, Vincent Caldwell, he gave two hundred acres adjoining the glade. It subsequently passed into the hands of Caleb Peirce, and is now in possession of the latter's great-grandchildren, bearing the name of Cox. Longwood Meeting House and Cemetery are situated on this tract. The children of George and Ann (Gainer) Peirce were: Betty, born September 18, 1680, married Vincent Caldwell; George, February 23, 1682; Joshua, mentioned below; Ann, March 8, 1686, married (first) James Gibbons, (second) William Pim; Margaret, October 25, 1690, married Joseph Brinton; Caleb, December 21, 1692, married Mary Walter, died January 22, 1797; Gainer, February 1, 1695, married Sarah Walter; Hannah, February 21, 1696, married Edward Brinton; John, February 15, 1704, died before 1720.

Joshua Peirce, second son of George and Ann (Gainer) Peirce, was born January 5, 1684, in England, and died September 15, 1752, in the eastern part of East Marlboro township, where he made his home through life. He married (first) August 28, 1713, Ann, daughter of Thomas and Mary Mercer, of Westtown, Pennsylvania, and (second) September 15, 1722, Rachel Gilpin, of Birmingham, that State. She was descended from Richard de Guylpin, who became the owner of the Manor of Kentmore in 1206, during the reign of King John. The family was long resident in Maryland. Children by first marriage: George, born May 5, 1714, died October 2, 1775, married Lydia Roberts; Mary, March 3, 1717, married William Cloud; Ann, October 20, 1718, married (first) Caleb Mendenhall and (second) Adam Redd. Of second marriage: Joshua, mentioned below; Dr. Joseph, a distinguished physician, born October 16, 1725, died March 9, 1811; Caleb, December 2, 1727, died October 12, 1815, married Hannah Greaves; Isaac, who married Hannah Sellers.

Joshua (2) Peirce, second son of Joshua (1) Peirce, and eldest child of his second wife, Rachel Gilpin, was born January 22, 1724, and married **Ann Bailey.**

Isaac Peirce, son of Joshua (2) and Ann (Bailey) Peirce, was the ancestor of the Maryland branch of the Peirce family. In 1760 he came into possession of a large tract of land in the present District of Columbia, now known as Rock Creek Park, which was purchased by the Government some years since as a national park. This was a portion of land known as "Gift." Soon after settling in Rock Creek valley, he began the construction of a mill for grinding cereals, which became one of the landmarks of the locality. The first mill, of frame construction, was erected about 1790, and some thirty years later this was replaced by a stone mill which still stands, a stalwart example of the solid architecture of the early nineteenth century. This quaint old landmark, with its slow moving waterwheel of past days, has been restored by the Government, and is now a picturesque feature of the park. The Peirce mill was always a popular place for the farmers to bring their grain. Sometimes as many as twelve teams could be seen at the stone building waiting for the corn to be ground into meal and the wheat kernels into flour. A like number of horses or mules could also be seen tethered near by, the farmers or their sons having ridden to the mill with the bags of grain slung across their animals' backs. The Peirce mill once brought what was almost a fabulous rental of $125 a month, or $1,500 a year, the owner leasing the property to a tenant and miller. Soon after settling in Rock Creek valley, Isaac Peirce married Elizabeth, daughter of ———— and Amy (Pyle) Cloud. Joshua (3) Peirce, a son of Isaac, built the large mansion on the estate, which has been preserved by the Government as a museum for exhibition of a collection of flora and mineral

treasures of the park. Joshua Peirce was an enthusiastic horti-
culturist, and made a specialty of raising camelias, which at
that time were exceedingly rare, and sold for one dollar and
two dollars a flower. Both father and son accumulated large
fortunes that enabled them to keep the proprety intact until
sold as a Government reservation. Another son, Job Peirce,
married Sally Harvey. They had but one child, Elizabeth
Cloud Peirce, who was the ancestress of numerous residents
of Baltimore. Her father died when she was a little girl, so
she resided with her grandparents on the Rock Creek estate,
and rode to and fro in an ancient coach, whose doors are said
to have borne the blazoning of the Peirce arms. She was an
heiress, and bewitchingly pretty, and it was during the War of
1812 that she met her fate in the person of a young Englishman, Henry L. S. Ould, whom she married, as above noted.
Five children were born to them: Elizabeth Jane Peirce, born
April 12, 1822, died November, 1825; Pauline Gaither, born
September 24, 1823, died March 31, 1826; Henry Peirce, born
February 24, 1827, died January 13, 1829; Charles Eugene
Eckle, born February 21, 1830, died unmarried, November
16, 1863; Marion Hall, mentioned below.

Marion Hall Ould, youngest child of Henry L. S. and
Elizabeth C. (Peirce) Ould, was born July 14, 1834, and died
April 24, 1909. He was one of the foremost citizens of Balti-
more, and became prominent in business and financial circles.
He was second vice-president of the Commonwealth Bank,
and vice-president of the Game Wardens' Association.
Though he never took active part in politics he always showed
great interest in the political happenings of the day and was
a lover of sports. He was a member of the Independent Order
of Odd Fellows. Mr. Ould married, June 28, 1855, Mary
Susanna Swift, daughter of Daniel Swift of Bucks county,
Pennsylvania, and Mary Martin, his wife, of Harford county,

Maryland. Their children were: Mary Elizabeth, born April, 1856, died May, 1856, and Margaret A., mentioned below.

Margaret A. Ould, child of Marion H. and Mary S. (Swift) Ould, was born June 7, 1857, married, August 1, 1877, Walter B. Swindell, born June 21, 1850, son of William and Henrietta (Mullard) Swindell. Children: 1. Marian Ould, born May 19, 1878, died December 22, 1884. 2. Walter B., born April 1, 1880; married, October 26, 1901, Gertrude Haldane de Valasco, daughter of Charles Fernandez and Elizabeth (Reed) de Valasco, son of Rafael Fernandez and Sarah Jane (Haldane) de Valasco; children: Walter B., born November 14, 1903, died November 16, 1905; Robert Haldane, born January 6, 1907; Margaret, December 20, 1909. 3. Sue Ould, born November 15, 1881; married, April 28, 1906, Claude Carlyle Nuckols, born February 26, 1880, son of Samuel Claiborne and Luella (Wasson) Nuchols, of Versailles, Kentucky; children: Claude Carlyle, born April 14, 1907; Margaret Ould, March 30, 1909; Walter Swindell, August 1, 1911; Susannah, November 1, 1913; Samuel Claiborne, October 15, 1915. 4. Jane, born January 8, 1884; married Charles Howard Smith of Seattle; children: Frances Townley, born July 30, 1910; Charles Jackson, December 9, 1912. 5. Margaret, born July 12, 1886, married Robert Quincy Baker of Coshocton, Ohio; child: Robert Quincy, born June 15, 1910.

JOHN ANTHONY LECOMPTE RADCLIFFE

THE BALTIMORE CLIPPER marks an era in the industrial life of Maryland, around which is the fascination of romance. The ships of Maryland sailed the Seven Seas and were found in every harbor in the world. Generations of ship-builders developed a craft which combined speed with sea-worthiness to an unusual degree. The accumulation of family and community experience brought ship-building along the shores of the Chesapeake Bay to an extraordinary state of perfection. The industrial life of tide-water Maryland was dominated by this activity. The successful planter or farmer was usually a ship builder, or at least a ship owner. The slave was frequently useful, not only in the field but also in the ship-yard. The magnificent quantities of virgin oak and other forms of timber afforded sufficient suitable building material. The profits from the sale or rental of the vessels were large since the builder owned often the laborers, and the building materials, and raised nearly all of his food on his plantation or took it from the adjacent waters. The result was production at a minimum cost.

An excellent representative of this type of combination of shipbuilding and planter was John Anthony LeCompte Radcliffe. In 1687 Richard Radcliffe, a young Quaker, came to Talbot county, Maryland, via Pennsylvania, from Rosendale, Lancashire, England. He soon became active as a land-owner and ship-builder. In time his grandsons went west or south, and one of his great-grandsons, John Ratcliffe, or Radcliffe, there was the customary early Colonial doubt or indifference as to method of spelling proper names—came to Dorchester and there married Fannie LeCompte, the great-granddaughter of Anthony LeCompte, one of the first settlers in Dorchester county, who had received a patent for land there in 1659.

This section of Dorchester county lying between the Chesapeake Bay and the Choptank River early attracted settlers. The records all indicate that the colonists who came there furnished a commingling of types unusual even for those days when the spirit of adventure was uppermost. These first settlers intermarried, and to a very large extent their descendants continued to live in or near the homes of their fathers.

Fannie LeCompte was descended from a number of these early settlers in this section. For instance, from Dr. Robert Winsmore, presiding justice of the county and probably the first physician or "chyrurgeon" in the county; from Stephen Gary, a man of unusual characteristics to whom reference will be made later; from Charles Powell, son-in-law of Stephen Gary, first lawyer in Dorchester county, and through her mother, Mary Sewell, from a famliy which had been actively connected with the affairs of the county. Their only son was James Sewell Radcliffe, who married Margaret Harris, a descendent of Henry Beckwith, another pioneer of that section of the county. Their oldest son was John Anthony LeCompte Radcliffe, the subject of this sketch.

John Anthony LeCompte Radcliffe was born on February 6, 1818, on a farm which had been inherited by his father from successive generations of LeCompte owners. He inherited the advantages and disadvantages resulting from the fact that his family had lived for generations in a community somewhat isolated, but with traditions of a vigorous and active participation in the affairs of the county. He also inherited a magnificent physique and unusual vigor and strength of mind and body. In spite of the fact that one Hill, a few years after the county was settled, had left a small provision in his will for the endowment of a free school in the community, the educational facilities one hundred and twenty-five years later were restricted to the rather scanty opportunities offered by private tutors or by teachers paid jointly by a combination of neighbors. John Anthony LeCompte Radcliffe's opportunities for education were very limited, but his mind was naturally studious. Throughout his lifetime a considerable part of every day was spent in reading, especially of books on history, theology, philosophy, etc.

Almost every ancestor of John Anthony LeCompte Radcliffe had combined farming and ship-building. It would have probably been impossible for him to realize when he first acquired a taste for, or a knowledge of, these occupations. While still a young man he acquired Spocot, a few miles from his birthplace. This had been patented by his grandfather in the seventh generation, Stephen Gary, in 1662. Stephen Gary had selected Spocot from his thirty or more holdings in Maryland, Virginia and England, as his "home plantation," as he termed it in his will. From there his restless spirit directed his numerous activities. Besides the constant patenting and developing of land, he was always active in the affairs of the colony, several times as high sheriff, as commissioner to organize the county, as judge, etc. He was one of the most vigorous and striking characters in the early history of the county. Spocot has continued to this day in the possession and ownership of his descendants.

John Anthony LeCompte Radcliffe brought Spocot to a high state of development. He owned a considerable number of slaves and large tracts of timber land, and Spocot illustrated to a remarkable extent the type of a self-sufficient little community. Its cotton and wool supplied clothing. Its fertile fields afforded an unusual wide variety of food. The waters of Gary's Creek upon which it bordered furnished sea food of many kinds. Saw and grist mills, iron forges, carpenter shops and a commissary helped to care for the needs of the family and the slaves and for the ship-yard located at Spocot.

In its shallow river vessels of surprising seaworthiness were built. At least one of the vessels launched there in not over six feet of water is known to have circumnavigated the world.

The work of his farm, the ship-yard, the demands of his family and his lifelong fondness for reading were absorbing, but his contributions to the political life of the community were not unimportant. Each time that he ran for office he was elected by majorities which were unusually large in his county. As president of the Board of County Commissioners, as member of the Legislature, and in many other political capacities, his services were helpful.

John Anthony LeCompte Radcliffe was saturated with the traditions of his community, and his lifelong effort was to perpetuate and develop **the best of these in harmony with the** march of progress. He tried to give his children the advantage of opportunities similar to those which he had received and better whenever possible. Possibly the predominating characteristic of his life was the desire to be truly helpful to those around him. He was the last in his community to continue the old-fashioned hospitable but expensive method of keeping "open house" throughout the year to which his relatives and friends were at all times welcome. It is undoubtedly true that during his lifetime there was no place in Dorchester county where hospitability was so freely, so cordially and so generously extended as at Spocot. On June 8, 1901, he died, full of years, beloved by the community whose interests he had served so well, in fact, better doubtless than by any man who has ever lived there.

He was married twice. His first wife was his cousin Rebecca Beckwith. Three children by that marriage survived him: Laura, widow of William H. Travers; Nellie wife of Nicholas Goldsborough Henry; and a son, William W. Also he left a grandson and granddaughter, John Ram say and LeOlin, the son and daughter respectively of a son who pre-deceased him. His second wife was Sophie D. Robinson, widow of A. J. Robinson, and daughter of Thomas Broome Travers, born September 18, 1802, died June 25, 1875. Three children were born to his second marriage, all of whom survived their father, namely: Thomas Broome Travers, James Sewell, and George L. Radcliffe.

THOMAS BROOME TRAVERS

ON the map, the western part of Dorchester county seems to be a part of the mainland. However, for a long time, and in fact so long that the "memory of man runneth not to the contrary," most of this section has been an island separated by a narrow stream called Slaughter creek from the mainland. One of the early settlements in the county was on this island, then considerably larger than at present since much of it has unfortunately been washed away by the stormy waters of the Chesapeake bay. The pioneer settler on this island was Thomas Taylor, after whom the island was named. Shortly afterwards his cousin, William Travers, came there to settle. William Travers died in 1701, devising by his will a considerable amount of real estate. One of his sons, Matthew, became one of the wealthiest and most prominent men in the county. He married Elizabeth, daughter of Henry Hooper, the second in line of successive generations of Henry Hoopers, who furnished probably the most striking illustration in the history of the county of the passing not only of the surname but of a marked degree of prominence from father to son. A brother of this Elizabeth was Henry Hooper, owner and builder of Warwick Fort Manor. Another sister married John Broome, sometimes spelt Brome, whose prominence personally and that of his family are well known to students of Maryland Colonial history. From both of these daughters of Henry Hooper, Thomas Broome Travers, the subject of this sketch, was descended.

Successive generations of Traverses and other allied families continued to live on Taylor's Island. The status of island, the distance from Cambridge, the county seat, and the almost impossible roads prohibited easy communication with Cambridge and other parts of the county. This isolation

and the unusual industrial advantages of Taylor's Island resulted in the development of a community unique in many
respects. Fertility of the soil, large holdings of slaves, big
profits from shipbuilding, ownership of vessels trading with
"Brazil and The Indies," produced a state of considerable
prosperity. The water as well as the land furnished food
in abundance. The houses were commodious, although a
simple style of architecture prevailed even in the homes of
the richest. The dominant families were closely bound together by blood and almost daily association. House parties
were large and frequent. Educational provisions were quite
good. The children were usually sent to school in Baltimore
or taught by tutors in private homes. It is doubtful whether
any section of Dorchester county, or of any other county in
the colony or State, had in proportion to population so many
men of wealth. The loss of slaves, injurious tides, the wash
of the sea and other causes brought about serious changes for
the worse in the community life of Taylor's Island. In recent
years a new era of prosperity has begun to develop.

Thomas Broome Travers was born in 1702, the son of
Thomas Broome and Delia Travers. He was born in one of
the Travers' homesteads which had been in the family for
many generations. He increased his inheritance, which was
considerable, by industry and excellent judgment, so that at
the time of his death he was one of the wealthiest men in the
county. His many farms were well handled. Throughout
his life he was constantly building vessels, which from their
ocean and bay trade brought in considerable revenue.

Thomas Broome Travers was an excellent representative
of the type of business man which in many respects has per-
force ceased to exist. Since not a bank existed in the county
until the latter part of his life, all of his various operations
were conducted without the use of bank checks. Payments

running up in the thousands of dollars were made and received in gold. Large quantities of gold were frequently kept on hand. For instance, a package containing $4,000 in twenty dollar gold pieces was allowed by him in one case to remain unopened for a period of at least fifteen years. He loaned many thousands of dollars to his friends, always without any form of note or written acknowledgement or receipt.

He was an Episcopalian throughout his life and furnished the larger part of the funds for the building of the Episcopal church now standing on Taylor's Island. This church with its solid walnut pews and other unusual features is an interesting survival. It took the place of one of the old Colonial "Chapels of Ease" which had been a matter of interest to students of history. The dramatic scenes illustrated on the coast of Taylor's Island during the Revolutionary War, and especially during the War of 1812, and which have never found proper place in history were matters of keen interest to him, and he endeavored to preserve fitting mementoes of these times, especially in so far as members of his family had participated.

He married his cousin, Elisabeth Travers, who died at the age of twenty-two, leaving three little daughters. These three daughters survived him. They were Sophie D., widow of John Anthony LeCompe Radcliffe, a sketch of whom precedes this; Mary, widow of William Cator, and Addie, wife of E. L. Griffith. Thomas Broome Travers never married again, but devoted the best of his time and energy to the welfare of his daughters. It was his aim to bridge over the loss to his children of their mother by assuming personally as many as possible of maternal duties and responsibilities. In spite of the engrossing nature of his business enterprises, he followed most closely the details of the daily lives of his daughters. He provided private instruction for them at his home, and as soon as they were large enough, he sent them to private school. A little instance illustrating his efforts to see that their desires and plans were properly looked after is seen in the arrangements which he made in regard to the wedding cake of his oldest daughter. To insure as much as possible against accident, he sent one of his best sailing vessels to bring the cake from Baltimore and permitted the vessel to have no other mission. Possibly the most distinguishing characteristics of Thomas Broome Travers were the personal attention and interest which he gave to the daily life of his daughters, and his constant efforts to give them the best of training and education. This was carefully done in spite of engrossing business cares.

He died in 1875, leaving one of the largest estates in the county. The best heritage to his many descendants was, however, his reputation for integrity, ability and general worthiness.

WILLIAM HADDON MARRIOTT

A TINY miserable-looking stream running through the heart of the City was one of the odd features of Baltimore. This little stream, known as Jones' Falls, was not large enough to be of any commercial value, or to afford any of the simplest advantages or pleasures of a water front. There was enough of it, however, to cause it to be regarded as a general nuisance. From time to time efforts were made by the erection of walls, etc., to protect the adjoining property from the spasmodic tendency of Jones' Falls to overflow its banks. Eventually a more or less comprehensive scheme of retaining walls and bridges was decided upon by the city. The work was entrusted to a young architect and engineer of the city, William Haddon Marriott, who, with his partner, Charles H. Latrobe, prepared and put into successful execution plans for the work. Imposing bridges, especially at St. Paul and Calvert streets, etc., crossed Jones' Falls and massive retaining walls eventually removed the barrier to traffic which Jones' Falls had occasioned, and attractive terraced gardens designed by Mr. Marriott took the place of the dreary looking shores which had fronted the Falls. The most important growth of the city, that to the north, resulted.

Many other public works for Baltimore and various other cities throughout the State of Maryland requiring engineering and architectural skill were designed and constructed by Mr. Marriott. Among these are the Casino and Observatory at Patterson Park, Baltimore. To the successful accomplishment of work on behalf of the city Mr. Marriott devoted many years of his life. The utility and general excellence of this work have always been universally recognized. Also a number of the churches in the City and large private buildings were constructed by him.

Mr. William H. Marriott was born September 23, 1849.

Through his mother he was descended from a family of Wilsons, whose business activities have been an important factor in the development of Baltimore. His paternal grandfather, William H. Marriott, Collector of the Port of Baltimore, once candidate for Mayor of Baltimore, was for many years a prominent figure in the political, social and financial life of Baltimore. General Marriott married Jane McKim, a member of the Baltimore family of that name which has played such a prominent part in the history of Baltimore since the early days of the nineteenth century. Mr. Marriott was also descended from General John Hammond, of Colonial and Revolutionary War fame. His Marriott ancestry in Maryland ran back to John Marriott, one of the earliest settlers on the Severn river in Anne Arundel county, Maryland, who arrived there about the middle of the seventeenth century. John Marriott was one of the strenuous type and an interesting account of some of his experiences with the Indians in 1681 is given in the Archives of Maryland. The Marriotts intermarried with the Sewells and other early settlers of Colonial Maryland.

Mr. Marriott married Mrs. Aline T. Marriott, nee Bracco, who, with one daughter, Mrs. George L. Radcliffe, survived him.

The prominent position which Mr. Marriott early in life acquired in his profession promised a brilliant career therein. In early middle age, however, he was attacked by a severe illness and remained a partial invalid for fourteen or fifteen years, that is, until his death on December 18, 1912. In the work of his profession Mr. Marriott showed marked ability. Possibly, however, his most distinguishing characteristic was a judicial cast of mind, exhaustive and impartial in its workings, combined with a spirit of toleration, gentleness and patient endurance.

ABIJAH H. EATON

IN the year 1877, Baltimore first knew Abijah H. Eaton as a young man of fine points, who had come out of the west via the maritime Provinces of Canada, gathering during the years 1867 to 1877, considerable reputation as a promoter of business schools, and as the joint author of a text book on arithmetic. Baltimore quickly endorsed the young educator, and until his death forty years thereafter, he was the head of the leading business college of that city, a member of the bar, and an author of standard textbooks. He passed from manhood to the prime of life, reached the crest, and for several years walked amid lengthened shadows, but his ambition did not abate, although the physical man weakened, neither did his mental power deteriorate, and during his seventy-sixth summer, 1916, he revised and enlarged a work on bookkeeping, corporation voucher, and cost accounting. He was widely known as the founder of Eaton and Burnett's Business College, and in Grace Methodist Episcopal Church as the faithful, devoted member of thirty years standing.

Mr. Eaton came from one of the oldest Colonial families, his ancestor, Francis Eaton, a passenger on the "Mayflower," his name on the list of Signers of the "Compact," the first form of government under which the Pilgrims lived. From Francis Eaton sprang a distinguished line of descendants, soldiers of the Revolutionary War, and in every war their country has ever waged, leaders in the professions, in public life, and in business. Abijah H. Eaton was a grandson of Nathaniel Eaton, of Boston, Massachusetts, and a son of Friend and Mary (Law) Eaton, who moved to Akron, Summit county, Ohio.

Abijah H. Eaton was born in Akron, Ohio, April 26, 1840, and died in Baltimore, Maryland, December 29, 1917.

A. H. Eaton

In 1845, his parents moved to Doylestown, Wayne county, Ohio, and there he attended public and private school, and took special business courses under private teachers. When the Civil War called the manhood of the north to the "colors," he, with three brothers, enlisted, Abijah H. safely passing the perils of war and returning to his family. In 1865, in company with Joel Warner, he opened an English school in Chatham, capital of Kent county, Ontario, Canada, and at the same time entered as a special student in the British-American Business College at Toronto, completing a business course of study which he needed in the career he had marked out for himself. He taught in Musgrove and Wright's Business College in Ottawa, capital of the Dominion of Canada, for one year (1866), going thence to St. John, New Brunswick, in the winter of 1867. There he founded Eaton's Business College and began his half a century connection with business college promotion and management. Eaton's Business College of St. John prospered, and in 1868 a college of the same name was founded in Halifax, Nova Scotia, and in 1870, a similar institution was opened by Mr. Eaton at Charlottetown, capital of Prince Edward Island, Canada. The same year the Eaton and Frazee's Commercial Arithmetic, the first of his series of text books, was published. He placed Eaton's Business College at St. John under the management of Samuel Kerr, in 1876, and entered Harvard Law School, completing a law course. He closed out his Canadian interests in 1877, and located in the city of Baltimore, and there purchased a half interest in Bryant, Stratton and Sadler Business College. The same year he was admitted to the Baltimore bar, and for a season practiced his profession and taught in the business college. In 1878, he opened a school for business instruction, was joined by Professor E. Burnett, the result of this connection being the founding of Eaton and

Burnett's Business College, a school which drew its patrons from all parts of the United States and from Mexico. The proprietors published that standard text book which went through three editions, Eaton and Burnett's Theoretical and Practical Bookkeeping, and in 1881 Mr. Eaton wrote and published Eaton and Burnett's Commercial Law, a third edition of that work being issued in 1887. In 1891, he began preparation of Eaton and Burnett's Practical Banking, based on the National banking system. His last work, completed during the summer of 1916, was on "Bookkeeping, Corporation Voucher and Cost Accounting." He continued the able head of the institution for forty years, succumbing to the "last call" at the age of seventy-seven years. He was an educator of learning and skill, infinitely kind, patient and conscientious, holding high ideals of his responsibilities, and very faithful in the discharge of every duty. The value of his life cannot be estimated, but must be found in the lives of the thousands of young men who have passed from under his instruction out into the world of business. He lived worthily and well, bequeathing to the city of his adoption an educational institution of merit, and to posterity an honored name and a record of usefulness.

Mr. Eaton married (first) in 1868, Emma Andrews, of Milltown, Canada, who died in 1884, leaving three sons: John Bernard, born in 1869, died March 17, 1891; Clarence Jackson, born in 1875, a resident of Baltimore; Donald Law, born January 14, 1878, died August 9, 1902. Mr. Eaton married (second) Harriet E. Smith, of St. John, New Brunswick, Canada, who died in 1914.

ALFRED DUNCAN BERNARD

ALFRED D. BERNARD, lawyer and political economist, was born in Baltimore, Maryland, March 25, 1868. He was the son of Richard Bernard, born in Bandon, County Cork, Ireland, 1840, and Frances Duncan Bernard. He was educated in the grade schools, Baltimore City College, Loyola College, and the University of Maryland, from which he graduated in 1889, receiving the degree of LL.B.

Through his connection with the law firm of Richard Bernard & Son, Alfred D. Bernard became an ardent student of political economy. The real estate transactions of the office naturally led him to the study of real estate values in Baltimore and the counties. But the study soon spread and he became interested in land values all over the country. In conjunction with his profession, Mr. Bernard continued the study of real estate, as an avocation, for many years, until 1904, when the great Baltimore fire brought about the need for a Burnt District Commission, upon which Mr. Bernard was appointed. Mr. Bernard served so efficiently in this capacity that when the work of the commission was completed, he was retained by the city officials as real estate expert for the Appeal Tax Court. While holding this position, Mr. Bernard, with his colleague, Mr. Thomas J. Lindsay, devised a system of real estate valuation known as the Lindsay-Bernard Rule, which is employed exclusively by the Baltimore Tax Court.

As the real estate officer of the United States Fidelity and Guarantee Company, Mr. Bernard found the opportunity to publish a book entitled "Some Principles and Problems of Real Estate Valuation." The book was written as a guide and text for appraisers, and has received favorable comment and praise from some of the foremost real estate experts in the country. Through the fame of his book Mr. Bernard's ability attracted widespread attention throughout the country, and he was called into consultation by the officers of the city of Cambridge, Massachusetts, in regard to their assessment methods, while at Harvard University for the purpose of lecturing.

Following the death of Mr. Bernard the Mayor of Baltimore said: "We will not be able to replace him. His experience was invaluable to us. Mr. Bernard saved the city not thousands but millions of dollars." In speaking of Mr. Bernard's ability and character, Judge John Gill, president of the Appeal Tax Court, said: "The city could always rely upon his work. He was peculiarly fitted to the work of the department, patient, and without prejudice of any kind. He was a man of even temper, and mature judgment, quiet, industrious and painstaking. His death is a distinct loss to the city, and to the Appeal Tax Court especially." Aside from real estate and law, Mr. Bernard was much interested in patriotic work. He was a member of the Society of the Sons of the American Revolution, and was president of the Society of the War of 1812 at the time of his death.

During his career as a real estate expert, and as a member of several patriotic societies, Mr. Bernard made many speeches and wrote many essays on various subjects. Notable among these are his essays on taxation, published in the "Annals of the American Academy of Political and Social Science."

Aside from Mr. Bernard's reputation as a business man, he also had an enviable reputation as a fine character. Throughout his life he was temperate, broad-minded, kind-hearted, affectionate and patient. He was noted for the beautiful attitude he maintained toward his father, it being more like that existing between two affectionate brothers than between father and son. So great was the attachment between them that upon the death of Alfred D. Bernard his father was unable to resume business, and died a few months after, grief-stricken over the death of his beloved son. Mr. Bernard was married twice, and was survived by his second wife, Theresa Elizabeth Bernard, and his only son, Richard C. Bernard.

The news of Mr. Bernard's death, on April 19, 1916, was a shock to all his friends and associates, as he was thought to have been in good health up to the time of his death. In his honor the flag on the city hall was placed at half mast, and the courts adjourned with appropriate eulogies by prominent lawyers and judges.

SAMUEL KIRK

TO the Quaker family of Kirk belongs the honor of establishing in Baltimore one of the first manufactures of silverware in this country, and that city owes much of its moral worth and commercial standing to the high character of this family. The Kirks were silversmiths in ancient times in England, and the ancestry has been traced to Godfrey Kirk, a member of the Chesterfield Monthly Meeting of Quakers in England.

(II) John Kirk, son of Godfrey Kirk, was born June 14, 1660, at Alfreton, Derbyshire, England, and came to America about 1682-83, locating in Darby township, in what is now Delaware county, Pennsylvania. He was an extensive land owner, and died 8th month (October), 1705. He married, about the 2nd month (April) 1688, Joan, daughter of Peter Ellet, who survived him, as she did also a second husband, and was living in 1735. Children: 1. Anne, born 1688-89, in Darby, married Benjamin Peters. 2. Godfrey, born November 27, 1690, married, February 17, 1725, Rachel Ellis. 3. John, mentioned below. 4. Samuel, born November 11, 1693, died unmarried. 5. Mary, born February 17, 1695, died January 11, 1782; married, October 20, 1715, John Warner. 6. Elizabeth, born May 9, 1696, died November 8, 1774; married, January, 1719, John Twining. 7. Joseph, born September 1, 1697, married, September, 1723, Ann Hood, died November 16, 1773. 8. Sarah, born February 23, 1699, married, July 23, 1723, Nathaniel Twining, died 1775. 9. William, born October 31, 1700, married (first) May, 1723, Elizabeth Rhoads, (second) June 9, 1747, Mary Ellis, died May 8, 1749. 10. Isaac, born April 23, 1703, died about 1781; married (first), December 9, 1730, Elizabeth Twining, (second), September 4, 1746, Rachel Kinsey. 11.

Saml Kirk

Thomas, born February 26, 1705, died February 14, 1752; married, October 28, 1731, Mary Shaw.

(III) John (2) Kirk, second son of John (1) and Joan (Ellet) Kirk, was born March 29, 1692, in Darby, Pennsylvania, and died in Abington township, Philadelphia (now Montgomery) county, August 9, 1759. He married at Abington Meeting, October 17, 1722, Sarah Tyson, born November 12, 1698, buried June 19, 1780, daughter of Reynear Tyson and Mary (Roberts) Tyson, of Abington. Children: 1. John, born September 30, 1723, died in childhood. 2. Reynear, born June 28, 1725, died 1799; was a farmer in Abington township and Upper Dublin; he married (first), May 24, 1748, Mary Michener, who died in 1766; (second), Elizabeth Wilkins. 3. Margaret, born September 7, 1727, married Nathaniel Loofborrow, Jr. 4. Elizabeth, born September 25, 1730, died January 10, 1820; married, November 21, 1752, John Spencer. 5. Mary, born October 29, 1732, died February 22, 1761; married, August 19, 1753, William Loofborrow. 6. Isaac, mentioned below. 7. Jacob (twin with Isaac), born September 30, 1735, died October 13, 1829; was a farmer in Abington; was born, lived and died in the same house; he married, May 14, 1760, Elizabeth Cleaver. 8. Sarah, born October 12, 1737; married (first), December 23, 1761, her brother-in-law, William Loofborrow, for which she was disowned by Abington and Philadelphia Friends' Meeting; (second) Samuel Spencer.

(IV) Isaac Kirk, third son of John (2) and Sarah (Tyson) Kirk, was born September 30, 1735, died June 17, 1826. He resided in Upper Dublin township, Montgomery county, Pennsylvania, where he was a farmer. His will was proved at Norristown, July 6, 1826. He married, June 20, 1756, Mary Tyson, born April 28, 1733, died June 1, 1828, daughter of John and Priscilla (Naylor) Tyson. Mary

(Tyson) Kirk died intestate, and letters of administration were granted June 5, 1828, to Isaac Tyson, John Child, John Kirk and John Tyson. Children: Priscilla, born about March 13, 1757, died April 3, 1834; married, May 25, 1780, Absolom Michener. 2. Sarah, born February 10, 1759, died October 12, 1815; married, May 22, 1788, Henry Child. 3. Elizabeth, born April 11, 1761, died December 10, 1849; married, January 22, 1784, Jesse Cleaver. 4. John, born February 29, 1764, died July 7, 1813; married Mary Dungan. 5. Joseph, mentioned below. 6. Susanna, born November 18, 1767, died April 5, 1838; married William North. 7. Mary, born June 25, 1770, married Isaac Tyson. 8. Isaac, born June 4, 1773, died April 5, 1827; married, October 1, 1807, Sarah Rush. 9. Margaret, born July 18, 1775, died November 12, 1852; married Thomas Marple.

(V) Joseph Kirk, second son of Isaac and Mary (Tyson) Kirk, was born April 12, 1766, died August 1, 1829. He was a carpenter by trade, and lived in Doylestown, Pennsylvania, and later at Philadelphia. He married, July 5, 1787, at the Presbyterian church in Philadelphia, Grace Child, born December 26, 1765, daughter of John and Sarah (Shoemaker) Child. Children: 1. Eliza, married James Warner. 2. Priscilla, died young. 3. Isaac, married Margaret Stinson, and resided in Baltimore county, Maryland. 4. Joseph, died 1812, in United States Army, in Canada, unmarried. 5. Samuel, mentioned below. 6. Absolom, died in infancy. 7. Sarah, married Dr. John S. Rich, who practiced in Doylestown, Pennsylvania. 8. Mary, died 1845, unmarried. 9. Hannah, married John T. Smith. 10. Robert Sherman, born June 23, 1800, died in Baltimore county, Maryland, June 24, 1872; married Ellen Alvira Waters. The Child family, like that of Kirk, was for many generations engaged in the manufacture of plate, and has been traced to Sir Francis Child, a goldsmith of London. The banking business originated with the goldsmiths of London, with whom people of property kept running accounts for safety rather than keep their valuables at home. The Childs for generations were first goldsmiths and then bankers. In the latter capacity they reached great prominence. The famous banking house of Child & Company is still in existence, and for more than two centuries has played an important part both in the financial and political history of England. Child & Company are inserted in the little London Directory of 1677 as "goldsmiths keeping running cashes." They were the first to separate the two callings. There is an account of their ledgers opened in 1669, before they divorced the two vocations, under the head of "Pawn," changed a few years later to "P," which has been brought forward from ledger to ledger under this title as their collateral loan account for over two hundred years.

The record of this family of bankers is so interwoven, warp and woof, with that of the Temple Bar, the Marygold and their environs, that any narrative of either, without frequent reference to the others would be incomplete. Many of their customers addressed their cheques to "Mr. Alderman Child and partners, at ye Marygold, next door to Temple Bar; sometimes next door to the "Devil Taverne." When the head of the firm was Lord Mayor of London, the Earl of Oxford addressed his cheques "To the Worshipful the Lord Mayor & Co., at Temple Bar." Like most of the distinctive appellations of the goldsmiths of London, the sign of the Marygold originated in that of the tavern. It was the usage for succeeding occupants to retain the sign, without reference to the vocation. "Messrs. Child's banking house was in the reign of King James First, a public ordinary, the sign being the Marygold." When it came into the occupation of the goldsmiths is not definitely known, but probably about 1620, as the last mention of it as a public house was on St. Thomas' day, December 21, 1619, when it was presented to the ward-mote "for disturbing its next neighbors late in the nights, from time to time, by ill disorders." The goldsmiths held it on a ground rent. Sir Francis Child put the present front to the Marygold in 1666, the year of the great fire of London, although the conflagration did not reach it. An old document, still extant, shows that Sir Francis renewed his lease of the Marygold from the "Feast of St. Michael," 1707, and the Sugar Loaf and Green Lettuce, 1714, at a yearly rental of £60 for sixty-one years. The Sugar Loaf was an old tavern directly in the rear of the Marygold. Sir Francis repaired it in 1707 and added it to his banking premises. He subsequently purchased for £2,800 the famous tavern popularly called the "Old Devil," which adjoined, and erected a block of houses, later known as "Child's Place." The "Old Devil" was the favorite of Ben Johnson, where he lorded over his confreres that were "sealed of the tribe of Ben." Here he sometimes met Shakespeare. Child & Company have, with characteristic conservativeness, preserved many very interesting relics of these three historical houses. They have the original sign of the Marygold and Sun, made of oak, stained green, with gilt border, with the motto *Ainsi mon ame,* now put over the door between the front and back office, and retain it on the watermark of their cheques.

The old passageways of the Sugar Loaf with their wooden hat pegs, the old dining rooms, kitchens and larders, with their wooden meat hooks, are preserved as they were two and three centuries ago. In one of the rooms over the old kitchen may be seen the bust of Apollo, and the tablet on which the lines of welcome to the Apollo Room, by Ben Johnson, are engraved in gold letters. When Sir Christopher Wren rebuilt Temple Bar, in 1666, Child & Company rented the chamber over the arcade adjoining their premises, of the city of London, at a yearly rental of £20. This they used as a sort of muniment room for the safe keeping of their old papers and books of accounts, until the excavations for the foundations of the new Inner Courts of Law, in 1875, caused Temple Bar to settle so much that, in 1877, the city gave them notice to vacate. The widening of Fleet street demanded for public convenience the demolition of the time-honored banking house, and the erection of another one door east, covering the site of Child's Place, to which the firm moved April 15, 1879. They are still on ancestral ground. Dickens describes Childs & Company characteristically in his "Tale of Two Cities," under the appellation of Tellson & Company as they were in the days of the French revolution.

Child & Company had had a branch house in Paris, with the accounts of the noblesse, which were transferred to London during the Revolution, together with their valuables to be used to eke out a miserable existence, or to be settled *sans compte rendu par les Etats executifs,* the guillotine. The Marygold became the headquarters of the Emigres during the reign of terror, and its secret couriers were constantly passing between the two cities. The banking firm retains many old time usages, probably inherited from their ancestors, the goldsmiths. They call their front office "the shop," and that in the rear, where the ledgers are kept, "the counting house," where they "cast up the shop" once a year.

The family was founded in this country by Henry Child, of Hertfordshire, who resided in Coldshill, in the parish of Rindersham, and had several children. The family was identified with the Society of Friends. On the twentieth of January, 1687, Henry Child purchased five hundred acres of land in Plumstead, Bucks county, Pennsylvania, near the headwaters of the Neshaminy river, for which he paid ten pounds.

He brought his son, Cephas, to America, and soon after returned to England. In 1715 Henry Child "for the love and affection he beareth to his son, Cephas," gave the five hundred acres to him. Before attaining his majority, Cephas Child was placed for a time with a family in Philadelphia, where he was taught the carpenter's trade. He came to America in 1693, and married, in February, 1716, Mary Atkinson. They were the parents of John Child, born June 14, 1739, in Plumstead, died in 1801, at Frankfort, Pennsylvania. He married, September 19, 1751, Sarah Shoemaker, daughter of George and Grace Shoemaker, of Warrington, Pennsylvania. They were the parents of Grace Child, who became the wife of General Joseph Kirk, as previously related.

(VI) Samuel Kirk, third son of Joseph and Grace (Child) Kirk, was born February 15, 1793, in Doylestown, and died July 5, 1872, in Baltimore. He was educated at a Friends' school, and at the age of seventeen years was apprenticed to James Howell, a silversmith of Philadelphia, to learn the trade. At this time his parents took up their residence in the Quaker City. At the end of his apprenticeship he was offered an interest in the business of James Howell, but decided to embark on an independent career, and removed to Baltimore. In August, 1815, he purchased an account book, and from this is learned the date of his beginning business. The first entry was made in August, 1815. His establishment was on Market street, and spoons, tea urns and pitchers made by him in 1816-18-19 are preserved by his descendants. For about one year he had a partner named Smith, and many pieces bearing the stamp of Kirk & Smith are still in existence. Multitudes of samples bearing the stamp of Samuel Kirk are among the treasures of his successors in business. His partnership with Smith continued about a year, and he subsequently carried on business alone until 1846, when his son, Henry

Child Kirk, became a partner, and the firm name was Samuel Kirk & Son. In 1861 two other sons were admitted, but withdrew about the close of the Civil War. After the death of Samuel Kirk, his son, Henry C. Kirk, continued business under the same name, until 1890, when his only son, Henry Child Kirk, Jr., became a partner, without change of the name. In 1896 the business was incorporated under the title of Samuel Kirk & Son Company. Samuel Kirk married, March 18, 1817, Albina Powell, born October 28, 1796, died December 23, 1865, daughter of Joshua and Margaret (Carpenter) Powell. Children: 1. Eliza Grace, born January 13, 1818, married, January 5, 1845, Seth Hance, who died May 2, 1884; children: Franklin, Emma and four others, all deceased. 2. James Howell, born May 24, 1821, died August 22, 1822. 3. Hannah Jane, born May 24, 1821, died July 22, 1822. 4. Henry Edgar, born September 24, 1822, died July 11, 1823. 5. Margaret Jane, born December 26, 1823, died July 11, 1882; married Jesse Hunt. 6. Henry Child, mentioned below. 7. Amanda Victoria, born December 28, 1828, died February 4, 1850. 8. Benjamin Powell, born April 28, 1830, died June 26, 1834. 9. Helen Albina, born February 28, 1835, unmarried. 10. Charles Douglas, born February 27, 1840, died January 5, 1880; married, April 2, 1861, Cassandra Ashton Anderson. 11. Edwin Clarence, born April 28, 1842, died July 11, 1876, unmarried.

(VII) Henry Child Kirk, third son of Samuel and Albina (Powell) Kirk, was born February 9, 1826, in Baltimore, and became a practical silversmith under his father's instructions. In due course of time he was made head of the corporation of Samuel Kirk & Son Company, and though eighty-nine years of age at the time of his death was actively interested in the business. In his time the volume of business transacted was very greatly increased, and he was brought into prominence in the silver world, having many friends throughout the country. For more than fifty years Mr. Kirk was treasurer of the Franklin Street Presbyterian Church, of Baltimore. During his presidency the company suffered two fires, the first on June 30, 1903, and the second in the great Baltimore conflagration of February 7, 1904. In the latter fire the building was totally destroyed, but all the original drawings, designs and patterns were preserved. He married (first) Virginia E. Hardesty, born in 1831, died August 21, 1855. He married (second) Lucy Strother Buckner, daughter of Bailey and Mildred (Strother) Buckner. He married (third) Eliza Hollins, daughter of George and Lydia (Campbell) Hollins, died April 22, 1900. Children by first wife: 1. Olivia Hardesty, married William Higgins Conkling; children: William, deceased; Elizabeth Baldwin; William Higgins; Olivia H. 2. Alice Virginia, married Martin L. Millspaugh, and had children: Alice Virginia, Laurence, and Henry Child Kirk Millspaugh, deceased. Children by second wife: 3. Mildred Buckner, married William Thomas Walter Mc-Cay, deceased, and had one child, Mildred Buckner. 4. Henry Child, born December 16, 1868, succeeded his father as president of Samuel Kirk & Son Company; he married, October 22, 1891, Edith Huntemuller, born March 26, 1872; children: Edith Buckner, born December 20, 1892; Mary Huntemuller, March 21, 1896; Ann Strother, August 29, 1901. Child by third wife: 5. Lydia Hensworth, married Roderick D. Donaldson; two children.

JAMES H. SMITH

SEVENTY-SIX were the years allotted James H. Smith, of Baltimore, and many of those years were spent in the public service of his city, the most important office held being that of comptroller of the city. His life until 1870 was a continual endeavor to "find" himself, and as a machinist, merchant and justice of the peace, those years wers spent. Finally he became a law student, was admitted to the Baltimore bar, and in law study, practice and public service the last half century of his life was passed. He was a man of ability and high character, having important relations with many of the interests of his city. In the annexation fight of 1886, he made common cause with the annexationists, and was a powerful advocate of that cause. He was fearless in public action, and in the office he held stood only for that which was right, good and true. He descended from that strictest of sects, the Scotch-Irish Presbyterian, and those North of Ireland ancestors were not more loyal in their faith than he.

James H. Smith was a son of Henry Smith, and a grandson of Rev. Alexander Smith, Scotch-Irish by parentage, and by profession a Presbyterian minister, of County Donegal, Ireland. There, Henry Smith was born, and resided at the Manse until eighteen years of age, then coming to the United States and locating in Howard county, Maryland. There he learned the machinist's trade, later came to Woodberry, Baltimore county, becoming clerk, later general bookkeeper for the McVernon Manufacturing Company, continuing with that corporation until his death at the age of sixty-eight. He was an elder of the Presbyterian church, and a man highly respected. He married Sarah Ayler, born on the eastern shore of Maryland, who died in Baltimore, aged forty-five, daughter of Henry Ayler. They were the parents of three sons and a daughter: James H., of further mention; William O., who succeeded his father as general bookkeeper of the Mc-Vernon Manufacturing Company; Joseph M., a merchant of Baltimore, and Sarah E. Smith, deceased.

James H. Smith, son of Henry and Sarah (Ayler) Smith, was born in Baltimore, March 17, 1841, died in his native city, August 20, 1917. He was educated in the city public schools and Newell's Commercial Institute, completing the regular course at the last named institution at the age of sixteen. He then determined to learn the machinist's trade, and for five years he was apprentice and journeyman with Poole & Hunt, of Baltimore. He did not longer pursue that calling, but became a merchant in Woodberry, at the same time holding office of Justice of the Peace, which office he held for ten years. His experiences as justice turned his thoughts to the law as a profession, and finally he began a regular course of legal study under L. P. D. Newman. He continued a student until 1870, then was admitted to the Maryland bar, and began practice, opening an office at No. 11 East Lexington street. He developed strong qualities as a lawyer, and continued in practice until his death. For many years Mr. Smith was the legal adviser of Dr. David H. Carroll, of Woodberry, and associated with the doctor in much of his real estate dealings. He took an active part in securing the annexation to Baltimore of that portion of the city lying north of North avenue in 1886, and when the subject was brought before the people for decision his voice was a potent one in favor thereof. He was a director of the Provident Savings Bank, and had other important business interests.

A Democrat in politics, Mr. Smith first entered the public service in 1889, being in that year elected to represent the twenty-second ward in the first branch of the City Council.

Three times he was re-elected, his entire service covering a continuous term of seven years. Three of those years he was chairman of the Committee of Ways and Means, and at all times an influential member. In 1893 he was elected in the second branch of the City Council, serving for two years in that body, and during the entire period was its president. In 1896 he was again elected from the twenty-second ward to the first branch of the City Council, again serving on the Committee of Ways and Means. He was also at one time County Commissioner; President of the Baltimore Association for improving the condition of the poor; president of the commission for opening streets under Mayor Timanus, and comptroller of the city under Mayor Hayes. He was an elder of the Maryland Avenue Presbyterian Church, and a long time member of that congregation.

Mr. Smith married in Baltimore county, May 27, 1873, Frances R. Gibson, born in Harford county, Maryland, who survives him, daughter of James F. Gibson, a former merchant of Baltimore county. Two children: Emma B. and Franklin Howard Smith, also residents of Baltimore, survive their father.

DAVID HUTZLER

MERCHANT, citizen, friend, showing in each capacity an exalted conception of duty, David Hutzler was a notable example of the right-thinking, far-seeing men who contribute largely to communal and municipal progress. It was characteristic of the solid quality of the business with which he was connected, Hutzler Brothers, that it should have been conducted for over half a century on the same spot where in 1858 it began. The business expanded of course, modern methods and inventions were adopted as they showed their value, but the foundations were laid broad and deep at the beginning and were adequate to carry the imposing structure erected thereon.

Early in his career, David Hutzler displayed his interest in public affairs and there were few movements for civic betterment, for the advancement of education, art, and music with which he was not intimately connected. Indeed, when a non-professional man was required for public service, his name perhaps rose oftenest in the mind of the citizens of Baltimore as the person best fitted for the place, both by reason of his ability and through his well-known, strong desire to be of service to his city and fellowmen; yet he resolutely refused political office, but was always willing to serve city or State on commission or committee for a stated purpose, and was connected with some of the most important movements instituted for the public good.

He was a notable figure in social life, and his friends and acquaintances were drawn from an unusually large field. In appearance he presented a striking and dignified figure, revealing to the observer at a glance a man devoted to the higher interests of men and affairs. He was affable and most

David Hutzler

considerate, though tenaciously maintaining the opinions formed after mature deliberation. He held to high ideals, vigor and alertness, mental and physical, distinguished him, and although he exceeded the Psalmist's "three score years and ten" he never created the impression of an elderly man. On the contrary he maintained to the last a zest and enthusiasm for public problems, travel and literature. He was keenly alive to the trend of events, absorbed their meaning, and vigorously championed the cause he approved.

The business of which David Hutzler was the executive head at the time of his death was founded in 1848 in a two-story building at the corner of Howard and Clay streets, Baltimore, the site of the present magnificent building occupied by Hutzler Brothers, dry goods merchants. The firm name was originally M. Hutzler & Son, the father, Moses Hutzler, allowing his son Abram G. to use his name as he was a minor and could not obtain credit on account of his youth. With him was associated his brother, David Hutzler, then a lad of fifteen, who acted as clerk. The business prospered and until 1861 the brothers were together. Then Abram G. and another brother, Charles G. Hutzler, who had been in the jobbing business, joined forces and opened a wholesale notion business on Baltimore street. This left the youngest brother David in sole charge of the original store on Howard street, and so well did he manage and develop it that in 1884 the two elder brothers gave up their wholesale business in order that the three might devote their combined energies to the Howard street store which in 1874 had been enlarged to five times the original size. Adjoining property was bought and enlargement followed enlargement until in 1886 the present main building was erected, while the last annex was constructed immediately after the great fire of 1904.

In the course of half a century there were few changes in the firm and none save those caused by death. In 1907 Charles G. Hutzler died, after devoting his life to the up-building of the business. This left David and Abram G. sole owners of the business. Later Edwin B. and Louis S., sons of Charles G. Hutzler, Albert D., son of David Hutzler, and Henry Oppenheimer, his son-in-law, were admitted. With the death of David Hutzler in 1916, Abram G., the founder, was left as head of the business, which strictly speaking is not a department store, but has been maintained according to the intent of the founder as a high class dry goods store. Founded on a conservative basis it has ever been conducted in sympathy with the high ideals and principles taught by the father, Moses Hutzler, to his three sons. At the top of the capstone on the Howard Clay corner of the store building, the face of his father is carved in stone by the express order of the son who thus testified his appreciation of his father's help and guidance. When, in 1908, the house celebrated its fiftieth anniversary, so thoroughly had they won the good will and confidence of the city that the anniversary partook of the nature of a public occasion.

David Hutzler, youngest son of Moses and Caroline Hutzler, was born in Baltimore, June 13, 1843, and died in the city of his birth, January 21, 1915. From the age of fifteen years he was connected with the business of which he was president at his death, Hutzler Brothers, and while there was the warmest feelings existing between the brothers that between the elder, Abram G., and the younger, David, was most remarkable. The boy David was first the elder brother's clerk, then his partner, then his ranking partner, and finally, after fifty-seven years closest intimacy, passed on leaving the elder of the brothers the last survivor. In addition to his

presidency of Hutzler Brothers Company, David Hutzler
was a director of the Merchants-Mechanics National Bank,
the Eutaw Savings Bank and the Fidelity and Deposit Company.

While as president of Hutzler Brothers his name was
a household word in Baltimore, and he was a life-long and
potent factor in the business world, his public spirit and
thorough familiarity with all the stages and phases of Baltimore's development made him a most valuable counselor and
helper in civic affairs, and several city administrations called
upon him to aid in smoothing out intricate problems or in
dealing with special emergencies. On the numerous occasions upon which he served the city and the State officially,
as a member of various commisions and committees, he
brought to his task a soundness of judgment and a resourse-
fulness which materially aided in the solution of the problems
under consideration. He was a constructive force in the true
meaning of the term, and his value was nowhere more apparent than, after the great fire, on that splendid body of
men who formed the Emergency Committee.

Mr. Hutzler was vice-president of the Baltimore Board
of Trade and chairman of its committee on Municipal Affairs;
committee chairman of the National Board of Trade; director
of the Merchants and Manufacturers Association. After a
defalcation was discovered which discredited city methods
of accounting, the four principal trade boards of the city, the
Board of Trade, the Chamber of Commerce, the Merchants &
Manufacturers Association, and the Clearing House, formed
a committee of municipal research for protection and elected
David Hutzler chairman of that committee. After six
months' work the committee gave to the city a fine system of
accounting which was afterward accepted by the New Char-

ter Commission of which Mr. Hutzler was a member, he being the only active merchant serving on that commission which was composed mostly of professional men. For fourteen years he represented the Baltimore Board of Trade on the National Board of Trade. In that body he took a deep interest in postal affairs, and in his effort to secure one cent postage framed a resolution which brought to light the fact that magazines paid but one cent per pound for the delivery that cost the government eight cents per pound. Mr. Hutzler showed that the profit of first class mail matter was 275%, but that profit disappeared by the loss on second class matter. He estimated that loss at $50,000,000 annually. President Taft, in his special message to Congress, showed the loss to be $63,-000,000, while the Postmaster General's report places it at $70,000,000. He was also chairman of the Parcels Post Committee of the National board and labored to secure the passage of the Parcels Post law. Mr. Hutzler was also a member of the committee, active in recommending the establishment of the Department of Commerce and Labor as a part of the National Government, a department whose usefulness to the country has been abundantly proven.

When the great fire of 1904 left Baltimore the gigantic task of rehabilitation, Mayor McLane sought for the best men to aid him in solving the difficult problems which followed each other in quick succession. One of the first to whom he turned was David Hutzler, whom he named a member of the State Special Relief Committee. Out of $158,000 placed to the credit of that committee but $23,000 was used, the remainder being returned to the state treasury. It is also notable that no monetary assistance was accepted from out-of-town, although the Trade League of Philadelphia invited Mr. Hutzler to draw upon them for $50,000. A similar public spirit prompted him to become at the request of Sir William Osler the first treasurer of the Maryland Society for the Relief and Prevention of Tuberculosis. For twenty-seven years he was a director of the Hebrew Orphan Asylum, also its president; a member of the National Conference of Charities and Correction; the United Association for the Study and Prevention of Tuberculosis (a special committee of the International Tuberculosis Congress); life member of the National Red Cross Association; the State Aids and Charities of Maryland; and the Federal Charities of Baltimore. He was also a member of the executive committee of the Red Cross Association of Maryland, and at the time of the San Francisco fire served on the special committee appointed to render assistance.

At the Chicago Columbian Exposition of 1893, he represented Maryland, and in 1901 acted as a delegate to the Peace Conference between Great Britain and the United States held in Washington. In April, 1907, he represented Baltimore at the Peace Conference held in New York City. He was an ardent lover of music and one of the supporters of grand opera in the city. As a boy he aided in organizing the Harmony Circle, was the master of ceremonies when but a youth, and afterward served as its president, as he also served Mendelssohn Literary Association of which he was a charter member. He earnestly worked for and generously contributed to the support of Johns Hopkins University endowment fund, and for a similar fund for Goucher College; interested himself in the Municipal Art Society, and the many organizations the object of which was to make Baltimore a better, more beautiful residential city. He was a member and an ex-president of the Phoenix Club, member of the Suburban and of the City Clubs, all of Baltimore, and of the City Club of New York City. In the Masonic order he was a past master of Arcana Lodge, No. 110, Free and Accepted Masons, having been master of that lodge several terms; and was past high priest of Adoniram Chapter, No. 21, Royal Arch Masons. For many years he was one of the active members of Hao Sinai Congregation, and in the closing passage of his address at the funeral of his parishioner, Dr. Ruhenstein, of Hao Sinai Temple, said:

No man needs a eulogy whose life was so well spent as that of our lamented friend. Besides our sacred dead are beyond both our praise and our blame. They dwell where the Eternal abides and our human judgment avails not. If I speak of the good works of this truly exemplary man now gone to his reward it is an incentive for us, the living, who mourn him, to see in life a constant opportunity for service, a means of realizing the higher ideals. Like our lamented friend, let us endeavor to make our life a benediction.

So his useful life was passed, the foregoing being little more than an outline of his life and work and of the influence he exerted. His genial, generous disposition won him many personal friends, but as a loyal son of Baltimore the city claimed him. In his home the natural dignity of the man relaxed and there he was at his best. His life was well spent and it may be truly said of him that "the world is better for his having lived in it."

Mr. Hutzler married, February 25, 1874, Ella J. Gutman, daughter of Joel Gutman, of Baltimore. They were the parents of two sons and three daughters: Albert D., married Gretchen, daughter of Max Hochechild, of Baltimore; Joel Gutman David; Cora, married Henry Oppenheimer; Theresa, since deceased, married Professor Jacob H. Hollander; and Mabel.

WILLIAM SHEPARD BRYAN, Jr.

TO HAVE achieved eminence at the Baltimore bar argues in itself a man of highest attainment, and no higher eulogy of William S. Bryan, Jr. is possible than to state that he was one of the brightest legal lights of that bar and at one time attorney general of the State of Maryland. Brilliant, learned, he was a formidable, aggressive adversary, but honorable in his legal controversies, holding sacred the highest ideals of the profession he honored. Keen and caustic in his wit, but lovable and warm-hearted, his nature a true gentleman under every condition.

He was extremely independent in thought and action, conservative rather than radical, but despised vascillation or indecision. His mind was a storehouse of facts, legal principles, adjudicated cases, historical and classical allusions, upon which he drew freely. He also possessed a fund of illustrations which were neither historical nor classical, but always conveyed the idea he was seeking to illuminate. He was so positive in his own nature that he had no patience with lawyer or judge who, to use one of his own favorite illustrations, concluded that "two and two made *about* four." Few men in the State were more successful than he in the practice of their professions, and no man in the State had so wide an acquaintance. He knew men in every walk of life and his interest in the public welfare was keen and unremitting. He was adviser to the Democratic party of Maryland, and himself, a Democrat of the highest type, he fought for political honesty and integrity, hating the shams of pretense, judging men of his own party as well as the opposition, not by their own claims for preferment, but by their true merit to serve the people well in the office to which they aspired. He loved the excitement of a close political contest and was at his best when

pleading with an audience of voters to support the principles
and the candidates of his party. His wit and readiness at
repartee charmed his friends and made him ever a most welcome guest, and he was the most loyal of friends.

William Shepard Bryan, Jr., son of Judge William S.
Bryan, of the Court of Appeals, was born in Baltimore in
1859, died in the city of his birth, April 3, 1914. His father,
a native son of North Carolina, and a warm southern sympathizer, married Elizabeth Edmonson Hayward, of Talbot
county, Maryland, and located in Baltimore, where he became an eminent member of the bar, and judge of the Court
of Appeals. After leaving St. Michael's School, Reisterstown,
the son attended Bethel Military Academy, at Farquier
county, Virginia; later entered the law school of the University
of Virginia, having previously read law in his father's office,
whence he was graduated. He returned to Baltimore,
office, whence he was graduated. He returned to Baltimore,
was admitted to the bar and began practice, and but a few
years passed ere he had assumed an important position among
the rising young lawyers of the city. During those first years
he was at one time a partner with George R. Gaither. In
1891 he formed a partnership with Edward N. Rich, an old
school chum, and for about eleven years he practiced in partnership with A. deR. Sappington. He became one of the
foremost lawyers of his day and could have become a judge,
but he never desired to be, saying that he was not suited
temperamentally for the bench.

Mr. Bryan was eminently fair in his conduct of law cases,
this endearing him to his opponents in the face of the fact
that he often lost his temper, saying or doing things that would
ordinarily offend. At times he incurred criticism for seeming
to be in contempt of court. One judge remarked upon one
occasion that Mr. Bryan "was not in contempt of court be-

cause he did not mean to be." In his conversation out of court he generally worked around to a legal question, his mind trained in that channel so thoroughly that he could not help himself. But he was a wide reader of other than law books; biography, history and mythology interested him, and he was well informed on general literature. His power of concentration was wonderful. When he read any judge's opinion he studied beyond the point decided, to learn something of the character of the man who rendered the decision. He was essentially a controversialist, a lover of debate on public questions, a critic of legislators, editors, and reformers. Conservative in his own views he was opposed to men of the Roosevelt and Bryan type, saying of the latter, "His name is too much like my own for me to like him."

It was not long after Mr. Bryan's admission to the bar before he was discovered by the Democratic party organization as of superior merit, and he became one of the party leaders and counselors. He was elected counsel to the board of election supervisors, the first city attorney, city counselor, first city solicitor and was attorney general of the State of Maryland during Governor Warfield's administration, that being the last public office he held. He did not seek office, neither did he decline it, believing that it was every man's duty to stick to his party through thick and thin, and he hated a "bolter." He was chief adviser to I. Freeman Rasin when he was at the head of the party in Baltimore, and was held in high esteem by Mr. Rasin's friends, from the fact that his opinions and advice were found to be sound. Mr. Rasin did not always follow Mr. Bryan's advice, but heeded it very often to his own advantage.

About a year prior to his death, Mr. Bryan decided to enter the race for United States senator, to succeed Senator Lee, and wrote to President Wilson stating that fact. Although encouraged by his friends to make the attempt, he finally decided not to do so. Although he had many warm friends he cared little for society and always remained a bachelor. He was extremely fond of baseball and attended as many games as he possibly could and delivered the address of congratulation to the "Orioles," in October, 1894, the year they first won the championship. The death of Mr. Bryan called for expressions of regret and eulogy from the bench and bar, and the State of Maryland officially recognized the blow which had fallen upon the commonwealth through the following resolutions, offered and adopted by both Houses of the Legislature.

Resolved by the General Assembly of Maryland, that in the death of Mr. Bryan the state has suffered the loss of a conscientious, able and devoted official who, as attorney-general of the State of Maryland, rendered to this commonwealth services of the highest value. An eminent and distinguished lawyer, a man of the highest integrity, of great energy and industry, he was ever interested in the public welfare and was always faithful to the best interests of the State.

Resolved further, that this resolution be found in the acts of the year nineteen hundred and fourteen.

As soon as Governor Goldsborough learned of the death of Mr. Bryan he ordered the national flag placed at half staff on the State House dome and to remain so displayed until after the funeral.

The American Historical Society.   Eng by W.T.Bather N.

Daniel Donnelly.

DANIEL DONNELLY

HARDLY a man now alive, then of mature years, who can recall the period of excitement which swept over this country in 1848 when gold was discovered in California in the race of the mill owned by John A. Sutter. By 1849 the news of the wonderful discovery was well disseminated throughout the United States, and in every part of the country parties were formed, bound for the land of gold, some going overland, some by the isthmus route, land and water, and others by the all water route around Cape Horn. Many of those who set out full of hope and courage perished miserably on the plains and in the mountains from exposure and hunger, or by the hand of a savage foe; many others perished at sea; only a small proportion ever reached the mines, only a still smaller proportion ever returned, and but a very, very few returned with the gold they sought. Among the cities over which this excitement swept was Baltimore, where dwelt Daniel Donnelly, then a young man of twenty-two years, making his way upward in the world by hard work. With all the impetuosity of his youthful, ardent nature, he plunged into preparations to join the mad rush, sold all he possessed and finally on a sailing vessel set out on the long voyage "around the Horn" a veritable "soldier of fortune."

There were fifty-eight other Baltimoreans who joined in the California gold hunting excitement who lived to return to the city from which they started. Later they formed themselves into the California Pioneer Society and for many years held meetings at increasingly longer intervals. One by one the members departed for another "Golden Shore," until only Elken Drey and Daniel Donnelly were left. In 1914 Elken Drey succumbed, and on August 1, 1915, at his country home, "Hilltop," Mt. Washington, Maryland, Daniel Donnelly, the last survivor of that band of "Forty-niners," then a man of eighty-eight years, breathed his last, passing away honored and respected as business man, citizen and neighbor. There was a sentimental interest attached to the passing of this old pioneer, for he was a link in other chains that connected the far away past with the present. He saw the upbuilding of that great fleet of clipper ships which in their sailing qualities eclipsed the ships of all maritime nations of the world, and in their prime carried the ocean commerce between the ports of the old and new worlds, and he saw that fleet swept from the seas by the introduction and development of steam sea going vessels. He saw Baltimore grow from a small to a great city, and in that growth bore an important part. When that sterling financial institution, The Metropolitan Savings Bank, was organized, the name of Daniel Donnelly was on the list of incorporators. One by one those names were marked "died," with the date of death, until but one name remained, Daniel Donnelly.

There was a sentiment about the business Mr. Donnelly founded and conducted for so long which, in later years, was known as Daniel Donnelly & Son, brick manufacturers. Old methods gave way to the newer, even shapes and uses changing to meet modern conditions. After his retirement from business, in 1892, he did not cut asunder the ties which bound him to the scene of his business successes, but retained the keenest interest in all its movements.

A review of the life story of Daniel Donnelly reveals that he was born in Hagerstown, Maryland, in 1827, and that he attended school in Pennsylvania until thirteen years of age, when he started out from home to seek his fortune, Washington being his objective point. He had very little money, and the journey was by stage and canal boat. After a short time spent in Washington he came to Baltimore, where he passed through all the hardships of a country boy in a strange city, but he was built of true pioneer material and he won a foothold. Life was fairly opening before him when, after nine years in Baltimore, he decided, in 1849, to relinquish all he had gained and join in the quest for gold. Selling his possessions of any value, he sailed from the wharf at the foot of Broadway, in October, 1849, and after six months of seafaring, arrived at the Golden Gate opening into San Francisco bay. There was little then about the collection of small houses, tents and cabins to foreshadow the San Francisco of today, but rough as was the population, and crude as were the conditions, Mr. Donnelly there saw opportunity and instead of going on into the mining region, opened a small general store, his customers, the miners, who were outfitting for the mines, the transients, the Indians, and some of the permanent inhabitants. He made money and had accumulated a snug little fortune, when one day the settlement was destroyed by fire, and although he suffered loss in this disaster, Mr. Donnelly had sufficient means to open another store, this time at Weaverville, but not meeting with as great a degree of success as at San Francisco, he closed his store, then spent a few months in actual gold digging at the mines, finally returning to Baltimore in 1854 after an absence of five years.

From that year until his retirement, Mr. Donnelly was engaged in successful business as a brick manufacturer, founding the business later known as Daniel Donnelly & Son, and acquired other important business interests, ranking with the leading men of his city. He was a keen, sagacious business man, careful and deliberate, but each move was a step in advance, difficulties not deterring, but rather nerving him to their overcoming. He built upon the solid rock, integrity, and the spirit of fair dealing which actuated every transaction won him the unvarying confidence, esteem and personal regard of all who deal with him or knew him. He was member of the Hibernian Society of Baltimore and a devout member of the Roman Catholic church. He was one of the incorporators of the Old Town Bank of Baltimore and for many years one of the directors of that institution. In 1856, two years after Mr. Donnelly's return from California, he married Mary H. Milholland. For forty-five years they resided in their home, 1418 East Chase street, Baltimore. His children were his two sons, Francis X. and Edward A. Donnelly, who succeeded their father in business, and his two daughters, Mary Agnes, wife of Joseph A. Moore, and Genevieve, wife of Thomas G. Fink. He also left surviving him five grandchildren.

WILLIAM FRANCIS CLAUTICE

IN the passing of William F. Clautice, the last member of the well known firm, Brooks, Rogers & Company, wholesale shoe dealers, in 1913, Baltimore lost one of its most able merchants and highly esteemed citizens, one whose integrity and honor had never been challenged during a long and successful business career. He was a native son of Baltimore, and through his wife, Alice Sweeney, connected with one of those admirable characters of the long ago, Peter Sweeney, a wholesale pork packer, and an excellent citizen, born in Ireland, in 1820, a man of sturdy character and rugged honesty.

William F. Clautice was a son of George and Catherine (Fitzgerald) Clautice of Baltimore, and grandson of Peter and Mrs. (Adelsberger) Clautice. Catherine Fitzgerald was a daughter of John and Mary (Drake) Fitzgerald. She married George Clautice, May 23, 1826, and they are the parents of Emily Clautice, married John A. Irvin; Alexina Clautice, married James Donnelly; Catherine Victoria, married Thomas Hill; George; Mary Elizabeth; Edward, and William Francis Clautice. Mary (Drake) Fitzgerald, who married John Fitzgerald, June 2, 1795, died October 22, 1850, aged seventy-six years, daughter of Francis Drake, who came from Devonshire, England, and married about 1775, Ann Slowey, who came from Ireland. Francis and Ann (Slowey) Drake were the parents of: Mary, who married John Fitzgerald; Elizabeth, married in 1800; Thomas Fletcher; William Francis, married June 7, 1800, Catherine Leckler.

William Francis Clautice was born in Baltimore, November 24, 1838, died in his native city, July 12, 1913. He was educated in St. Mary's Seminary, Knapp's Institute, and Loyala College, beginning business life upon completing his studies at the last named institution. He began his business

career as office boy with Brooks, Rogers & Company, wholesale shoe dealers, a firm located in Baltimore, on Baltimore
street, between Howard and Eutaw streets, for seventy-seven
years. He proved his adaptability and business ability very
quickly, and being active, and in earnest, gained quick and
continued promotions, his record showing that during his long
and active business career he was never connected with but
that one firm. He at one time had charge of the firm's branch
office, at Zanesville, Ohio, which was discontinued during the
time of the Civil War, when Mr. Clautice returned to Baltimore. In 1867, he was admitted to a partnership, and for
many years his duty was as a salesman in the mountain towns
of Virginia, Maryland and West Virginia. He became well
known to the mountaineers, gained their respect and confidence to a remarkable degree, his visits being looked forward
to by the natives with even a greater degree of interest than
by the merchants to whom he sold goods. In time, Chauncey
Brooks the senior partner, was called to his reward, and later
David Rogers closed his earthly career, leaving Mr. Clautice,
the last of the trio, who had so long conducted the business.
The junior, then the senior and only owner, continued the
business until 1906, then the weight of years prevailed, and he
retired, spending the last seven years of his life in contented
ease. He was a member of the Church of the Immaculate
Conception, and at the time of his death, the oldest member
of that parish. He was also a member of the Young Catholic
Friends' Society.

Mr. Clautice married, November 17, 1870, Alice
Sweeney, daughter of Peter Sweeney (q. v.). They were
the parents of William S., married Elizabeth Kroeger; Edward C.; Emily Maude; Alice Jenkins; Mary Loretta;
George J., married Janet Harwood Wellmore; Francis Albert, married Jamima Disney, and Dr. Charles P. Clautice.

PETER SWEENEY

A YOUNG man of twenty when he left England, and came to Baltimore, Peter Sweeney, in the land of his adoption, proved his ability as business man, and in Baltimore took an active part in many movements designed to advance the interests of the city. Peter Sweeney was born in Ireland, in 1820, but when a lad, was taken by his parents to England, and there was educated. In 1840, he came to the United States, coming of course on a sailing vessel, the passage being unusually long and tedious. He landed in New York City, there entering the employ of Charles Taylor, a pork packer, from whom he acquired a thorough knowledge of the business. Having possession of the requisite capital after a few years in business, he left New York, and established a wholesale pork packing house in Baltimore, his plant located on then, Louisiana avenue, now, Lexington street, on the site now occupied by Jacob C. Schafer Company. He prospered abundantly, his business being a most extensive one, and he the leading man of his business in the city. He executed large contracts with the English Government, shipping large quantities of meat to England, and to the British Army in Russia.

During the Civil War Mr. Sweeney warmly sympathized with the South and aided the Confederate cause all in his power without actually taking part in the conflict. Just after the war was declared, one Sunday morning while walking along Fayette street on his way to the postoffice, Mr. Sweeney was pointed out as a "Southern Sympathizer." This was in the days of the "Bloody Tubs," the "Rip Raps," and the "Plug Uglies," therefore a crowd quickly gathered, ripe for anything. Bricks were thrown from the piles around the old Court House, then being torn down to make way for the new

City Hall, Mr. Sweeney taking refuge in Barnum's Hotel. As he was going up the steps one of the gang kicked at him, but Mr. Sweeney caught the rowdy's foot and sent him sprawling. In the hotel his injuries were given care by the ladies who knew him, and two hours later, he left the hotel to be immediately arrested upon a warrant sworn out by the man who had come to grief at his hands. Influential friends soon secured his release and the affair blew over. On one election day, when going to Perkins drug store on Howard street, near Franklin, to cast his vote, a ruffian sneaked behind to stab him, but a friend interfered with a knockout blow which gave Mr. Sweeney time to escape to the drug store. But these were war times and when the conflict was over all was well again and the wounds of war soon healed.

Mr. Sweeney was a Democrat in politics, and a devout Catholic, a member of the Cathedral congregation. He was a liberal contributor to church and charity, a founder of the Society of St. Vincent de Paul, member of the Young Catholic Friends' Society, the Hibernian Society, and a member of other organizations. He married Miss Chatterton, who died in England, they the parents of: Alice Sweeney, who married William Francis Clautice (*q. v.*). He later married Margaret Hart, May 4, 1853, to which union was born Mary Maud, and she married William K. Miller, November 13, 1883.

WILLIAM KEALHOFER

PRIOR to the Revolution came Theobald Kealhofer, from Alsace, France, to Hagerstown, Maryland, where a son was born, who was the father of William Kealhofer of Hagerstown, Maryland, whose death, November 13, 1916, extinguished the male line and left no one of the Kealhofer name in the section in which Theobald Kealhofer, the Alsatian, came. Henry Kealhofer, son of the founder, was born in Hagerstown, June 28, 1776, died there October 21, 1851. His son, George Kealhofer, was born in Hagerstown, June 4, 1803, died, November 28, 1866. A merchant in early life, George Kealhofer afterward became cashier of the Hagerstown branch of the Washington County Bank, located at Williamsport, Maryland. It is said of him that when the Confederates under General Imboden came to Hagerstown, they found that the cashier had so securely safeguarded the funds of the bank that but sixty-seven cents was found in the vaults. George Kealhofer married Mary E. Hanenkamp, daughter of Dr. Arnold Hanenkamp, a student under and a contemporary of the famous Dr. Rush of Philadelphia; they were the parents of William Kealhofer to whose memory this review of a valuable life is dedicated.

William Kealhofer was born in Hagerstown, Maryland, September 2, 1842, died in the city of his birth, November 13, 1916. His early and preparatory education was obtained in private schools and St. James College, his classical education at Franklin and Marshall College, whence he was graduated with the Bachelors degree, class of 1862. He then became a law student under the preceptorship of the eminent Judge Richard H. Alvey, and on March 22, 1865, was admitted a member of the Washington county bar. His connection with that bar was lifelong, and he rose to a commanding position, but his business interests were also large and his public service important. He was prominently mentioned as a successor to succeed to the judgeship made vacant by the death of Judge Edward Stake, but he would not allow his name to be presented. For a number of years Mr. Kealhofer was city attorney of Hagerstown, and in the early eighties assisted in drafting the city charter. In 1884, he was appointed school commissioner for Washington county, by Governor Frank Brown, and re-appointed by Governor Lloyd Loundes. In 1881, he was the Democratic candidate for the Maryland house of delegates from the Hagerstown district. This was the only excursion he ever made into political life as a candidate, but he was ever an ardent Democrat and deeply interested citizen. As a lawyer he always adhered closely to the best traditions of his profession, and his long and honorable career earned an endearing place among the men of his day whose lives added brilliant pages to the history of the Washington county bar.

Mr. Kealhofer was for many years a director of the Western Maryland Railroad, director of, and attorney for, the Hagerstown Bank until his death, declining the presidency; president of the Hagerstown Ice Company; trustee of the Washington County Free Library from its foundation, and was closely identified with the social and literary life of Hagerstown. He was one of the founders and charter members of the Concocheague Club, and for a long time its president. In religion he was a communicant of the Roman Catholic Church, strong in the faith and mindful of his religious obligations. He was not only learned in the law but was a wide reader, deep thinker, and a scholar of attainment. His knowledge of European history, its political and racial problems of his own, was a source of amazement, not only to his friends, but to the many learned foreigners he met in his frequent and extended tours of European travel. His conversational gifts were rarely equalled, pleasure and profit attending his listeners who were always closely attentive. He rarely made a statement on any subject, the truth of which he had not first verified, and never one of importance without knowing it was founded on incontrovertible facts. His disposition was lovable, his companionship charming, and all who knew him were well bound to him in real affection. Modest to an extreme, he seemed perfectly unconscious of his own merits and talents, but this but added to the charm of his personality. He was a good man in all that the term implies, and his memory will ever remain green.

Mr. Kealhofer married Elizabeth Lane Smith, who survives him, daughter of Dr. Josiah F. Smith, an eminent physician of Washington county, in the long ago.

HENRY WILLIAMS

A COURTLY Maryland gentleman of that type lovingly referred to as "the Old School," Henry Williams passed his mature years in the city of Baltimore, an honored resident and exceedingly prominent in the public life of city and State, and no less prominent as a business man. His lineage was ancient and honorable. He was the son of the Rev. Henry Williams, a clergyman of the Episcopal church, and Priscilla Elizabeth (Chew) Williams, a grand-daughter of the Rt. Rev. John Claggett, the first Protestant Episcopal bishop of Maryland, the further line of descent being traced to Thomas Claggett, who from 1640 until 1703 was one of the honored men of Calvert county, Maryland. He was county commissioner in 1680, coroner in 1683, and in the same year was commissioned a captain of militia. His grandson, Samuel Claggett, son of Richard and Elizabeth (Dorsey) Claggett, born 1718, died 1756, was rector of Christ Church, Calvert county, Maryland, and of St. Paul's Parish, Prince Georges county, and William and Mary Parish, Charles county, Maryland. He married Elizabeth Gantt. His son, Thomas John Claggett, born 1743, died 1816, was rector of St. James, Anne Arundel county, and All Saints, Calvert county, Maryland, 1769-76, and was consecrated the first bishop of the Protestant Episcopal church in Maryland in 1791. He was chaplain to the first Congress that met in the capitol in Washington and opened the first meeting of the Senate there with prayer. He married Mary Gantt. His daughter, Priscilla Elizabeth Claggett, born 1778, married Colonel John Hamilton Chew and was grandmother to Henry Williams. Their daughter, Priscilla Chew, married the Rev. Henry Williams. Their son was Henry Williams, to whose memory this tribute of appreciation is dedicated.

Henry Williams was also descended on the maternal side from Colonel John Chew, born 1590, died 1668. Colonel John Chew was a member of the House of Burgesses of Virginia from Hog Island, Virginia, 1623-24, 1629; from York county, Virginia, 1642-44; Justice, York county, 1634-52; removed to Maryland about 1653. His son, Samuel Chew, born 1634, died 1677. He was burgess for Anne Arundel county, Maryland, in 1661; member of the Council and justice of Provincial Court, 1669-77; colonel of Anne Arundel county militia in 1675. Colonel Chew married Anne Ayers, daughter of William Ayers, of Nansemond county, Virginia. His son, Samuel (2) Chew, born 1660, died 1718. He was commissioner of the peace for Anne Arundel county, Maryland, in 1683. He married (first) Anne ——, and (second) June 29, 1704, Mrs. Eliza Coale. His son, John Chew, born April 8, 1687, married Eliza Harrison, 1708. His son, Samuel (3) Chew, died in London, England, in 1749. He married Sarah Locke, born 1721, died February 1, 1791. His son, Samuel (4) Chew, born 1737, died 1790. He was commissioner of the peace for Calvert county, Maryland, 1765-73; a member of the Revolutionary Convention of 1775, and first lieutenant, Third Battalion Flying Camp, June to December of that year; captain, Third Maryland Regiment, December 10, 1776; resigned February, 1777. Captain Chew married (first) Sarah Weems, and (second) Priscilla Claggett, daughter of Rev. Samuel and Elizabeth (Gantt) Claggett, a descendant of Colonel Edward Claggett, of Canterbury, England, who married Margaret Adams, daughter of Sir Thomas Adams. His son, Colonel John Hamilton Chew, born September 14, 1771, died March 22, 1830. He married his cousin, Priscilla Elizabeth Claggett, born 1778, died September 20, 1843, daughter of Rt. Rev. Thomas J. Claggett, D.D., and Mary Gantt, his wife. Thomas J. Claggett was first bishop of Maryland and

first bishop of the Protestant Episcopal church consecrated
in the United States. His daughter, Priscilla Chew, born July
25, 1809, died July 6, 1881; married, October 11, 1839, Rev.
Henry Williams, born January 25, 1812, died April 8, 1852.
Rev. Henry Williams was son of Philip and Elizabeth Williams, of South Carolina.

Henry Williams, son of Rev. Henry and Priscilla
(Chew) Williams, was born at the rectory of All Saints
Church, Upper Calvert county, Maryland, October 9, 1840,
died in Baltimore, Maryland, March 20, 1916. The rectory
was his boyhood home and until thirteen years of age he
studied in private schools near by and under private tutors
who came to the rectory for his instruction. In 1854 he was
sent to Baltimore for better educational advantage, entering
the Toppings' private school, whence he was graduated. During the years he was a student in Baltimore he was a guest
at the home of his uncle, Dr. Samuel Chew. After graduation he returned home and pursued a course of law study, and
in 1860 finished his preparation under the direction of Charles
J. M. Gwinn, one of the ablest lawyers of Baltimore. In 1861
he was admitted to the Maryland bar and began practice at
Prince Frederick, Calvert county, Maryland, in association
with James T. Briscoe. He soon afterward located in Baltimore, his residence until death. In addition to his law practice, Mr. Williams became active and prominent in business
and public life. For thirty years he was executive head of
the Weems line of steamers running from Baltimore to Chesapeake bay and Virginia points. The Weems line, which was
founded in 1817, was sold to the Pennsylvania Railroad Company and later Mr. Williams was interested in the Baltimore
& Carolina Steamship Company, founded at an earlier period
by the sons. During the latter years of his life his chief business connections were as a member of the board of directors of

the National Bank of Commerce, the Colonial Trust Company and the Central Savings Bank. The only director of the National Bank of Commerce whose term of service on the board exceeded that of Henry Williams was Eugene Levering, whose service yet continues.

From the beginning of his residence in Baltimore, Mr. Williams was genuinely interested in the city government and one of the loyal, devoted citizens who could be relied on to support measures intended to benefit the public while advancing city interests. He was a Democrat in politics, and in 1864 was elected to the Maryland House of Delegates by a practically unanimous vote of the district, but one vote being recorded against him and that in all probability his own. In 1866 he took active part in the legislation which followed the Civil War, and in 1872 and 1874 was state senator. In 1895 he was the candidate of his party for mayor, but in that year the entire city ticket went down in defeat. In 1897 he was again a candidate, but failed of an election. In 1901 he was elected president of the Second Branch of City Council and largely through his personal work and interest, the Fuller bid for the city holdings of Western Maryland Railway stock was accepted. In 1903 he was appointed collector of taxes by Mayor McLane, serving the city in that capacity for four years, winning the approbation of the officials and business men of the city and the esteem of the employees of the tax department, who, on his retirement, expressed that esteem by presenting him with a silver platter and carving set.

In 1907 his name was before the Democratic State Convention for the Gubernatorial nomination, and up to the very day the convention met he had been virtually accepted as the most available man for the honor and was the choice of a majority of the delegates who assembled in the hall prepared to cast their ballots for him. But over night the powers that rule selected another and the nomination went to Austin L. Crothers, of Cecil county, who was elected.

True to the tenets of the faith of his fathers, he was all his life a devoted churchman, serving the Episcopal church by faith and works. He was a vestryman of St. Peter's Church, president of the Churchman Club for thirty years. Tall in stature, of dignified yet kindly democratic bearing and nature, he was one of the most distinguished men in appearance, and his deeds and his character were in proportion with the physical man. He was vice-president of the Southern Maryland Society.

Mr. Williams married, June 11, 1868, Georgeanna Weems. Their children are Mason L. W.; Henry, Jr.; George Weems; John H. C.; Elizabeth Chew, and Matilda Weems Williams. Absolutely devoted to his family, Mr. Williams saw his sons grow to prominence as business and professional men, and rejoiced that in them his name and virtues were perpetuated. Mrs. Williams continues her residence at the family mansion, "Woodcliffe," on Thirty-ninth street, near University parkway, Baltimore.

James Preston

JAMES PRESTON

SIXTY-SIX were the years of the life of James Preston of Baltimore, Maryland, and of these, forty-two were spent in association with the dry goods firm, John A. Homer & Company, of which he was a member until his retirement four years prior to his death in 1917. He began at the bottom of the ladder and through sheer ability won his way to the top. He was one of the oldest members of the Merchants and Manufacturers Association, was one of the oldest directors of the National Western Bank, and in all his long and useful life there was no duty refused or left unperformed. He met every demand of good citizenship but had no taste or desire for public position, and never held a political office. He was of Pennsylvania birth, but a descendant of the Preston family, one of the oldest in Maryland, springing from Thomas Preston, born in 1650, died in 1710. Prestons were identified with Harford county, Maryland, from its earliest settlement, but James Preston's father, also James Preston, located in Pennsylvania, at Seven Valley, where he died March 30, 1852, aged forty-one years. James Preston, Sr., was a son of John and Rebecca Preston, and was married May 25, 1847, in old St. Paul's Church, Baltimore, by Rev. Dr. Wyatt, to E. Adelaide Jenkins, born November 22, 1821, died June 25, 1908, daughter of Robert Jenkins, owner of Locust Vale Farm, Baltimore, Maryland, and his wife Jane Dart. Robert Jenkins and Jane Dart were married May 30, 1820. He died April 28, 1879, and his wife, Jane, September 7, 1864.

James Preston, son of James and E. Adelaide (Jenkins) Preston, was born at Seven Valley, Pennsylvania, April 21, 1851, died at his home, No. 2210 Eutaw Place, Baltimore, Maryland, November 10, 1917. He came to Baltimore in early youth, and after completing his studies in the public schools and in City College, Baltimore, he entered the employ of John A. Homer & Company, dry goods and notions. He evidenced unusual aptitude for business, was rapidly advanced, and soon admitted to a partnership. He continued a member of the firm until 1913, then attempted to withdraw, but his partners persuaded him to reconsider. Six months later, however, he announced his positive withdrawal, and for the remaining four years of his life he lived practically retired from business cares, although he was interested in real estate operations and other investment activities. He was a man of excellent business, sound in judgment, progressive in method, upright in all his dealings, careful always to wrong no man by word or deed.

Early in Mr. Preston's business career he became a member of the Merchants and Manufacturers Association of Baltimore, and was ever one of the most active workers and useful members of the Association, only surrendering his position as chairman of the Publicity Committee, and member of the Executive Board a few weeks prior to his passing away. He was very earnest in his association work and took great pride in its accomplishments. He was president of the Merchants Hotel Company, from the time of its organization, and there was no member of the board of directors of the Western National Bank of Baltimore, who was his senior in point of years of service. He was also a member of the Baltimore Credit Men's Association for more than twenty years, a charter member of the Fidelity and Deposit Company, which he also aided to organize, and was a member of the Atlantic Deeper Waterways Association.

A meeting of the Merchants and Manufacturers Association was called the day of Mr. Preston's death at which the following resolutions were passed:

It is with feelings of regret that the Executive Committee of the

Merchants' and Manufacturers' Association meets today to honor the memory of their long-time associate and former treasurer, James Preston. Mr. Preston appreciating the value of the Association in advancing the business interests of our city became an important factor in its activities, serving for years as treasurer, member of the Executive Board and chairman of one of our most important committees, which positions he held at the time of his death. There was no duty required of him to which he did not respond promptly, always giving much of his time and energy to the accomplishment of good results. He was an active and public spirited citizen. Sorrowfully we bid him farewell, but his memory will linger a long time with us.

After the great fire the Merchants Hotel Company was formed, which built the New Howard Hotel, and of this company he was president. He was a member of Kedron Lodge, Free and Accepted Masons; Baltimore Chapter, Royal Arch Masons; Beauseant Commandery, Knights Templar; and in Scottish Rite Masonry held the degrees of Baltimore Consistory. He was also a Noble of Boumi Temple, Nobles of the Mystic Shrine. In religious faith he was a member of the Methodist Episcopal church, affiliated with the Madison avenue congregation. His funeral was attended by members of the various organizations with which he was identified, and after the religious services had been conducted by Rev. R. J. Wyckoff, pastor of Madison Avenue Methodist Episcopal Church, the beautiful burial service of the Knights Templar ritual was rendered by the Templars of Beauseant Commandery. The honorary pall-bearers were: Mayor Preston, Charles E. Falconer, William C. Rouse, Charles E. Rieman, Captain Samuel D. Buck, Jacob Epstein, James M. Easter, Frederick H. Gottlieb, Franklin P. Cator, Samuel E. Reinhard, Judge Walter I. Dawkins and Frank N. Hoen. The burial was in Druid Ridge cemetery.

Mr. Preston married, in 1874, Emma L. Meakin, daughter of Samuel and Mary Irene (Whitely) Meakin, who survives him with one son, James Oscar Preston, born December 23, 1879.

ROLAND BRIDENDALL HARVEY

ROLAND B. HARVEY was born in Baltimore county, Maryland, October 12, 1870, son of William Pinkney and Virginia (Jordan) Harvey. He was educated in private schools in the United States until he was sent abroad for study and travel. Over three years were spent in Switzerland, France and Germany with tutors, special attention being given to languages. After his return home he entered Johns Hopkins University, whence he was graduated Bachelor of Arts, class of 1895; University of Maryland, Bachelor of Laws, 1896. He was admitted to the Baltimore bar in 1896, and to the bar of New York in 1897. He practiced law in the office of Elihu Root during the years 1897-99, then returned to Baltimore, and was made assistant State's attorney, an office he held three years, 1904-07. He made a strong record for efficiency and was urged to continue in politics, but declined further honors, and resigned the office in 1907, and in 1909 after passing the examinations, he entered the diplomatic service. During this career he was considered one of the best qualified men in that service, and his efforts attracted much favorable comment.

Mr. Harvey's first appointment was in July, 1909, when he was appointed to Roumania, and consul-general to the Balkan States, to act as charge d'affairs on arrival in Roumania. This he did for several months, later being made charge d'affairs to Bulgaria. The special pleasure he found in his two years' work in the Balkans was the meeting of prominent diplomats sent by European countries to guard their Balkan interests. Although a staunch American and firm believer in his own country, Mr. Harvey had a keen and unprejudiced interest in the world at large. His unusual knowledge of the history of nations and their rulers aided him in coming very near to those he met, and added greatly to the pleasure and benefits of his career. After more than two years in the Balkan States, he received in February, 1912, his appointment as Secretary of Legation to Peru. It was expected his knowledge of international law would be valuable in the law cases of long standing in that country. On his arrival at Callao, May 13, 1912, he was, however, greeted with the cable order from the Department of State, "Proceed to Chili without delay. In charge on arrival," and on May 13, 1912, he arrived at his post, for the second time "charge" on arrival. His stay in Chili, from May 13, 1912, to February 25, 1914, was full of varied events of unusual interest. Among the most noted while Mr. Harvey was in charge, were the great receptions tendered to former President Roosevelt on his tour of South America, and the visit of Hon. Robert Bacon, representing the Carnegie Peace Commission. The opportunity also to visit Peru long enough to make the ascent of that world wonder of switch-back engineering, the Auroya railroad, the work of an American engineer; and later the tour of Chili down its coast to the Straits of Magellan; on to Punta Arenas, the most southern city in the world; on through the Straits to the Falkland Islands, that rocky bit of the British Empire, and then up the east coast of South America to Buenos Aires, crossing the great range of the snow-capped Andes back to Chili.

When his appointment to Berlin as Second Secretary of Embassy came it was received with mixed feelings, his comment being: "Germany is a history-making country"—and he loved work. With keen interest in the new duties before him, he sailed for Liverpool, February 26, 1914. Going via Liverpool he arrived in Berlin, March 29, 1914, a post full of interest, but almost from arrival Mr. Harvey thought clouds of war were hanging low. How soon the storm would break he realized when, at Kiel to see the great regatta, and expecting to be present at the reception given by Prince Henry, news came of the murder of the Archduke Ferdinand. At once all gaiety stopped, the Kaiser left Kiel, as did all the German notables. Excitement ran high until the evening of July 28, when word was received that war had been declared. Immediately the work of the United States Embassy increased tenfold, the thousands of Americans making a mad rush to get out of Germany. Mr. Harvey had entire charge of the passports, and his strength and sympathy were taxed to the limit. Not in good health, the strain proved too much and he was obliged to seek rest for a short time at Hamburg, Bavaria.

Returning to Berlin with renewed strength and energy, Mr. Harvey went once more into the rush of his post, the absence of Counselor Grew on a short leave, causing him to assume much additional labor. While Mr. Grew was absent in the United States, the following order was received from the State department in Washington: "Harvey transferred Buenos Aires in charge indefinitely." The promotion to the most important post in South America and to be "charge" on arrival was so exactly to his liking and so suited to his capabilities that Mr. Harvey was delighted. He hoped to spend only two weeks in the United States, but his health demanded a longer leave, and two months were granted. At its end he realized he was not in condition to be "charge indefinitely" of so important an embassy, and decided to spend one year devoted to his health, expecting by so doing he would be fit for any post. His hopes seemed to be realized until July, 1917, when he had a bad fall and sustained a fracture of the hip. The long operation made necessary, with his already depleted condition, made his recovery almost impossible, and on November 14, 1917, his life passed away, one so full of promise and high ambitions, a mind clear and full of interest in his country to the very last. His approachable manner, lovable disposition, and high sense of duty gained for him the affections as well as the esteem of all with whom he came in contact. In his official capacity he was ever ready to lend a helping hand to those of his countrymen who found themselves in difficulties in foreign lands, often going beyond the official requirements to do so. Many there are to-day of these who will have a lasting sense of obligation to the kind-hearted young diplomat, who smoothed things out for them, setting aside in his capable way the difficulties that beset them when the great war broke out, and helped them to reach the frontier, and neutral lands, in ease, comfort and security. But this was his way, and he took no credit to himself for the thousands of acts of kindness and courtesy that characterized both his official and social life.

DAVID MARION NEWBOLD

AT the age of seventy-three, prominent in the business and financial life of two cities, David Marion Newbold closed a long and honorable career, his business life covering a period of half a century. He was a direct descendant of that Thomas Newbold who came to this country, from Derbyshire, England, prior to 1665, and settled in Somerset, Maryland. This is abundantly proven by the following record in the Annapolis Records (Rent Rolls of Somerset County, Maryland, Book 1-61): August 26, 1665, "Acquintico" surveyed by George Watson, on the north side of Pocomoke River, then in possession of Mr. Thomas Newbold, to Samuel Wilson, February 2, 1667; October 20, 1665, three hundred acres surveyed by Jenkins Price for Thomas Newbold of Pocomoke. The records also show that he received in 1678 a grant of land of four hundred and fifty acres for transporting Adriana, his wife, two children, Murphy and Sarah Newbold, and five servants. Rent Rolls and Deed Books of Somerset county show several large tracts of land taken up by Thomas Newbold; "Acquintico" surveyed August 26, 1665, for George Watson on north of Pocomoke River in possession of Thomas Newbold; 1678, "Friendship" and "Content," on north side of Pocomoke River; 1684, "Bashan" surveyed for Thomas Newbold of Pocomoke River. Deed Book B. L. (folio 404) Princess Anne county: November 8, 1696, Thomas Newbold and Jane, his wife (second wife) sell two tracts of land "London's Adventure" and "Blackridge" to Samuel Handy.

Thomas Newbold was evidently a man of substance. The fact that he was financially able to transport a considerable retinue of "servants" and had very large land holdings show this. He was also a gentleman with rank of esquire, and bore arms as is shown by a "gold seal ring" he left in his will to his

W. M. Newbold

son Thomas. He took a very prominent part in the affairs of
Somerset county, both civil and military, from 1678 to 1713.
He was a "Member of the Councill," 1684-89; commissioned
"Lieutenant of Horse," Colonial Militia, Somerset county,
1689; one of the "Gentlemen Justices for Tryall of Cases,"
1679; "Thomas Newbold, Justice," 1694-97 and "Vestryman
of Coventry Parish."

Thomas Newbold married twice. His first wife was
Adriana; his second wife, Jane. Children by first wife:
Murphy; Thomas, married a Joyce; Sarah, married Thomas
Hearne; William, died about 1720. Children by second wife:
Francis, see forward; John, married (first) Rachel, (second)
Naomi. Thomas Newbold died in 1713.

His will, probated in 1713, is as follows:

"I, Thomas Newbold, Gentleman, weak and infirm of
body but sound in mind. To eldest son, Thomas, 2500 acres
of land; 'Acquintico,' 'Friendship' and 'Gift.' Second son,
William, 2500 acres of 'Acquintico.' To Thomas, gold seal
ring, waistcoat, East India Chest, feather bed, hay horse, with
pistols and holsters and one gun. To son, William, silver
Tobacco box, bed and household furniture and one gun and
a bay mare. To daughter, Sarah, wife of Thomas Hearne,
three hundred acres of 'Bashan.' To youngest son, Francis, 500
acres of Tract called 'Bashan.' Wife, Jane, Executrix.

THOMAS NEWBOLD.

June 5th, 1713."

As Murphy Newbold is not mentioned in his father's
will, it is supposed that he died young.

Francis Newbold, son of Thomas Newbold, of Pocomoke River, Somerset county, Province of Maryland, and
his second wife, Jane, was born about 1698. He inherited

with his brother, John, a large tract of land called "Bashan," or "Bushan," which was surveyed for Thomas Newbold in 1684 by George Layfield in Somerset county, Maryland, but by removal of boundary line became situated in Sussex county, Delaware. Francis Newbold died in 1777.

Francis Newbold and his wife Sarah had issue: Francis, Jr., see forward; Thomas; John, married Rachel Newbold, his cousin.

Francis Newbold, Jr., son of Francis and Sarah Newbold, married, about 1775, Sarah Owens, daughter of David Owens. The Owens were among the early settlers of Somerset county, Maryland, and were closely associated with the Colonial history of the Province. Thomas Owens, one of the progenitors of the family, took up land prior to 1673. His son, William Owens, married Mary ——, and was prominent in the affairs of Somerset county, being a member of the "Providence Councill," and a Provincial Commissioner in 1675. He received grants of land from the Lord Proprietary, called "Owen's Venture," and "Morgan's Venture." By his wife, Anna, he had four children: William, John, Robert and Somerville. His son, William Owens, who died in 1743, had issue by his wife, Sarah: William, David, Robert, Samuel and four daughters. His second son, David Owens, inherited from him "Morgan's Venture," in 1775, and was the father of Sarah Owens, who married Francis Newbold, Jr. Francis Newbold, Jr., died in 1776, leaving one son, David.

David Newbold, son of Francis, Jr., and Sarah (Owens) Newbold, was born in 1776, in Sussex county, Delaware, and died in 1852. He removed in 1803 to Missouri, and, in 1810, married Sophia Robinson, born in Fredericksburg, Virginia, 1787. Children: Theophilus, David Owens, John, Wesley, Newton, James Francis, see forward.

James Francis Newbold, son of David and Sophia

(Robinson) Newbold, was born, October 16, 1816, in Scott county, Kentucky, and died June 3, 1902, in Baltimore. Being possessed of an adventurous spirit in his younger days he joined that celebrated band, known as the "Forty-Niners," and twice made the long and tedious journey, so full of danger at that time, to California. His first trip, in 1849, was across the plains; again in 1851 he went back to the gold fields by the way of Panama, being one of the first to go by that route. In a short time he amassed a considerable competence and returned East, settling in Baltimore, where he continued to reside until his death. There he founded, in 1852, the well known wholesale glass concern of Newbold & Sons, the other partners being David M. Newbold and James Francis Newbold, Jr. This business had a long and successful career of more than fifty years, and only terminated with the death of his son, James Francis Newbold, Jr., February, 1902, when the firm closed its doors permanently.

In politics James Francis Newbold was a Democrat. He took considerable interest in local politics, serving several terms in both branches of the City Council. He was a good Christian and a devout member of the Bethany Independent Methodist Church of which he was one of the founders.

James Francis Newbold married, March 18, 1841, Mary Elizabeth Bowen, born 1823, died March 10, 1849, daughter of Richard and Maria (McGregor) Bowen, of Harford county, Maryland. Children: Elizabeth Ann; James Francis; David Marion, subject of this sketch.

David Marion Newbold, of the sixth American generation, son of James Francis and Mary Elizabeth (Bowen) Newbold, was born in Boonesville, Missouri, June 4, 1843, died in the city of Baltimore, at his home in Eutaw Place, April 22, 1917. After his years of educational preparation had ended, he entered business life in Baltimore, becoming a member of the firm of Newbold & Sons, a famed business house, dealing in wholesale glassware and crockery. He continued an integral part of that firm until its dissolution, after a successful career covering half a century, and henceforth David Newbold confined his activity to real estate and public utilities. His connection with real estate resulted in his becoming known as one of the largest operators of the city, a man whose vision was broad, and judgment sound. With the development of the city and the increasing need of better transportation system, city and inter-city, Mr. Newbold became interested in that great problem which confronts all cities; took an active part in the building of the electric lines between Baltimore and Washington; acquired large traction interests in Washington; was president of the City and Suburban and of the Eckington and Belt Line street railway companies of that city; also a member of the Elkins-Widener Syndicate of Philadelphia, whose operations extended to many cities. He was for a time largely interested in the American Street Lighting Company, of which his sons, Eugene Saunders Newbold, of Philadelphia, is president, and David M. Newbold, Jr., vice-president and general counsel.

A Republican in politics, Mr. Newbold took an active interest in city and national affairs, and as the candidate of his party, ran for Congress from the Third Maryland district. During his more active years he was a member of the leading clubs and fraternal organizations, but in his latter years he withdrew from all but the Park Place, Shawbridge Church, there continuing an active member. He was highly regarded by those who were acquainted with the strength of his ability as a business man and executive, and that respect he never forfeited.

Mr. Newbold married, in November, 1865, Eliza Boyd,

daughter of William A. Boyd, a prominent and successful wholesale tobacco merchant in Baltimore before the Civil War. They were the parents of three sons, James Boyd Newbold, David Marion Newbold, Jr., and Eugene Saunders Newbold.

CHARLES E. WAYS

THE death of Charles E. Ways, the Nestor of American railway officials, removed from the scene of human action one of the historic landmarks of the nation. To the younger generation it seems incredible that there was living in their midst, so recently as 1914, the man who opened the first telegraph office in the capital of our nation and who prior to that was operator at Harper's Ferry during the John Brown raid. But those were some of the interesting facts in Mr. Ways' life and he was not a boy when he linked his career with those most dramatic events. From 1855 until about six months before his death he was continuously in the employ of the Baltimore & Ohio Railroad Company, rose to important position, and was one of the oldest if not the oldest railroad official in the United States in point of years of service, witnessing and aiding in the development of the Baltimore & Ohio from a short single track line to a great modern railroad system. During his last years he received from the management, in appreciation of his long service, a perpetual pass made of silver in card form, designed and authorized by President Williard and Vice-President Randolph, the only one of its kind ever issued by the road. He held personal as well as business relations with former presidents of the Baltimore & Ohio—John W. Garrett, Samuel Spencer and John K. Cowan. The old veteran was a thorough railroad man and loved his work; in fact, when obliged to retire from active service, the great interest of his life departed, and he only survived his retirement six months. He was a boy of thirteen when he entered telegraph employ as a messenger boy, a year older when he came to the Baltimore & Ohio Company, a man of seventy-five when he retired as assistant general freight traffic manager. His railroad career linked him with some of the 'dramatic events of the anti-Civil War period. He was at Harper's Ferry when John Brown made his famous but insane raid into Virginia, and when troops, under Robert E. Lee, then a colonel in the United States army, stormed the old armory and captured the Abolition leader, Mr. Ways sent the message to the world announcing that event. When in 1861 it was necessary for the protection of President Lincoln on his journey from Springfield, Illinois, to Washington, D. C., that a telegraph office be opened in Washington, Mr. Ways was selected to open and operate it, the first in the city, his choice for the honor testifying to the confidence reposed in his ability, loyalty and faithfulness.

Charles E. Ways was born in 1839, died January 2, 1914. His parents lived in Frederick during his boyhood and there he went to school, and at the age of thirteen became messenger boy in the commercial telegraph office. He picked up a knowledge of telegraphy at the same time and when shortly afterward his parents moved to Ellicott City he was so expert that he took the place of the regular operator for a month, while he was away on a vacation, and received the regular salary. That was his first introduction to railroad telegraphic work and the beginning of his sixty years connection with the Baltimore & Ohio. Shortly after the regular operator returned to his duties, a vacancy occurred at Frederick Junction, and the young operator, then fifteen years of age, was offered the place. His mother objected to his leaving home on account of his youth, but finally gave way, and the position was accepted. The little office and bedroom at a lonely junction told on the boy's nerves and his first night there was a sleepless one. In the morning his feelings were not soothed by learning that a man had died of cholera in the bed the morning before he occupied it at night. But he stuck to his post and performed his duty well, as he stuck to every post and performed every duty required of him until he laid down for final rest. From Frederick Junction he was sent to Martinsburg. In 1859 he was made payroll clerk at Cumberland; in 1861 was placed in charge and opened the first telegraph office in Washington; in 1863 was made chief telegraph operator of the Baltimore & Ohio, with headquarters at Baltimore; in 1867 was promoted general agent at Hagerstown; was promoted division freight agent in 1878; assistant general freight agent in 1888. He was appointed in 1897 to the position he held until his retirement six months prior to his death, assistant general freight traffic manager. This record of service brought him into intimate relation with two of the important departments of the Baltimore & Ohio—telegraph and freight. Beginning at the bottom, he thoroughly mastered every detail and developed quick decision, sound judgment, wisdom, initiative and ready resource. The way of the Baltimore & Ohio official was not a smooth, easy one in the early years of his connection, but he overcame every discouraging circumstance and became one of the men whom the management of the road trusted implicitly with weighty responsibilities and were never at fault in so doing.

Fortunately Mr. Ways was induced to write a very complete account of his early experiences and so valuable is the story from both a historical and human interest view that it is here reproduced in part:

I was operator at Martinsburg, West Virginia, at the time John Brown captured the Government armory at Harper's Ferry. Having nothing to do after the wires were cut I went with the Martinsburg militia to the scene of action. The second day after the arrival there, I was instructed to open an office, which I did in a one-story brick building located alongside the Winchester Branch track and directly facing the engine house, or fort as it was called, in which Brown and his men were barricaded.

My selection of a location for the instrument table was in the middle of the room, and the door being open all the time, I had a full view of the

Brown fort, and it appears he had a full view of me and my instruments, for it was not more than twenty mnutes after I had gotten to work before two Sharp's rifle balls in quick succession passed within six inches of my head and buried themselves in the wall back of me. I can recall very vividly the whistle of the balls as they passed my head, and it did not take me very long to move my instruments to a safe place. Brown had portholes on all sides of the building and his men shot anything that came in sight.

It was this recklessness that caused the death of old Mr. Beckham, the agent at Harper's Ferry at that time. He walked out of his office up the platform and put his head out to look at the fort when a Sharp's rifle ball put an end to his life in a moment. He was a well beloved old gentleman and his death caused much greater ill-feeling toward Brown and his men. From a point on the platform near where Mr. Beckham was killed I witnessed the storming of the fort by the United States troops commanded by General Robert E. Lee, then a colonel, and the capture of Brown after he and his men had fired half a dozen volleys through the doors of the fort into the troops, only one of them was killed, as I recall it, though I saw several fall wounded and carried away. The old man looked the picture of misery as he was dragged out to a spot under the Star-Spangled Banner which floated from a pole in the middle of the armory yard.

I witnessed a curious incident in connection with the John Brown raid. He had imprisoned some of the citizens of Harper's Ferry in the western part of the engine house, and among them was "Daddy Malloy," a simple-minded native of Harper's Ferry, who had been run over by trains and had fallen off the bridge wall into the Potomac without being hurt, besides having other narrow escapes at various times. He saw an opportunity to get out of one of the windows and escape, which he took advantage of. That side of the engine house was in full view of the steep road or street that led up to Bolivar, and the side of the road toward the engine house was lined with armed militia and citizens, all looking toward the engine house. All of them saw Malloy getting out of the window and mistaking him for one of Brown's men, probably three hundred shots were fired at him without one of them taking effect. This would seem to verify the saying that it takes half a ton of lead to kill one soldier in battle.

I opened the first telegraph office at Washington, D. C., which was for the protection of Mr. Lincoln's train when he was brought to Washington to be inaugurated. My instruments were set up in a watchman's house about one hundred yards outside the shed of the old depot. This was one of the precautions taken by the Baltimore & Ohio Company to insure safety to the train on account of the rumors that it would be attacked.

When the Civil War broke out I was at Harper's Ferry and witnessed the massing of the Confederate soldiers getting ready to march up the valley. When the Confederate flag was hoisted, to the tune of "Dixie" on the same flagpole from which had waved the Star-Spangled Banner at John Brown's capture, the enthusiasm was beyond description. After the Confederates abandoned the armory building and moved up the Valley, the United States troops occupied the place for a time, but later abandoned it and blew up all the armory buildings.

Having had notice of this movement I was detailed to go with the general supervisor of trains to open an office in his car at Sandy Hook, if necessary. He went over to Harper's Ferry and left me alone in the car. At about eight o'clock at night I was startled by a terrific noise of explosions like thousands of cartridges, and looking in the direction of Harper's Ferry I saw the light from the burning buildings. Just then a man whom I did not know opened the door and calling me by name, said: "If you attempt to cut the wires here you will be killed." With the delivery of that pleasant message he disappeared. Perhaps it is because I did not have to cut the wires that I am enabled to write this.

While at Martinsburg, West Virginia, during the Civil War, the railroad officials had advance notice from Winchester of Banks' retreat from the Valley and instructions were given to remove all the engines and equipment to Cumberland. One engine was held on the track in front of my office for the master mechanic, supervisor of engines and myself to go on as soon as everything had been started away, which had been accomplished just as the troops began coming into town. I notified Camden Station and the other offices, disconnecting my instruments; carrying them away with me, and started the engine for Hancock, where we were to cross the Potomac river, the engine going to Cumberland. We went from Hancock to Hagerstown in a wagon, and the same night went to Williamsport and saw Banks' army retreating across the Potomac river into Maryland.

Mr. Ways was president of the Baltimore & Ohio Relief Association; a member of the Masonic order, the Independent Order of Odd Fellows; the Royal Arcanum and the Maryland Club, being one of the oldest members of the last named. He was a man of warm human sympathies and the number of his friends was "legion."

He married Elizabeth Virginia, daughter of Dr. Frederick Byer, of Leitersburg, who bore him two sons and a daughter: Thomas F. Ways; Max Ways, well known as one of the Democratic leaders in Baltimore; and Margaret E. Ways.

JULIEN P. FRIEZ

PROBABLY no single word so well classifies Mr. Friez as the title "Scientist," but that word indicates only the scope of his wondrous life of activity. He was a skilled worker in metals; an inventor; a maker of fine instruments used in telegraphy and meteorology; maker of the first telegraph key and sounder used by the Western Electric Company; spun the first watch case made in this country; made the first musical telephone while associated with Professor Gray; aided in perfecting the Mergenthaler typesetting machine, and devoted the last sixteen years of his life wholly to the science of meteorology, perfecting during that period countless numbers of recording instruments, the appliances and apparatus made at his Belfort plant, now being in use by the United States government, municipal governments, colleges and universities all over this and every country of the world. He was not a scientist of the type which investigates only, but his studies seemed but the preliminary work to the perfecting of scientific instruments or apparatus. He was of that exceptional type of scientist who, after investigation, research and study of a subject, could discern just what instruments would be necessary to give practical value to his discoveries, then evolve the instrument from his inventive brain, then produce it in metal worked by his own hands or under his supervision. So as scientist, inventor and mechanician his work was so interwoven that while his fame might safely rest upon either title, in combination they form a record of achievement marvelous in scope and value.

Julien P. Friez was born at Grandvillars, near Belfort, France, August 16, 1851, and died at his home, "Belfort," Central avenue and Baltimore street, Baltimore, Maryland, March 9, 1916. He was the son of Joseph Friez, born December 13, 1818, died February 21, 1891, and his wife, Marguerite (Roy) Friez, daughter of Francis Roy, of the house-

Julien P. Friez.

hold of Louis XVI., of France, and a grandson of Jean Jacques and Marie (Moine) Friez. Joseph Friez (father) was for many years a manager in a manufacturing establishment at Grandvillars, or near there.

Julien P. Friez obtained his early education under the private teaching of Professor Rose, in the village of Geromany, France. At an early age he came to the United States, locating in New York State, entered the New York University, pursuing courses there until graduation. For a time thereafter he taught French, during his residence in New York State, and when about sixteen years of age went west, locating in Ottawa, Illinois, the residence of some of his relatives. In 1868 he became an apprentice under Robert Henning, a machinist and maker of telegraph instruments, located in Ottawa. There he acquired his expert mechanical skill, and developed the inventive genius hitherto laying dormant. He became foreman of the Henning factory, and was one of the pioneers in the work of perfecting the telegraph. This establishment was the first in the west to become interested in the development of the telegraph, and during his apprenticeship Mr. Friez aided in completing the first telegraph line in the west, a line about ten miles in length, connecting the factory and shops with the residence of Mr. Henning. During his four years residence in Ottawa, Mr. Friez met the early telegraph workers, and later came in direct association with Professors Morse, Knox and Shane. At Ottawa he made the first telegraph key and sounder for the Western Electric Company, that corporation having taken over the Henning plant.

From Ottawa, Illinois, Mr. Friez removed to Philadelphia, Pennsylvania, where he began the manufacture of telegraph instruments, but the great panic following the failure of Jay Cooke, the Philadelphia financier, so completely paralyzed the business interests of that city that he soon closed his shops and removed to Baltimore, Maryland, that city henceforth to be the scene of his life work. During the time spent in Philadelphia, he was employed in a watch case factory and he devised means by which cases could be "spun" instead of being stamped, and for this achievement was presented with a watch. In Baltimore he soon became associated with A. Hall & Company, manufacturers of electric clocks, in the capacity of manager, and while serving in that capacity made the acquaintance of Mr. Mergenthaler, who was employed in the same shop. One of the clocks installed by this company, under Mr. Friez's management, is still marking the hours in the city hall, another in the Rennert hotel. Mr. Friez was next connected in an official capacity under the Brush Electric Company, and later was superintendent of the Baltimore works of the Mergenthaler Manufacturing Company, and was of especial aid in inventing and perfecting that wonderful piece of machinery which revolutionized the printing business of the world—the linotype. He was also associated with Professor Gray at one time, and built for him the first musical telephone, and with Professor Henry A. Rowland in instrument manufacture, Professor Rowland bearing testimony to the high quality of his partner's scientific attainment. About 1876, Mr. Friez established the business that was to win for him world-wide fame, a business which was not to pass away with him, but is still conducted by the founder's sons, Julien M. and Lucien L. Friez, whose natural ability was carefully developed and trained by their father.

His first plant was located on West German street, but prior to this he worked at his home, in the evenings, developing and improving, also manufacturing meteorological instruments, all this work being done by Mr. Friez with a foot lathe. In 1896, he removed to the present site of the Belfort Observatory, Baltimore street and Central avenue. He became known as one of the foremost manufacturers of meteorological instruments and apparatus in the world, and volumes could be filled with descriptions of his life's work. He perfected and completed the first heliograph, a great improvement over the cumbersome English instrument. He also invented the quadruple register, which records on a single sheet the velocity and direction of the wind, the sunshine and the rainfall for each minute of the day. Another of his chief inventions was the soil thermograph, by which the temperature beneath the earth's surface can be obtained; another, the Friez water-stage register, which records the stages or levels of the water in rivers and reservoirs, and the movements of the tides. He built instruments of the most delicate nature for scientists in every field, but the public knew of his work more through the perfecting of the Rowland Multiplex Telegraph, the linotype, the making of the dies and punches for the old Baltimore Oriole souvenir pins, and for his imposing residence, "Belfort," a great old-style mansion, spacious and comfortable, surrounded by terraces, arbors and flower-beds, where hundreds of varieties of flowers, shrubs and trees flourish in succession throughout the year, the grounds presenting a most beautiful spectacle during the summer months. The name he gave his home and observatory, "Belfort," was in remembrance of his native Belfort, in France, the Chateau of Belfort, the scene of some of the deadly conflicts of the present European war, overlooking the place of his birth, and during the Franco-Prussian war, of 1870, Belfort was the only French fort which did not surrender.

During the years 1900-16, Mr. Friez personally devoted himself to meteorology, a science in which he was a pioneer. The value of the work of those years cannot be computed for the records he made are preserved and the instruments he invented and perfected to aid the work of the meteorologist are almost without number. He established his observatory at "Belfort" and made his retreat so difficult of entrance to strangers that it was surrounded by a certain air of mystery. There Mr. Friez pursued his study, investigation and invention, his only diversion outside the laboratory being an occasional fishing trip and the beautifying of his grounds with all varieties of roses, shrubbery and trees. Rather a remarkable fact was that although a Frenchman, nearly all of his friends were Germans or of German descent, and he was connected with the leading German singing societies of this city and others he resided in, being at one time an active member of the Germania Maennerchor, of Baltimore. His manufacturing business was conducted under the corporate name of Julien P. Friez & Sons, and The Belfort Meteorological Observatory.

Mr. Friez was the friend of young men seeking to make their way in the scientific world, and in all parts of the country there are heads of departments of large manufacturing companies, men who served an apprenticeship under his guidance. When a young man completed his course and passed from under his control, Mr. Friez presented him with a gold watch, this applying even to his own sons, the youngest of them being the last to receive this reward. His sons, Julien M. and Lucien L., received their reward in 1913-14, the last to receive instruction under their father. This instruction fitted the sons, even at an early age, to successfully conduct the wonderful business so well established. In 1913, Mr. Friez, in company with his youngest son, Lucien L., toured the cities and countries in which he had studied and labored, he describing and illustrating his entire life for the benefit of the son.

Mr. Friez married Cordelia Schimff, of Philadelphia, Pennsylvania. Three sons were born to them: Frederick J., a resident of Atlantic City, New Jersey; Julien M. and Lucien L., successors to the business of Julien P. Friez & Sons; and three daughters: Sister M. Pierre, a Sister of Mercy; Alice J., wife of M. J. Jennings; and Louise M., wife of Burns Hyland.